MAN OF WAR

Richard Ollard has written a number of books on seventeenth-century subjects. He is past Vice-President of the Navy Records Society. In 1992 he was awarded the Caird Medal by the Trustees of the National Maritime Museum.

Also by Richard Ollard

This War Without an Enemy

The Image of the King (Phoenix Press)

Pepys

Fisher and Cunningham

Clarendon and his Friends

Cromwell's Earl: A Life of Edward Montagu,
First Earl of Sandwich

Dorset

An English Education

A Man of Contradictions: A Life of A.L. Rowse

MAN OF WAR
Sir Robert Holmes and the Restoration Navy

Richard Ollard

**PHOENIX
PRESS**

5 UPPER SAINT MARTIN'S LANE
LONDON
WC2H 9EA

To Michael Lewis

A PHOENIX PRESS PAPERBACK

First published in Great Britain
by Hodder & Stoughton in 1969
This paperback edition published in 2001
by Phoenix Press,
a division of The Orion Publishing Group Ltd,
Orion House, 5 Upper St Martin's Lane,
London WC2H 9EA

A CIP catalogue record for this book is available
from the British Library.

Printed and bound in Great Britain by
Clays Ltd, St Ives plc

ISBN 1 84212 236 3

Contents

Acknowledgments

To ACKNOWLEDGE all the kindness and courtesy that I have met with in writing this book, though pleasant to me, would be tedious to the reader. But some debts are too large to leave unrecorded. The two leading authorities on the seventeenth-century Navy, Dr. R. C. Anderson and the Rev. J. R. Powell, have been unstintingly generous of their learning. How much I am indebted to their published work will be clear from the references.

I wish also to record my gratitude to Mr. Alan Pearsall, the Curator of Archives, and to his colleagues in other departments of the National Maritime Museum; to Mr. Kenneth Timings of the Public Record Office; to Mr. E. L. C. Mullins of the History of Parliament Trust; to Mr. Pepys Whiteley of the Pepys Library; to Mr. J. D. Jones of the Isle of Wight Museum at Carisbrooke and to Mr. E. G. Earl, the Honorary County Archivist of the Isle of Wight. I must also thank the Marquess of Bath and the Master and Fellows of Magdalene College, Cambridge, for the use of manuscript material in their possession, the Controller of H.M.S.O. for permission to reproduce Crown Copyright material from the Public Records, and Mr. Patrick E. M. Holmes for his kindness in supplying me with genealogical information. To the British Museum and to the London Library my debt is great.

Finally, I wish to thank those who have been so kind as to read my manuscript: Dr. R. C. Anderson, Professor Michael Lewis and my brother Christopher. They have saved me from some errors of fact and interpretation, and those that remain are all my own.

Illustrations

Between pages 128 and 129

KEY TO ACKNOWLEDGMENTS

1 National Maritime Museum. 2 By gracious permission of Her Majesty the Queen. 3 Boymans Museum, Rotterdam. 4 Guildhall Museum. 5 British Museum. 6 Carisbrooke Castle Museum. 7 Christie, Manson and Woods. 8 Author; photo, Sheila Kearns.

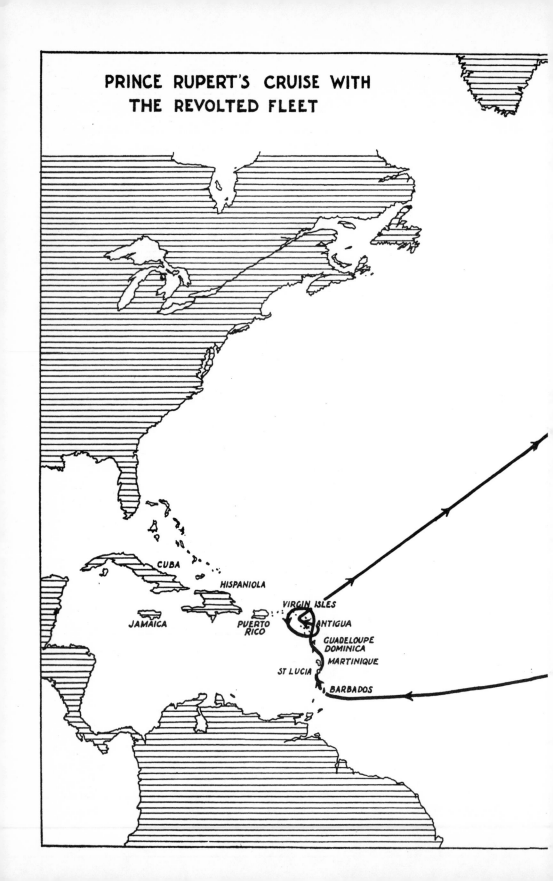

PRINCE RUPERT'S CRUISE WITH
THE REVOLTED FLEET

CUBA

HISPANIOLA

JAMAICA

PUERTO
RICO

VIRGIN ISLES

ANTIGUA

GUADELOUPE
DOMINICA

MARTINIQUE

ST LUCIA

BARBADOS

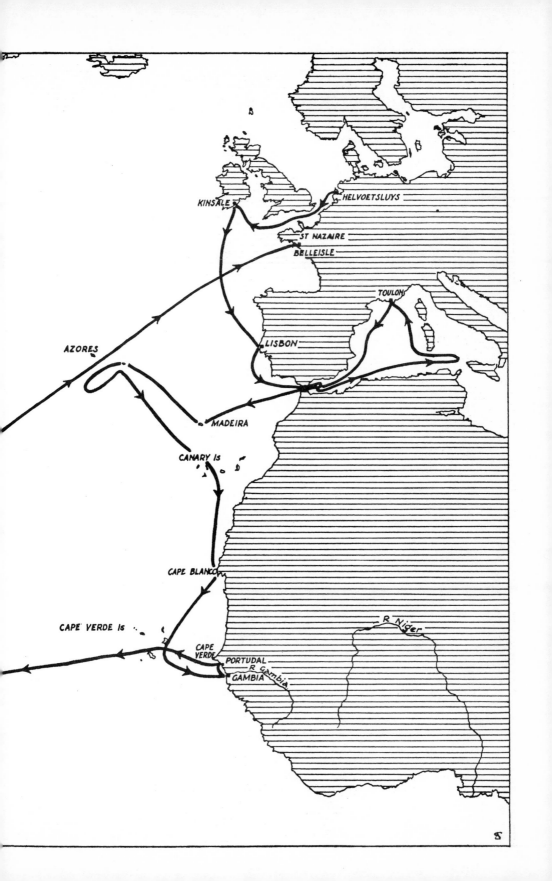

KINSALE

HELVOETSLUYS

ST NAZAIRE

BELLEISLE

TOULON

AZORES

LISBON

MADEIRA

CANARY Is

CAPE BLANCO

R Niger

CAPE VERDE Is

CAPE
VERDE

PORTUDAL
R Gambia
GAMBIA

9

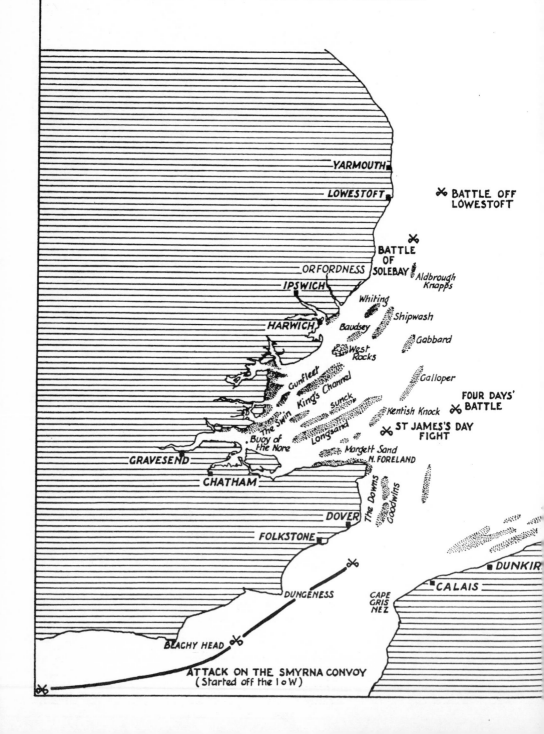

THE DUTCH AND ENGLISH COASTS

SHOWING THE BATTLES OF THE SECOND AND
THIRD DUTCH WARS IN WHICH SIR ROBERT HOLMES FOUGHT

YARMOUTH

LOWESTOFT

BATTLE OFF
LOWESTOFT

BATTLE
OF
SOLEBAY

Aldbrough
Knapps

ORFORDNESS

IPSWICH

Whiting

Shipwash

HARWICH

Baudsey

Gabbard

West
Rocks

Gunfleet

Galloper

King's Channel

FOUR DAYS'
BATTLE

The Swin

Sunck

Kentish Knock

ST JAMES'S DAY
FIGHT

Longsand

Buoy of
the Nore

Margett Sand

N. FORELAND

GRAVESEND

CHATHAM

The Downs

Goodwins

DOVER

FOLKSTONE

DUNKIR

CALAIS

DUNGENESS

CAPE
GRIS
NEZ

BEACHY HEAD

ATTACK ON THE SMYRNA CONVOY
(Started off the I o W)

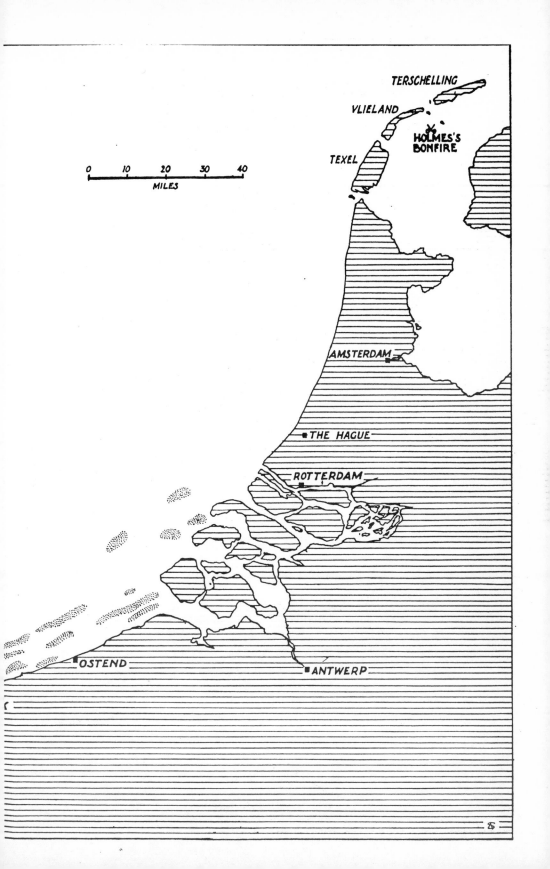

I

A Cornet of Horse

T O HAVE STARTED one war is generally accepted as an adequate
title to a place in the history books. To have started two and yet
to remain virtually unknown seems, in Lady Bracknell's words,
like carelessness. Everybody has heard of Captain Jenkins and the loss—
or alleged loss—of his ear; but if anyone has heard of Sir Robert Holmes
it is ten to one through familiarity either with naval history or with
Yarmouth, Isle of Wight, where Holmes, after so long and eventful a
voyage, came to his last moorings. There indeed he is conspicuously
commemorated by his statue with a chapel to itself in the parish church
by the castle which, as Governor of the Isle of Wight, he reconstructed
and put into good defensive order, and by the handsome house that he
built for himself next-door to it. Readers of Pepys's *Diary* may perhaps
remember him as one of the many villainous figures who excited alarm
and suspicion in that never too confiding breast. That these were of a
personal as well as a professional nature is early made clear: 'and then my
wife and I to church, and there in the pew, with the rest of the company,
was Captain Holmes, in his gold-laced suit, at which I was troubled
because of the old business which he attempted upon my wife.'[1] Five years
later, discussing Holmes's position and prospects in the Navy with his
colleague Sir William Coventry, he quotes with evident approval
Coventry's dark conclusion of the whole matter: 'a cat, says he, will be a
cat still'.[2]

The tides that erode or add to historical reputation are as strong and
persistent as those that reshape the coastline or redraw the channels of an
estuary. A few miles east of Holmes's seat at Yarmouth there stands, in
the middle of a country lane half of which has gone to grass, a handsome

town hall. It was built only a year or two after Holmes's death, and his nephew and heir, Henry Holmes, who sat for that very borough of Newtown and no doubt inherited his uncle's unashamed partiality for gerrymandering elections, must have heard himself declared member from its elegant upper chamber. But round it now are fields and hedgerows. A comfortable distance away there are a handful of houses standing by themselves. Beyond them again a large, rough stretch of undrained pasture has supplanted the harbour that made medieval Newtown the equal if not the superior of Portsmouth and Southampton and left it even in the seventeenth century some pretensions to wealth and importance.

So it is with the career of Sir Robert Holmes. The ablest of his contemporaries like Pepys and Coventry had a great deal to say about him, most of it hostile but all marked by a grudging respect, even admiration, for his courage and abilities. Of his seniors Clarendon, who by temperament, conviction and political connexion had every reason to find him unsympathetic, described him as a 'very bold and expert man'.[3] And Prince Rupert's opinion of him is eloquent from an association in the profession of arms that extended over nearly thirty years. This long comradeship probably sprang from the dash and courage that Holmes displayed as a cornet in Prince Maurice's regiment of horse during the summer of 1643. Certainly after the final defeat of the Royalists Holmes served Rupert as his page in the French Army. He was one of the adventurous spirits who in 1649 sailed with him on that most desperate of all maritime enterprises, a cruise without a base; a cruise that, astonishingly, lasted for three years, two of them in the tropics, and which gave Holmes his first experience of sea fighting, of sea-borne assault, and of command at sea. And Rupert, commanding the fleet against the Dutch in the last of a lifetime's campaigns, repeatedly asked for, and was refused, the services of Sir Robert Holmes.[4]

Perhaps the most pithy of contemporary descriptions of his career is that given in an anonymous pamphlet published in Amsterdam in 1677 and often attributed to Andrew Marvell.[5] 'Sir Robert Holmes, first an Irish livery-boy, then a highway-man, now Bashaw of the Isle of Wight, got in boons £100,000. The cursed beginner of the two Dutch wars.'

It omits much: but it does achieve the triumphant feat of telescoping a life that spanned the most eventful and exciting decades of the seventeenth century, and was largely spent in action and adventure that in turn led on to wealth and position. Its details, if unflatteringly presented, are on the whole accurate. Holmes's governorship of the Isle of Wight had a certain flavour of Turkish absolutism. Whether or not he got in boons—the writer presumably means rewards for service—as much as £100,000 there is no doubt that he died worth a great deal of money. And as the third son of an obscure English family settled in County Cork he can have inherited little, even if 'livery boy' overstates the simplicity of his origins. 'Highway-man' we may take as an economical allusion to his service with the Royalist cavalry during the Civil War and to his activities as an officer in the fleet under Rupert's command after the war was over. If that naval expedition does not wholly deserve the adjective 'piratical' there were many then and since who thought that it did. Holmes, who seems to have been little interested in questions of law or morality, would probably have found the imputation less offensive than the sneer at his breeding. What he thought of the final accusation, that of starting the two Dutch wars, we do not know; but everything about his life and about the way in which he chose to be commemorated suggests that he would have taken it as a compliment. The long Latin inscription on the plinth of his statue in Yarmouth parish church records a lifetime spent in war; it pretends to no piety; it owes, and claims, nothing to affection. The fine portrait of him together with his companion in arms Sir Frescheville Holles that now hangs in the Queen's House at Greenwich reveals the same overriding single-minded concern. Other admirals and generals might sit for their portraits without the cannon roaring in the background and without brandishing their weapons in the world's face. But Holmes was a professional and proud of it.

Temperament, talent and situation combined to enable him not only to fulfil himself but to stamp some of his own character on a long and interesting tract of history. The British Empire and the Royal Navy are economic, political and social forces of the first importance for the two and a half centuries that divide the period of Charles II and Louis XIV from that of the Second World War. It would, of course, be imbecile to argue that the whole course of English and European history would have been deflected if Holmes had been carried off by a stray shot in one of the many battles of his young manhood. But as a mere matter of historical fact Holmes appeared on the labour market just at the moment when there were openings for people like him, openings which he and others were to widen with incalculable effect. He lived and fought and argued and acted and wrote and spoke in such a way as to influence the course of events in his own time and to help shape the institutions and to colour the ethos of a great age that was to follow. And he did what he did both because he chose to do so and because it offered him a living and wide prospects of reward. The society depicted in Congreve's plays, or a century later in Jane Austen's novels, depends on Holmes (speaking generically) for its security and self-confidence and derives from him many of its unspoken assumptions and its judgments of value. He was among the early specimens, a hard and sharp-edged one it may be, of a type that was for many years and to many people to represent the image of England.

Large claims, it may be felt, are being made on behalf of one who was simply the unknown soldier of the British Empire. It must be the business of this book to substantiate them. But before going on to describe the character and achievements of Sir Robert Holmes it may be useful to say something of the Royal Navy of his day. It is a commonplace to say that Pepys is the architect of the Navy that won and kept maritime supremacy for Britain, the Navy in which Jane Austen's brothers—and many of her characters—made their careers and which, not so very long ago, Noël Coward portrayed in his film *In Which We Serve*. The keynote of this service is its professionalism, a professionalism which Pepys devoted his life to promoting. To grasp his achievement one has only to compare the eighteenth-century Navy, complete with its uniform, its cadres of officers, its standardised equipment, with the rough-and-ready, *ad hoc* force that defeated the Armada, officered by independent seamen such as Frobisher

and Drake, commanded by a grandee of no professional maritime experience and composed, mostly, of merchant ships commandeered for the
purpose. The Navy of Pepys's and Holmes's time was in transition
between the two. Pepys, a civil servant of genius, did more than any man
to mould, to shape, to regularise, to define. As he was also one of the most
articulate and self-aware Englishmen who ever lived we have a uniquely
vivid impression of him and his work. Holmes, a professional fighting
leader, was himself a part of the material and, by what he was, helped to
determine the nature and scope of the instrument of policy which Pepys
was fashioning. Pepys was, no question, a much more gifted, various and
civilised man than Holmes: this coupling of their names is not meant to
imply any equality. Rather it is to show in what respect, beyond its
intrinsic merit and interest, Holmes's career has any significance in the
evolution of a great service.

*　　　　　*　　　　　*

Sir Robert Holmes was born in or about 1622 the third son of Henry
Holmes of Mallow, Co. Cork. Nothing is known of his early life and
education—though the elegance of his handwriting and his vigorous and
correct use of language implies a degree of formal education sufficient to
disprove the suggestion that he had been a livery boy. His grandfather,
another Robert Holmes, is described in a grant of arms[6] as 'born in the
County of Lancaster and an officer in the Warrs against the Rebells in
Ireland in the reign of Queen Elizabeth'. He was in all probability the
Robert Holmes named as provost when the town of Mallow received its
grant of incorporation in 1612.[7] This suggests that the family was
comfortably off.

His service in the Civil War gives us the first authentic and appropriate
glimpse of him.[8] In the summer of 1643 Prince Maurice's regiment of
horse, one of the most active units in the Royalist Army, was taking part
in the Western Campaign that was to culminate in the taking of Bristol.
Early in the morning of June 10th the Royalist forces, tired after several
days hard marching towards Bath, ran into Sir William Waller's army at
the village of Chewton Mendip. The Parliamentarians got the best of the

ensuing skirmish in the course of which Prince Maurice was wounded and taken prisoner. One of his officers, Captain Richard Atkyns, determined to get him back in spite of the fact that he was disobeying orders and risking a court martial in so doing. He set off with his own troop (of which Holmes was the cornet) and, joined by a few fugitives, one of whom, conveniently, held field rank, soon found himself confronting two hundred dragoons and a regiment of horse. It was a clear, bright day but still early. Luckily for Atkyns down came a thick mist blanketing everything. The dragoons heard the Royalist horse coming towards them at a steady trot. There were only about a hundred of them: but each soldier waiting for them to burst on him out of the mist heard the jingling of a hundred bits, the treading of four hundred hooves, the snorting of the horses; and felt the ominous vibration of the ground under a large party of mounted men coming closer and closer. The dragoons fired one blind volley and then mounted their own horses and turned to retreat. At this moment the mist cleared and the Royalist charge knocked the dragoons into the cavalry that was covering them. A tight-packed struggling mêlée made it impossible for the Parliamentarians to deploy their superior force. They broke and ran. In the pursuit the Royalists retook Prince Maurice but, as so often in that war, exposed themselves to unnecessary danger by chasing the enemy too far. Captain Atkyns suddenly found that he had only thirty men with him to face three fresh troops of cavalry. He needed all his nerve and skill to extricate the remains of his troop from a very ugly situation.

Atkyns retired to his quarters much distressed at the disappearance of both his officers, most of his men and of the colours of his troop. However, early the next morning . . . 'Mr. Holmes my cornet brought my colours to me, which pleased me very well: but with this allay, that my Lieutenant Thomas Sandys, my near kinsman was taken prisoner . . . and that he [Holmes] with some few troopers took such leaps that the enemy could not follow them, else they had been taken also.'

A month later at the battle of Roundway Down the Royalist horse won one of the most surprising victories of the war against a much superior Parliamentary force under the experienced and highly successful Sir

William Waller. Atkyns, whose account of the battle is again the source for what follows, got the better of a hand-to-hand fight with the Parliamentary cavalry commander, Sir Arthur Haslerig, who abandoned his troops and fled. Atkyns followed, determined, if he could, to capture so well-known a figure; but Haslerig was very well mounted and even better protected 'having a coat of mail over his arms [armour] and a headpiece (I am confident) musketproof'. After sustaining several nasty knocks without being able to make any impression on his opponent Atkyns concluded that the only hope lay in attacking his horse.

> In this nick of time came up Mr. Holmes to my assistance, (who never failed me in time of danger) and went up to him with great resolution, and felt him before he discharged his pistol, and though I saw him hit him, 'twas but a flea-biting to him; whilst he charged him, I employed myself in killing his horse, and ran him into several places, and upon the faltering of his horse his head-piece opened behind, and I gave him a prick in the neck, and I had run him through the head if my horse had not stumbled at the same place; then came in Captain Buck a gentleman of my troop, and discharged his pistol upon him also, but with the same success as before, and being a very strong man, and charging with a mighty hanger,* stormed him and amazed him, but fell off again; by this time his horse began to be faint with bleeding, and fell off from his rate, at which said Sir Arthur, 'What good will it do you to kill a poor man?' said I 'Take quarter then', with that he stopped his horse, and I came up to him, and bid him deliver his sword, which he was loathe to do; and being tied twice about his wrist, he was fumbling a great while before he would part with it; but before he delivered it, there was a runaway troop of theirs that had espied him in hold; says one of them 'My Lord General is taken prisoner'; says another, 'Sir Arthur Haslerigge is taken prisoner, face about and charge', with that they rallied and charged us, and rescued him; wherein I received a shot with a pistol, which only took off the skin upon the blade bone of my shoulder.
>
> This story being related to the late King [Charles I] at a second, or third hand, his answer was, 'Had he been victualled as well as fortified, he might have endured a siege of seven years.'

Of his further service in the Royalist Army I have found no record (there is none of the vast majority of his fellow officers and soldiers) but some evidence: the inscription on his tomb, the military rank of Major by which Pepys and others constantly refer to him after the Restoration

* A sword.

even when he was in command of a ship or a squadron, above all the close
personal and professional relation to Prince Rupert already referred to. It is
here that we next catch sight of him.

Rupert had been granted a pass to go overseas with his servants and
goods as part of the terms on which Oxford had surrendered to the Parliament. On July 5th, 1646, he sailed from Dover: on July 10th servants and
horses followed him to Calais.[9] On his arrival in Paris negotiations were
opened for his employment in the French Army but Rupert was reluctant
to commit himself too deeply in case his presence might once again be
required in England by an unexpected revival of the Royalist cause.[10] By
the following spring satisfactory terms had been agreed. Rupert was made
Maréchal de Camp (equivalent in modern terms to brigadier) and was given a
regiment of foot, a troop of horse and the command of all the English in
France.* This enabled him to write to a number of ex-Royalist officers
inviting them to raise men for the French service or simply to engage in it
themselves under his command. Possibly Holmes was one of those
attracted by this offer but it is much more likely that he had crossed the
channel as a member of the Prince's entourage.

Anyway it is in action that his presence is first reported. In the summer
of 1647 the French Army was engaged in a not very successful campaign
against the Spanish and Imperial forces for the possession of a line of
towns, Arras, La Bassée, Armentières, that was to be disputed in many
later and bloodier wars. Rupert had been instructed to use his forces in
support of Marshal Gassion, a commander whose habit it was to observe
the enemy from close range. This had already nearly cost him his life at
the siege of Armentières and was to do so a few weeks later at the siege
of Lens. In July shortly after the capture of Armentières the Spanish
Army was marching to the relief of La Bassée, shadowed by the French.
Gassion, anxious as usual to take a close look at his opponents' dispositions:

> asked the Prince, 'Are you well mounted, sir? shall we go see the army?' The
> Prince agreed to it, and . . . with Gassion, and three or four men went up, and

* In January 1647 they mustered 1,372 men.

meeting two or three Croats, Gassion pressed upon them, and they ran away; but upon a pursuit, there started out an ambush of eleven more from behind a hillock, and a good troop of horse following them to cut off the Prince's and Gassion's retreat, they got over a little slough, and then Sir Robert Holmes, Mr. Mortaigne,* and several other volunteers that were left behind, came up to their succour. The enemy endeavouring to pass a little river that was betwixt them, three or four of them were got over, but beaten back again by Mr. Mortaigne . . . and Sir Robert Holmes, who was then Page to His Highness, together with some volunteers whom Gassion had employed to beat them over. Sir Robert Holmes's leg was shot in pieces just below the knee, and his horse killed under him where he lay upon the place, and Mortaigne also was shot in the hand. Sir Robert Holmes being left alone upon the ground, and the enemy firing hard from the other side of the river, his Highness, seeing that nobody would engage to bring him off, with a generosity peculiar to himself, went himself with Mortaigne (who, by reason of his wound in the hand, could give him but little assistance), took him up behind him with great danger and difficulty, and so carried him off; not a man of the French volunteers coming in to his assistance.

The breathlessness of the contemporary account—it was found among Rupert's papers and was probably written by his chaplain some twenty years after the event—reproduces convincingly the effect of skirmish and surprise. The nature of Holmes's wound must, however, be exaggerated. If his leg had really been shot in pieces no seventeenth-century surgeon could have restored the use of it to the degree that would have made it possible for Holmes to live the life he actually led. That he was wounded several times in his military career and that his health was permanently impaired as a result seems certain.[11] The wound was certainly severe enough to put him out of the campaign and to require a replacement in the office of page. The Thirty Years' War, of which these operations were part, had in any case almost dragged to a close. In the year that peace returned to Europe Holmes and Prince Rupert were to embark on an extraordinary series of adventures.

* Prince Rupert's Gentleman of the Horse. He sailed with Rupert's squadron and went down with the flagship in a storm in the Atlantic.

II

The Revolted Fleet

NEGLECT OF THE NAVY, or rather the taking it for granted, was a mistake made at different times by both sides in the Civil War. Had Charles I made sure of settling the command in safe hands instead of opening the question at the moment of acutest crisis and had he attached the loyalty of the seamen by paying their wages or even by providing adequate food, the Parliamentary cause could hardly have escaped military defeat. It could certainly be argued that this initial failure cost him the war. The Parliamentarians, as long as active hostilities lasted, were wise enough to learn from his mistakes. Warwick, who held the chief command at sea until April 1645, kept a sharp eye on the victualling and on all such matters as affected the welfare of his men.[1] But in the years of distrustful manœuvre that followed the Royalist defeat in the field the dangers of indiscipline and disaffection in both the Army and the Navy were much increased. The Government could not disband its forces until the King had been induced to accept the political verdict of the war; every month that passed made it harder to find the money to maintain them, let alone to pay off their arrears. In the Army this state of hesitation and uncertainty contributed to the sudden rise of radicalism, exemplified in religion by the Independents and in politics by the Levellers. The Navy, more isolated from currents of opinion and less accessible to press and pulpit, reacted more conservatively. It did not seek innovation in Church and State; it did not want interference from landsmen; it expected to be paid and fed.

This passivity may have misled the Government, hard pressed by the fierce and open controversies among its supporters, into judging the Navy more placid and biddable than it really was. After all it would have

required a very high degree of these qualities if it was to stand entirely
aloof from the struggle for power among the victors that was in effect
taking place. The political colour of the flag officers who had commanded throughout the war was that of the Presbyterian party, which, like
many political parties, is best defined negatively. The Presbyterians were,
then, at least as strongly opposed to Levelling and Independency as they
were to the policies of Laud and Strafford. It was from this party that
some among the defeated Royalists hoped to reconstitute an alliance that
would embrace the Scots, the lawyers, the merchants and the landowners,
united by the threat to property, law and religious uniformity. Warwick
in his days as Lord High Admiral had been closely associated with this
party; and Batten, his Vice-Admiral and successor, was certainly in
sympathy with it.

Throughout the summer of 1647 the tensions grew: between Army and
Parliament; between Independent and Presbyterian; between Radical and
Conservative. None of these sets of labels is strictly co-terminous with the
others but that this was a period of political polarisation is inescapable.
Batten, anyway, did not escape it. He incurred the serious displeasure of
the Government for permitting half a dozen Presbyterian members of
Parliament to resume their journey to France after their ketch had been
arrested by one of his frigates in August.[2] In September the Mayor and
Jurats of Sandwich reported a sworn statement of some indiscreet
apprehension for the King's safety that Batten had expressed in a pub. A
week later he was summoned before a Committee of both houses and
surrendered his commission.[3]

Reaction in the fleet does not seem to have been noticeable. But only
three weeks later there was a mutiny—over arrears of pay—in a vessel of
the Irish squadron.[3] As the ship had not come under Batten's command the
incident was probably unconnected with his supersession. It was none the
less a warning. So far from recognising its significance the two houses
nominated Colonel Rainsborough, an eloquent left-wing soldier who had
previously served in the Navy, to succeed Batten as Vice-Admiral. Before
he could take up his appointment, however, the Lords withdrew their

consent until his part in the recent revolutionary assemblies and disturb-
ances in the Army should have been thoroughly examined by a committee
of both houses. This brought on a tussle between Lords and Commons
which ended on January 1st 1648, in a Commons order to Rainsborough,
in peremptory defiance of the Lords, to repair at once to the Isle of Wight
there to take command of the fleet.4 The unwisdom of the appointment
was soon demonstrated. On May 24th Rainsborough expressed fears that
two of his ships might refuse to sail on a northbound convoy. On May 27th
he had to report that the crew of his own ship headed by his Lieutenant
had turned him off and that she and four others had declared for the King.
Three weeks later the sailors gave these three reasons for their decision.5

1. The Parliament, of late, grant commissions to the sea-commanders
   in their own names, leaving out the King.
2. Several land-men made sea-commanders.
3. The insufferable pride, ignorance, and insolency of Colonel Rainsborough, the late vice-admiral, alienated the hearts of the seamen.

By this time a sizable part of the fleet under his command had crossed
over to Holland and put themselves under the orders of the Prince of
Wales. Parliament, thoroughly alarmed, had recalled Warwick to the
supreme command and had ordered Batten to join him at Portsmouth.
Batten, however, had other ideas. After an unsuccessful attempt to
subvert the Portsmouth ships to the Royalist cause, he sailed for Holland
in a fast frigate of which he was part-owner. On his arrival the Prince of
Wales knighted him and made him Rear-Admiral, an appointment of
which Clarendon did not approve. The post of Vice-Admiral had already
been conferred on Lord Willoughby of Parham, whose military record as a
Parliamentary commander was a string of misfortunes and failures*
punctuated by quarrels with colleagues. But his prominence in the
Presbyterian party had already earned him a term of imprisonment and
driven him into exile. The Admiral was the Prince of Wales, later Charles
II, at that time a young man of eighteen.

* He began the war badly by arriving too late for the battle of Edgehill.

Small wonder if this curious command-structure seemed to offer an opening for the under-employed talents of Prince Rupert. He and his brother Prince Maurice left Paris on June 29th to join the fleet.[6] According to Clarendon he lost no time in intriguing against Batten, whose long and impressive record of command made him the only serious professional rival.[7] Indeed, the scene was set in that summer of 1648 for the conflicts of personality and the clash of interests that was to dominate the Restoration Navy. Even James, Duke of York, then only a boy of twelve or thirteen, made his entrance on the stage on which he was later to play so important a part. As he happened to be staying with his sister and brother-in-law when the revolted fleet came over to Holland he was the first member of the Royal family to go on board. It may be that the excitement and the cheering of the sailors turned his head. Certainly he took it upon himself to appoint Lord Willoughby of Parham Vice-Admiral so that when the Prince of Wales and the main body of excited cavaliers arrived from Paris it would have been a ticklish business to change. In fact it was only with difficulty that James was persuaded to stay on shore when the fleet put to sea. To risk both brothers on the same expedition would obviously have been unjustifiable; and it would have been unthinkable for the Prince of Wales not to lead in person when it suddenly seemed that the verdict of the war might be reversed.

The hopes that unexpectedly reanimated the Royalist exiles as they hurried to the Dutch coast were not unreasonable. Royalist risings had already broken out in Essex and Kent; the Scots under Hamilton were on the point of invading England; Ireland, torn and ravaged by a far crueller war than her sister kingdoms, could still produce men to fight for the King if ships could be found to transport them and money be raised to feed and equip them. All that was wanted to fuse these remote elements into victory was command of the sea, which brought with it the trade and wealth of London. This the Royalists were now in a fair way to possessing. In addition to a sizable part of the fleet—twelve ships out of just over thirty on the main home stations—the three forts in the Downs, Deal, Walmer and Sandwich, had declared for the King.

Ugly as the situation might look for the Parliamentary leaders the exercise of power to decide, to act, to select an objective and to coordinate the means to its attainment was an art they had not yet forgotten and the Royalists had still to learn. The rebellions in Kent and Essex were quickly stamped out or contained; Cromwell, despatched to the north, routed the Scottish army at the battle of Preston on August 17th, barely a month after the Cavalier fleet had weighed anchor and sailed for the Downs. The grand strategy of the Royalists began to take on its familiar battered unlucky appearance: the martial propensities of the Cavaliers revealed themselves, as so often before, principally in squabbling with each other and in deriding the decisions of their commanders.

What in fact was the fleet to do? To capture a port and hold it in support of an insurrection that showed signs of spreading? A half-hearted move to do this at Colchester was abandoned. To attack the main divisions of the Parliamentary fleet before they were able to unite their strength? This was strongly favoured by the exiles who had swarmed aboard the ships, men who had nothing to lose and everything to win;[8] but so desperate a gamble with the safety of their country could hardly commend itself to mere Englishmen such as Batten whose actions shewed them no sticklers for particular forms of government. Indeed, it was precisely to avoid rash and extreme policies that they had changed sides. Failing so dramatic an exertion of sea-power, there remained an obvious and superficially attractive use for it: to blockade London and to seize vessels entering or leaving the Thames as prize of war. This would deprive the Parliament of its chief economic resource, would alienate the city from a government that could no longer protect its interests and would at the same time happily provide a means of paying and victualling the fleet. On closer inspection this too had its disadvantages. The London merchants whose ships and goods were to be seized and sold to finance the operation might, almost certainly would, be antagonised: and the grand strategy of politics demanded that this should at all costs be avoided. And what was to happen when the Parliamentary fleet, which could hardly be expected to remain a spectator, tried to interfere?

True to form the Royalists hovered and dithered. They spent more than a month in the Downs, capturing ships and then letting them go again, to the disgust of the seamen, who were understandably anxious to secure the means by which they were to be paid and fed. They considered reinforcing the castles that had declared for them but postponed the attempt until what would have been easy had become difficult. Eventually they sailed uncertainly into the Thames and narrowly escaped being 'ground to powder', as one of them put it, between Warwick's fleet and the Portsmouth squadron that had sailed in to reinforce him. Short of food and water, the Royalist fleet returned to Holland early in September.

Holmes, almost certainly, sailed on this cruise as a member of Prince Rupert's entourage. Such glimpses as we catch of him throughout this period show him always as one of Rupert's closest and most active companions so that it is most unlikely that he would have missed so promising an adventure. Tame though it may have turned out it was an introduction to a career in which he was to make his name and fortune; and the waters through which he now sailed for the first time in a man-of-war were to be the scene of his most famous actions, the centre of his interest, familiar in every mood of wind and weather, scanned for approaching fleets or likely prizes. From the hot summer battles off the mouth of the Thames in 1666 to the anxious watching through the fog of a November afternoon for the invading fleet of 1688 making its way down Channel, Holmes was present, and not as a spectator, in the moments of climax through which Restoration England passed.

If his subsequent career is any guide no doubt Holmes joined as loudly as any in the uproar of accusation and dispute that broke out as soon as the hungry and thirsty Cavaliers came clattering out of the ships into the taverns of Helvoetsluys. Dissatisfaction with the conduct of operations was universal and a change imperative. Batten was accused by the sailors of having taken bribes from the London merchants to let their ships go free.[9] No doubt he was glad enough to make this insult a pretext for resigning his commission and retiring to The Hague. Shortly afterwards he availed himself of an amnesty offered to those who had taken part in the revolt of

the ships and returned to England where he lived as a private citizen until
the Restoration. Logically he agreed to transfer to the Parliamentary
authorities the frigate of which he was part-owner, the *Constant Warwick*,
reputed the best sailer of her day. This naturally annoyed the Royalists and
infuriated the Parliamentary agent in Holland: 'Batten, that arch-traitor
. . . made a fleet revolt and must be saved for part of a ship.'[10] His with-
drawal cleared the way for Rupert. As Clarendon who was by no means
well disposed towards him wrote: 'There was in truth nobody to whom
the charge of the fleet could be committed but Prince Rupert: for it was
well known that the lord Willoughby, besides his being without any
experience of the sea, was weary of it, and would by no means continue
there; and the seamen were too much broke loose from all kind of order
to be reduced by a commander of an ordinary rank.'[11]

The decay of discipline to which Clarendon refers was hardly surprising.
Pay and victuals remained the unsolved and apparently insoluble problems
of naval administration from the time of the Tudors down to the Napo-
leonic wars.[12] What was to prove beyond the capabilities of Elizabeth I
and Cromwell, of Pepys and of Pitt was bound to be too much for a
quarrelsome, impoverished and irresponsible group of émigrés. Indeed the
Parliament had proved much more satisfactory employers than any
preceding government so it was only to be expected that the ships, or at
any rate the sailors, should return to their previous allegiance once it was
clear that the revolt had failed to achieve a *coup d'état*. This probability was
increased by the arrival of Warwick's fleet at Helvoetsluys on September
19th.

The two fleets lay within sight of each other for more than two months.
Had Warwick violated Dutch neutrality and attacked the Royalist ships
straight away, as his political masters evidently wished, he would almost
certainly have made an end of the whole business. But he missed his
chance; and the Dutch, anxious not to give him another, sent in a powerful
squadron under Tromp which anchored between the two fleets. The
Royalists, protected by the presence of the Dutch, were none the less shut
in and thus prevented from taking the prizes which were the only means by

which they could pay and provision their fleet. Several ships reverted to the Parliament and more would have done so if Rupert and his followers had not prevented them by force.[13] With the approach of winter the outlook was discouraging. On the other hand Warwick could not risk being frozen in with a good part of the Parliament's total naval force. Early on he had sent in a frigate to try and obtain the berth highest up the harbour and nearest to the sluice or lock-gate that gave the place its name. If he could secure this he could deny access to the Royalists by mere obstruction and force them out to find a secure base elsewhere. The move almost succeeded: but Captain Allin, a Royalist frigate captain who was to share many of Holmes's adventures and to rise high in the Restoration Navy, acting the part of a helpful bystander ashore took hold of the mooring rope as though to make fast and then deliberately let it go again.[14] This respite enabled the Royalist ships, alive now to the danger, to crowd up to the top of the harbour where they lost no time in getting safe inside the sluice. Early in November Tromp's squadron left Helvoetsluys but Rupert had already constructed fortifications and landed some of his ordnance so that an attack would have proved costly. On November 21st Warwick, short of provisions and tired of a blockade that seemed to be achieving little, sailed for home and left the Royalists to their own devices.

Rupert had been confirmed as Commander in Chief with instructions that left him the widest scope. The first object of his activities was to make money, not only to keep the fleet in being but to meet the necessities of the exiled court. As a subsidiary aim he was to establish his base in the port of Kinsale and to do what he could to help the Royalist cause in Ireland. The question whether he should come under the orders of the Marquis of Ormonde, the Lord Lieutenant, was evaded in Rupert's favour.[15] The first task, however, was to get the fleet to sea. The new Admiral set about provisioning and manning the ships with characteristic energy and professionalism. A couple of frigates, sent out to take prizes, soon eased the problem of supply. But seamen were not so easily come by: in spite of constant vigilance and occasional violence a high proportion of the original

crews had managed to desert.[16] When on January 21st, 1649, the Prince
sailed for Ireland his fleet of seven warships was severely undermanned.

No lists of officers or men survive. But Holmes's presence with the
fleet is proved by his adventures on the Mauretanian coast and in the
Gambia recorded in Chapter IV. Rupert's own flagship the *Constant
Reformation* had a mere forty seamen and eighty soldiers aboard in place of
her normal complement of three hundred.[17] If the Parliamentary squadron of
four ships that sighted them off the Downs had brought them to action
there can be little doubt of the result. But at this stage of his career
Rupert enjoyed the luck without which no commander can succeed. By
the end of the month all his ships had arrived safely at Kinsale. The long
cruise that was to take him and his friend Holmes to strange coasts and
distant seas had begun.

III

Prince Rupert's Cruise—I

T HE FLEET, WHICH NOW represented the most formidable
military force at the disposal of the Stuarts, merits some description.[1] Rupert as Admiral flew his flag in the *Constant Reformation* a
52-gun ship; his brother Maurice was his Vice-Admiral in the *Convertine*
(46-guns) while the Rear-Admiral Sir John Mennes had the *Swallow* (40-
guns). These vessels were, on paper, among the most powerful units of the
Navy; but neither the *Convertine** nor the *Constant Reformation* was in her first
youth, and all the ships were hopelessly undermanned. Rupert and
Maurice had of course no experience at sea but both were military
professionals of high rank such as had traditionally been appointed to
command fleets. Sir John Mennes, on the other hand, was one of the most
experienced sea officers of his time. In the course of a long career—he was
just on fifty, twenty years older than his Admiral—he had fought the
Spaniards in the West Indies in the time of James I, he had commanded
the ship that brought Rubens across the channel to Charles I in 1629 and
had been constantly employed until, on the outbreak of the Civil War,
Warwick dismissed him together with two or three other captains who
refused the authority of Parliament. Already old to be facing the rigours
and squalors of life in a seventeenth-century ship, he survived into the
Restoration period, an amusing and convivial littérateur, whose obvious
incompetence as a naval administrator was, even in Pepys's eyes, almost
atoned for by the charm of his company and conversation.

If these three ships constituted a latent menace that the Parliament
could not neglect, it was the four frigates that did immediate and
extensive damage. Commanded by Captain Allin[2] they made use of the

* She had been built for Sir Walter Raleigh.

Scillies, still in Royalist hands, as well as the Irish ports to prey on the rich trade of the western approaches to the Channel and the Severn estuary. The prizes came in thick and fast; the garrison in the Scillies was supplied and reinforced; the exiled court was refreshed by remittances from the proceeds of these exploits.[3] But such a run of luck could not last for ever. Returning from a cruise, Captain Allin's ship was separated from her consorts in a storm and had the misfortune to fall in with two Parliamentary frigates who soon took her. In May a powerful squadron under the new Generals-at-Sea, Blake, Deane and Popham, arrived off Kinsale and forced Rupert to keep his ships in harbour. Prevented from commerce-raiding he seems to have used his enforced immobility to recruit for his undermanned fleet. Towards the end of June he brought down two hundred and sixty men from Waterford to Kinsale.[4] But the Parliamentary blockade undid his work. The Generals-at-Sea had departed to settle accounts with the Royalist privateers operating from the Scillies but they had left so strong a detachment under Ayscue, the Admiral of the Irish station, that the Royalists had had no chance of replenishing their stores or of making money from seizing merchant ships. Consequently they could not even pay the men they already had, let alone the new Irish recruits. By the end of July only one of Rupert's frigates, the *Blackmoor Lady*, was still active, and she had had to take refuge with her prize in a French port.[5]

Inaction destroys the value of any military force except the professional. It must have been clear to so seasoned a commander as Rupert that unless he got his fleet away from ports which were easily accessible to enemy blockade he was done for. In Ireland itself things were going from bad to worse; the total defeat of the Royalist cause loomed close; in so hopeless a situation despair or treachery could cut the few remaining strands in a matter of hours. Kinsale could no longer be counted a useful or even a secure base. As early as mid-March, within six weeks of arriving in Ireland, Rupert had written to the King of Portugal to sound his reaction to a visit from the Royalist fleet and had received two or three months later a friendly reply. By this time, however, the Generals-at-Sea had begun the blockade. At a council of war held about Midsummer Day Rupert was for fighting his way out and making for Lisbon without further delay. In the event, however, he accepted the more prudent advice of his colleagues to wait till bad weather should drive the blockaders off their station and then to make a dash for it. About the beginning of October it began to blow very hard, and by the middle of the month there was only one Parliamentary ship left in the offing. On October 20th the three flagships escorted by four frigates put to sea.

The voyage was a prosperous one. Although the ships were scattered by rough weather in the Bay of Biscay they reached their rendezvous safely and took three or four prizes in the approaches to Lisbon, including one stout vessel which was subsequently converted into a 36-gun warship. The force which sailed up the Tagus in mid-November thus appeared more formidable than anything the Parliamentary fleet had had to contend with since the original revolt in the summer of 1648. Even with all the difficulties of maintaining the ships without a base, of manning them without a body of seamen who could be enticed or brought on board by the press-gang, it was far too serious a threat for an English Government to leave suspended over its main trade-route to the Mediterranean and the Levant. And the English Government was not alone in such apprehensions. All the countries that lived by or depended on sea-borne trade had a common interest in keeping down piracy—and the contemporaries who viewed Rupert's activities in this light had not had the advantage of reading the rhapsodical representation of them achieved by the romantic Royalists of the nineteenth and twentieth centuries. Hardly had his ships come to an anchor in Cascais Roads before the Dutch and the Spaniards had lodged protests with the Portuguese Government. This was followed by legal action on the part of the English merchants resident in Lisbon whose goods had been seized in the prizes that now, thanks to the King of Portugal's kindness for the Stuarts, had come up the Tagus to Lisbon itself. To them it was as if protection were being afforded to criminals, and the English Government was not slow to support this view in the strongest terms. Luckily for the Royalists it was too late in the year for a

c

fleet to be sent against them. Rupert made use of the respite with his characteristic energy and efficiency. Two of the smaller frigates were sold, two, perhaps three, of the prizes were converted into well-armed ships, as was a Dutch vessel which he bought in Lisbon. The old *Convertine* was laid-up and her armament transferred to the newly commissioned frigates. Besides rationalising the fleet, victualling it, preparing it for action and disposing of the prize goods Rupert was also holding his own against the diplomatic pressure exerted on the King of Portugal. It was a good introduction to the many-sided resourcefulness and to the thorough attention to detail required of an independent commander.

Pleasantly as the winter passed in one of the most civilised of seventeenth-century capital cities there was no mistaking the signs that the government was beginning to wish itself well rid of such embarrassing guests. Just how embarrassing they might be was made plain one day early in March when Blake arrived off the Tagus with a squadron of eleven warships and four auxiliary vessels to demand the surrender or expulsion of the Royalist fleet. Although Rupert was by his own account now ready for sea[6] he knew that he was no match for a force on paper little stronger than his own but well-manned, well-found and officered by professionals. He played for time and was rewarded by the arrival of two French warships which shewed their sympathies by anchoring with the Royalist fleet. Blake's men grew impatient. In the middle of April some of them attacked Rupert and a party of his followers as they were returning from hunting. Rightly or wrongly Rupert chose to regard this an an attempt on his person which presumably entitled him to retaliate in kind. Never one to miss the opportunity of experiment he devised a primitive time-bomb concealed in a barrel which he gave to one of his soldiers, suitably disguised as a Portuguese, to smuggle aboard the *Leopard* the flagship of Blake's Vice-Admiral. The man was discovered and captured before he had planted the infernal machine, but incidents of this sort can hardly have reassured the unhappy Portuguese. Their fears were intensified by the arrival on May 26th of strong English reinforcements under Popham with clear and uncompromising instructions. No further prevarication

was to be tolerated; and if the French ships at present in Lisbon wanted a
fight they were very welcome. On June 6th the Portuguese were presented
with an ultimatum. On the 13th the English seized all Portuguese fishing
vessels off the mouth of the Tagus. Portugal was a small country with a
large, rich and vulnerable colonial empire from which the Dutch had
already begun to take what they wanted. A naval war with England in
support of the hopelessly defeated Stuart cause would have been disastrous as well as pointless. Politely but firmly Rupert was told that he
must sail at the first opportunity and he was promised the assistance of
the Portuguese fleet and the two French ships in obstructing any attack
that might be made on him as he came out of harbour.

Accordingly on July 26th Rupert hoisted the standard and weighed
anchor. The Portuguese admiral had some trouble, real or pretended, in
hauling in his anchor so that by the time the Royalists were in range of the
Parliamentary fleet he was just setting sail. At this point the wind shifted
and then failed. After a night and a day of inconclusive manœuvring the
sortie was abandoned. Much the same happened on September 7th, the
next occasion on which the Royalists tried to escape, except that in a brief
action Blake brought down Rupert's foretopmast. Tempers on all sides
were getting shorter. On September 14th Blake relieved the irritation of
his long vigil by attacking the Portuguese Brazil fleet, taking thirteen
prizes and sinking two more. This was but the first instalment of the
heavy damages exacted from the Portuguese for their ill-judged kindness
to Prince Rupert.

On October 12th, 1650, the Royalist fleet at last cleared the Tagus and
shaped a course for the Mediterranean. The fleet was now reduced to six
ships, two of the original three flag ships, the *Constant Reformation* and the
Swallow, two of the original frigates and two rather more powerful vessels
that had been fitted out in Lisbon.[7] How well they were manned it is not
possible to say except that they can hardly have had an adequate complement. Shortly after his arrival in Lisbon Rupert had written to the King
that he had twelve hundred men on board.[8] Evidently a good number of
the crews of the prizes had entered his service, as was the common practice

in the seventeenth century. Probably the arrival of the Parliamentary fleet
had attracted a good few of them back. Certainly disease would have
accounted for a number more. And it is difficult to see where any recruits
could have come from. At a guess, nine hundred to a thousand men would
probably be optimistic.

At first everything went swimmingly. There was no sign of Blake's
fleet. Two days out from the Tagus Rupert took a couple of prizes. One of
the frigates parted company from the fleet to chase a Frenchman, but this
proved an unfortunate exploit as she met Blake's fleet who promptly
captured the French ship themselves. What conceivable right either
Rupert or Blake had to attack and seize a ship belonging to a country with
which neither of them was at war and to which the Royalists indeed
were under considerable obligation is by no means clear. But as Hobbes
was to point out a few years later, ''tis not wisdom but authority that
makes a law'. One of the services rendered to civilisation by the establishment of powerful regular navies was the reduction of the more or less
permanent piracy in which even quite respectable governments had been
prepared to join. To read the memoirs of a foreign-going seaman of the
time such as Edward Coxere[9] is to be left wondering how men or money
could be attracted into so infinitely hazardous an undertaking. And yet,
against all odds, men signed on and ships sailed on voyages for which the
rewards were altogether disproportionate to the dangers. One of the prizes
taken by Rupert on his entry to the Mediterranean was the *Marmaduke* of
London bound from Archangel to Leghorn.[10] To reflect on the dangers
and hardships of that voyage is to understand something of the courage
and enterprise that have gone into the construction of an international
economy whose benefits we take for granted. Apart from what sea and
weather could do to a wooden ship in those cold, forsaken northern waters,
apart from navigating a sailing ship without any of the aids now regarded
as indispensable, the *Marmaduke* would have had to run the gauntlet of
Scandinavian privateers licensed to prey on shipping in the anarchy of the
incessant Northern wars, of the Dutch with whom a fierce and prolonged
struggle was on the point of erupting, of the Dunkirkers who swarmed in

the Channel, of the French who were at war with the Spaniards and of the Spaniards who were at war with the French. The *Marmaduke* survived all these perils to be chased and attacked and eventually captured, after a stout defence in which her captain was killed, by her own countrymen. She surrendered some thirty or forty miles from Tunis, not so very far from the port for which she was making. Perhaps if she had escaped Rupert she would have fallen a victim, as so many English ships and seamen did, to the Barbary pirates who infested the southern Mediterranean until the nineteenth century. But it is hard not to feel a sense of outrage at the wanton frustration of useful endeavour: and, more particularly, at the gilding of such acts with laudatory phrases about honour and the King.

Retribution came swiftly. On November 2nd Blake captured one frigate and chased three others into Cartagena where three days later their captains ran them ashore to avoid capture. It was a blow from which Rupert's fleet never recovered. The two flag ships were in any case separated by violent weather. Prince Maurice in the *Swallow*, reached Toulon with a prize on November 25th, but Rupert in the *Constant Reformation*, blown far to the eastward, only struggled in at the end of December. The friendliness of the French authorities enabled them to careen their ships and to fit out the prize as a man-of-war. By spending the last of his loot Rupert was able to buy and fit out a fourth ship; and a certain Captain Craven who had a ship at Marseilles volunteered to join the fleet. Thus by the summer of 1651 it again numbered five ships; but its effective strength is best indicated by Rupert's eagerness to leave the Mediterranean for remoter seas.

To trace the ups and downs of this vagrant force in every detail would be irrelevant to the purpose of this book which is only concerned with Rupert's fleet because it was there that Sir Robert Holmes served his apprenticeship to, and first exercised, command at sea. Readers who desire a fuller and more particular narrative are referred to Dr. R. C. Anderson's articles in the *Mariners Mirror* to which acknowledgment has already been made. The disaster at Cartagena changed the character of the force. One of the frigate Captains was accused of being on suspiciously good terms with Blake. Another, Allin, who had escaped from prison after his frigate was captured off Kinsale and had rejoined the fleet in Lisbon, was court martialled for cowardice and only avoided execution by escaping once again. Seventeen years later when Allin had become one of the most trusted and reliable senior officers of Charles II's Navy, Pepys as he sat over the wine after dinner was astonished to hear the story from Sir George Carteret, the Treasurer of the Navy, who had sheltered Allin in Jersey of which he had then been Governor.[11] Sir John Mennes also seems to have left the fleet about this time; indeed there is no mention of him after its arrival at Lisbon. Two other Captains quarrelled so bitterly that one refused to serve if the other were not dismissed. A third who had been given the command of a prize taken from the Genoese deserted taking ship and crew along with him. Nothing is recorded of what the men felt or how many of them took the first opportunity to desert. But it is hard to believe that the disintegrating morale of the officers left the seamen in good heart.

Rupert's ultimate objective was the West Indies, where several of the islands were still in the hands of staunch Royalists. To get there he proposed to sail down the African coast as far as the Cape Verde Islands and from there to stretch across the Atlantic. But his plans were flexible. He could not afford to loiter in the Mediterranean but he was in no hurry to arrive in the West Indies. He was in urgent need of prizes and any other loot he could pick up, and he wanted in particular to pay off a score or two against the Spaniards whom he held largely responsible for the loss of his ships at Cartagena. All these secondary objects were successfully accomplished. A number of prizes were taken, including a Spanish galleon homeward bound from the Indies, and the proceeds disposed of in Madeira, where the Portuguese governor received the two Princes with every civility. According to Rupert's own account[12] it was at this point that his officers got wind of his plan to make for the West Indies and at once divided into two parties, of which the stronger was against venturing so far from home. At a council of war which Rupert held in the hope of obtaining general assent to his proposal to sail southward to the Cape Verde

Islands to victual the ships, it was decided to make instead for the Azores where they arrived in July 1651. While they were victualling there, a process unnecessarily drawn out by the disaffected party, stormy weather forced them to leave harbour, hoping to return and take on the rest of their stores as soon as the wind and the sea had slackened. Instead of easing, it came on to blow a full gale and they had no choice but to run before it. Three days of this was too much for the timbers of the *Constant Reformation*. She sprang a bad leak which was with great difficulty stopped by forcing a hundred and twenty pieces of raw beef into the hole and stanchioning them down. The relief was short-lived, for the violence of the sea drove in the stanchion and the whole plank with it. This was on the morning of September 30th. It was clear that she could not last more then a few hours. Rupert, who must have seen that there was small hope of rescue, shewed his usual imperturbable courage. Only two ships, the *Swallow* with Prince Maurice on board, and the *Honest Seaman* had kept company with the Admiral and could be seen from time to time through the driving spray whipped off the wild seas. Both the *Constant Reformation* and the *Swallow* had lost their pinnaces early on. The captain of the *Honest Seaman* risked his ship by bringing her alongside the weather bow of the flagship but no one took advantage of this fine piece of seamanship, 'their resolutions being to die together'.[13] The difficulty of communication made things impossible for the rescuers. 'From the Admiral's deck they waved the ships so confusedly that they knew not what to do.'[14] At last from Rupert's gesticulations it appeared that he wanted to give his final instructions to his brother. Maurice told his officers to bring the *Swallow* under the stern of the *Constant Reformation* but they preferred to keep off a little, so that the brothers were unable to hear each other above the roaring of the wind and the sea. In spite of Rupert's determination to die with his men, he was at last induced to board a small boat from the *Honest Seaman*[15] which in the two trips it was able to make before it was swamped brought him off together with half a dozen of his personal attendants and the Captain of the ship. It is very possible that Holmes was among them. Certainly his successor as page was; and his companion in arms, Mortaigne, was one of those specifically named by Rupert for a place in the second, and final, trip though he declined the opportunity. In spite of the Prince's urgent efforts to save more of his shipmates it proved impossible to do so, as the *Constant Reformation*, her mainmast and all her sails gone, drove helplessly into those merciless seas. At nine o'clock that night the lights she had been burning suddenly went out. She took three hundred and thirty men with her to the bottom and a considerable treasure amassed from several months of commerce raiding.

The magnitude of this loss and the hard feelings caused by the apparent reluctance of the Captain and officers of the *Swallow* to risk anything for anyone except themselves reduced the strength and spirit of the fleet. It also had a marked and immediate effect on the attitude of the Portuguese authorities in the Azores. To make matters worse they found on their return that Captain Craven's ship which had joined them as a volunteer had dragged her anchors and been smashed to pieces in the storm. A change of scene became imperative. Early in December they sailed for the Canaries and after a short stay they anchored in a natural harbour on the African coast just south of Cape Blanco where they could careen the ships and fit them for the Atlantic passage without fear of being attacked unawares. The ships' companies lived ashore in tents while their vessels were heeled over on the ground to have the bottoms scraped free of weed and sheathed against the ship-worm. It was a long job—between four and five weeks—but they had a long voyage in front of them.

IV

Prince Rupert's Cruise—II

IT IS ALMOST AS DIFFICULT to overstate the expectation of easy
wealth with which a seventeenth-century European approached the
west coast of Africa as it is to find any rational basis for it. The
Portuguese, the Dutch, the English, the Swedes, the Danes and other less
considerable maritime nations competed keenly for the prizes it was
thought to offer.[1] The student of balance-sheets, in England at any rate,
might feel less sanguine. The first company that had traded along the
coast, the charmingly named Gynney and Bynney Company,* had made
spectacular losses. Over £7,000 had been invested in the first three
voyages of the years 1618, 1619 and 1620 on which the return was a loss
of £5,600.[2] The second company which received a charter in 1631
granting it a monopoly of trade between Cape Blanco and the Cape of
Good Hope showed no profit until 1636 when its first successful voyage
brought home £30,000 worth of gold.[3] This was one of the few winning
tickets in a large lottery of blanks.

One of the others was, in course of time, to be cashed by Sir Robert
Holmes. It must have seemed improbable in January 1652 that a man of
twenty-nine, no longer young as age was reckoned in the seventeenth
century, a penniless exile, a veteran of many battles who had been seriously
wounded once already and was now on a coast famous for its killing diseases,
should survive an expedition already tainted with disaster to achieve place,
prosperity and power. From the barren, friendless coast of Cape Blanco
to substantial estates in Wales and Ireland, in Hampshire and the Isle
of Wight was a strange voyage. To Prince Rupert perhaps it might not
have seemed so. Only three years older than Holmes as soldier, prisoner,

* Guinea and Benin, to use the modern forms.

Commander-in-Chief, as a Prince of the blood driven from his own country, as a favourite publicly repudiated and then recalled, he had experienced the vicissitudes of life. During the sunlit period of his first visit to England before the Civil War he had, as it happened, been appointed Governor of the African company founded in 1631.[4] He must therefore have been aware of the high hopes excited by the encouraging results for 1636. Even to less desperate men a visit to the fabulous Gold Coast would have seemed a worthwhile gamble. Small wonder, then, that he determined to find out all he could about the land and its inhabitants while his ships were refitting.

Unfortunately Cape Blanco was not the best place to do so. That part of the African coast had no communication or connexion with the rich, well-watered littoral between Cape Verde and the Bight of Benin. Empty and arid, its only visitants were the Dutch and Flemish fishermen who came there to catch mullet, and the Moorish nomads who found an exiguous pasture for their cattle. With these Rupert tried to converse but as they habitually fled at his approach he shewed his displeasure by shooting one of their camels. The rider and his wife easily got a lift on another but, in the confusion, left behind their little boy and a good number of cattle. Rupert hoped that these would prove a decisive bargaining counter but in the ensuing negotiations he obtained no intelligence and lost a couple of men. A day or two before the ships were ready for sea he determined on a final attempt to corner the Moors and make them talk. He accordingly landed sixty men under the command of Captain* Robert Holmes about twenty miles east-south-east of the Cape, marching to meet them himself with a rather larger body from the opposite direction. They were then to form a cordon tightening on the coast. Against slow-moving European troops this manœuvre might well have succeeded; but the Moors though caught unawares in the net slipped through without anyone so much as sighting them.[5] In this militarily insignificant incident Holmes, by holding his first recorded independent command, may be held to have served out his apprenticeship.

* His Captaincy referred to the rank he had held in the Army.

While in harbour at Cape Blanco Rupert had made contact with a Dutch fishing vessel whose master had contracted to supply him with fresh water and deal boards for his ships from a small Dutch station a few miles down the coast. Since the man proved trustworthy Rupert decided to freight his vessel with such prize goods as he had—mostly sugar and ginger from the captured Spanish galleons—and send her to a French port with letters to the King. From these we learn that the fleet that put out to sea 'cleansed, fitted, and new-rigged' on January 26th, 1652, consisted of three ships; the *Swallow* (40-guns), the *Revenge* (40-guns) and the *Honest Seaman* (40-guns).[6] Spending three weeks watering and victualling in the Cape Verde islands (the purchase of a thousand dried goats[7] throws a sombre light on the dietary of the expedition) they embarked some Portuguese soldiers and two Portuguese pilots to accompany them, at the Governor's suggestion, on a voyage up the Gambia River. Arriving off the river about February 26th, the Portuguese pilots contrived to run both the *Swallow* and the *Revenge* aground. Luckily they were got off without much damage: luckier still Rupert found a ship belonging to the Duke of Courland at anchor in the river, the *Krokodil*, whose Captain kindly offered his services as a pilot. Once inside the river they surprised and overwhelmed the English ships they found at anchor. The first of them, the *John*, a small vessel engaged in trading along the coast, yielded an invaluable and intrepid native interpreter known as Captain Jacus who attached himself to the expedition for the rest of its stay on the coast. The journal of the *Swallow* which records the capture on February 29th, adds: 'Mr. Holmes was sent aboard commander.' Thus he received his first command at sea only five or six weeks after his first independent command as a soldier.

The next day Prince Maurice captured the large ocean-going ship to which the *John* had acted as a coastwise tender.[8] A small Spanish ship and another English ketch that had fled up a creek for safety completed the bag. The value of the English prizes alone was subsequently estimated at £10,000.[9] Unhappily the blacks who had betrayed her hiding-place did not appreciate that Rupert was exercising a lawful authority over

rebellious subjects vested in him by his Sacred Majesty King Charles II.
Pardonably they had put him down as just another European cut-throat
and had darted off up the river to massacre the crew of yet a third small
craft. Rupert had it made clear to them that the shedding of Christian
blood was not a privilege to be usurped by infidels. His small craft
reached as high as Elephant Island, about a hundred and fifty miles up
the river, and returned to the fleet without further incident. A few days
later having incorporated the prizes in the fleet and re-arranged the
commands they cleared the river and set a course for Cape Verde.[10]

Apart from his prizes Rupert carried away from the Gambia certain
intelligence which made him anxious to return at the earliest convenient
opportunity. Since two or three months of violent weather was expected
on the coast at that season the safety of the fleet could not be put at risk
to indulge his curiosity for the present. But one can understand his
attraction. In addition to the pleasure of seeing the unicorns in which the
country abounded and of watching the other animals at the watering
places waiting respectfully until the horn had been dipped in the water as
a signal that they might drink,[11] there was, farther up the river, 'a
mountaine of gold', 'rather a firme rock of pure gould than mixed', 'the
whole discovery his Highness hath found amongs their [the Company's]
papers'.[12] No wonder that Rupert lost no time after the Restoration in
promoting an expedition to the Gambia. No wonder that, when ill-
health prevented his going in person, Holmes should take his place.

The immediate future, however, offered more danger than profit. As
they sailed back up the coast towards Cape Verde some of the slower ships
dropped astern. To give them time to catch up Rupert anchored off a small
town from which, as he had Captain Jacus aboard, he thought he might
buy some fresh provisions. This was arranged by Jacus to everyone's
satisfaction but in the comings and goings of the canoes an African member
of Prince Maurice's ship's company took the opportunity of going ashore
to visit his parents without the formality of asking leave. Worse, although
a convert to Christianity, he seems to have preferred home life among the
heathen to reporting back on board. Rupert, finding requests for his

return ineffectual, determined on force. He took a hundred men in a ketch close inshore off the town, sending a smaller boat to secure a landing place in a nearby creek. Unfortunately he had reckoned without the surf which tossed the boat over and tumbled her crew into the breakers. As they struggled up the beach winded and half-stunned they found themselves surrounded by an ever-increasing throng of excited and potentially hostile Africans. Never one to leave his men unsupported in a tight corner, Rupert ordered Holmes to take some musketeers in another boat and to cover them from the sea. But while he was trying to get close enough to the shore to give them some protection the surf caught him and toppled him and his musketeers out like so many matchsticks.

Things now looked very ugly. But the situation was transformed by the timely arrival of Captain Jacus whose attention had been aroused by the hubbub on the beach. He boldly undertook responsibility for all the Europeans and even induced his compatriots to hand them back their belongings. Rupert thereupon sent another well-manned boat which successfully re-embarked all the Europeans but, owing to a stupid misunderstanding of his orders, the officer in charge landed Holmes and another man to persuade Jacus to come off as well. At this point Prince Maurice's pinnace captured an African canoe that had ventured too far out. Most unluckily one of the Africans was shot and killed in full view of everyone. Naturally enough Holmes and his companion were at once seized, roughly handled and carried off under a strong guard. None of the watchers from the ships can have given much for their chances of survival.

Rupert, considering himself personally responsible for their predicament 'resolved to bring them off or perish'.[13] Wisely, his first expedient was the diplomacy of Captain Jacus. There was, after all, a canoeful of Africans to exchange against the two Englishmen. A day passed: a long day for Holmes and his companion held close prisoner by people with whom no communication was possible but who were clearly angry and probably savage. No result was achieved; no report reached the ships. Next morning Rupert manned all the pinnaces and took his own within hailing distance of the shore. Contact was established with Jacus who had

got his countrymen to agree to the release of the prisoners as soon as they
could see their own captured canoe clear of the English ships. Rupert
gave a signal, and a few moments later the canoe could be seen racing for
the shore. Jacus, realising too late that his own people did not mean to
keep their part of the bargain, rushed down the beach shouting to Rupert
to retake the canoe. But even without a long start a stout English sea-boat
had no chance against a lithe African canoe.

There was nothing for it now but a resort to force, culminating in all
probability in that tactical nightmare, an opposed landing on an exceptionally difficult coast. The chances of success were slight and of complete
disaster very high. The one advantage that the Europeans might be
thought to have, namely superior weapons, was nullified, if not reversed,
by the circumstances. The natives, who showed no sign of fear or reluctance,
sent a large party into the sea up to their necks to meet the pinnaces, so
that when the Englishmen presented their muskets—tricky work in the
lurching and tossing of a breaking sea—the Africans dived under water to
avoid the shot, reappearing a moment later to give the boats a volley of
arrows. Within a few minutes Rupert was hit just above the left breast.
Although it was a deep wound he asked for a knife and cut the arrow out
himself. The moral courage shewn in risking everything to save men who
had been endangered through carrying out orders was matched by the
physical courage with which the enterprise was executed. But where it
would all have ended, if at this point Jacus had not succeeded in
spiriting the two English prisoners away in the general excitement to a
bay the other side of the town and signalling to one of the other pinnaces
to pick them up, is a matter for speculation. Rupert sent Jacus a message
of thanks and an offer to take him on board at a harbour further up the
coast if he should think it prudent to leave the country. But Jacus, even
from so brief a glimpse a salesman of genius, politely refused, 'saying he
had done nothing he should fear to justify'.

Holmes's first visit to Africa had not been wanting in excitement or in
dramatic turns of fortune. No doubt at one moment it had looked as if it
was going to end very unpleasantly, but it had given him his first experi-

ence of command, the ambition and the business of his life. He had heard about the mountain of pure gold which was just the kind of mountain to appeal to him. There might be something in the story. But facts were facts: it was the deck of his own ship he was treading as he saw the African coast drop away from his starboard quarter and lose itself in the haze of the horizon.

At the Cape Verde Islands the fleet took in stores and provisions for the passage to the West Indies. Two English merchantmen came in and anchored close to the *Revenge*, never suspecting her true colours. They were taken at once and sent the next day, under the convoy of Holmes in the *John*, to join Prince Maurice in the harbour of Santiago, another of the islands. The limits to these successes were set by the small number of officers and soldiers who could command the prizes. To dilute beyond a certain point was to risk mutiny since most of the seamen in the captured ships wanted to get home to England at the earliest possible moment. A week after Holmes had sailed with the prizes, exactly such a result occurred. The seamen of the *Revenge* overpowered their officers and got clear away. On the balance of this transaction the Royalists had lost as the *Revenge* was a larger and better-found ship then either of the merchantmen, one of which was so sluggish that Rupert made a present of her to a religious community in Santiago. On May 9th, 1652, he sailed from that harbour for the West Indies. His fleet consisted certainly of five, perhaps of six, ships, among them the *John*. Designed for trading up the creeks and rivers of West Africa she can hardly have been comfortable in an Atlantic swell.

The course steered by the expedition should have brought them to a landfall in Barbados, an island which they knew to be staunch to the Stuart cause and from which the prevailing winds would carry them easily to such other of the West Indies as might be suitable for a base. About one hundred and fifty miles east of Barbados the *Swallow*, Rupert's flagship, sprang a bad leak, so bad indeed that she had to run before the wind, while pumping and baling left no time for navigation. As a result the fleet sailed past Barbados during the night of May 26th and first sighted land late the next afternoon. Finding that this was Grenada and St. Vincent and that Barbados must therefore be far to windward they stood for the then uninhabited island of St. Lucia where they anchored on the 29th. They found abundance of wood and fresh water and plenty of hogs and goats running wild which together with fresh fruit improved their health and spirits. Almost at once the leak was brought under control, 'insomuch that we gave over baling to the great ease of our men and the comfort of us all'.[14]

The political situation was less encouraging. A Parliamentary fleet under Ayscue had subdued Barbados as long ago as January 11th when Rupert and Holmes had been stalking the Moors of Cape Blanco. By March the last Royalist supporters in the other islands had capitulated. Ayscue had left for England taking with him a number of prizes on May 25th, a bare two days before the *Swallow* had limped in. Any hope of finding a base that could supply men and materials and a more than day to day security must be finally written off. On the other hand the steadily worsening relations of the English Republic with the other countries of Europe won the Royalist fleet a notably friendly reception from the French and Dutch possessions.

As soon as the *Swallow* was fit for sea and her men recovered from their exertions Rupert embarked on a characteristically active policy. On June 3rd he was at Martinique: on the 4th at Guadeloupe: on the 5th Montserrat where he did not let the fact of its being Whitsunday deter him from attacking and taking two small English ships. On the 7th he attacked some ships in the harbour of Nevis and took another prize. On the 10th he returned to Guadeloupe and proposed to the Governor that they should concert plans for an attack on the English possessions. The Governor declined. His backwardness made Rupert doubt the safety of a French anchorage. Accordingly he sailed a few days later for the Virgin Islands, a then uninhabited archipelago with a great number of natural harbours. Choosing one hitherto known by the homely title of Dixon's Hole but subsequently renamed Cavaliers Harbour or Rupert's Bay he careened and refitted the *Swallow*, the *Defiance* and the *Honest Seaman* and another vessel, stripping three of the smaller ships including the *John* of masts, spars and rigging to make good the defects of the larger. Though there was plenty of wood and water, food was short: everyone, including Rupert, was given a ration of four ounces of cassava bread per day. Some of the carpenter's party, sent to cut wood along the coast, stole the long-boat and deserted to the Spanish colony of Puerto Rico. At the end of August Rupert burned the hulks of the three ships he had dismantled and put to sea.

For the next fortnight the little fleet cruised off the Virgins. On September 13th disaster overtook them. Seventy miles north of Sombrero they were caught in a hurricane. In a few minutes it became impossible to see more than a cable's length ahead or to manage the ships. The *Swallow* miraculously escaped wreck, first on Sombrero itself and then on the rocks between Anagada and the Virgins. On the 17th, torn and battered, she reached a safe anchorage at St. Ann's Island, one of the Virgins. Next day she returned to Cavaliers Harbour where Holmes who was aboard the *Swallow*[15] could still see the charred remnants of the *John* and could thank his luck that her obsequies had been conducted in the nick of time. She would not have lasted many minutes in such a sea. The *Swallow* had been the only ship of the four to come through it. Captain Craven* of the *Honest Seaman* and his ship's company survived both shipwreck on the coast of Hispaniola and several weeks as castaways during which they kept themselves alive by hunting turtles. The *Defiance*, in which Prince Maurice was, and the merchantman were never seen again. Reports of their fate, and particularly of Maurice having escaped from the wreck only to be imprisoned, were not slow to come in and persisted for a decade. In a collection of statements on the subject made in the years 1662 and 1663[16] there is general agreement that the *Defiance* was wrecked on the Virgin Islands and that the Prince and a few of the crew survived and were taken prisoner by the Spaniards. Some say they were all massacred: but the

---

* The volunteer who had brought his own ship, the *Loyal Subject*, to join Rupert in the South of France. The *Loyal Subject* had been wrecked on the Azores in the storm that accounted for the *Constant Reformation*.

majority affirm that Maurice was imprisoned in Puerto Rico. A certain Thomas Masters swore to Sir William Coventry that he had twice met a Royalist survivor called Joshua Clarke at Caracas, 'where an English surgeon, taking good liking to this Clarke, preserved him'. The confused statement of an Englishman who was carried off and imprisoned by the Spaniards while turtle-fishing in the Virgins implies that he, too, was a survivor. But had there been any substance in the rumours about Prince Maurice Rupert would never have sailed away and left him in a Spanish dungeon. He had already risked the whole expedition to rescue Holmes on the African coast; he would certainly have done as much for the brother to whom he was most deeply attached. It was Holmes who, twelve years later, was to clear away the last shreds of mystery surrounding his death.*

The fleet was now reduced to one old, storm-beaten warship that had been too long in tropical waters for the health of her timbers. Even under a fighting leader of Rupert's quality it could not achieve any results proportionate to the risks. Quick prizes and the first fair wind for the French Atlantic ports were the aim. Although hardly yet fit for sea the *Swallow* was forced by shortage of supplies to leave her familiar anchorage on September 25th. Everything depended on meeting a well-found but not too powerful vessel that could be pillaged to supply every deficiency. But Rupert's luck was out. Last time there had been too much wind: this time there was not enough. For six broiling days they were becalmed off Montserrat. At last the wind freshened and they caught a small 10-gun ship, probably from New England, and took her into Guadeloupe. The Governor was most friendly, allowing them to buy whatever they needed, even wine, which was regarded as a great mark of favour. He also gave Rupert the news of the outbreak of war between Holland and the English Republic. A Dutch ship that came in while they were there told them of three English merchantmen lying in Five Island Harbour, Antigua, under the protection of a large gun mounted ashore. This was towards the end of October. Sailing at once Rupert entered the harbour on the 30th and

* See below p. 125.

landed fifty men under Holmes's command. The defence was soon overwhelmed whereupon the ships surrendered.

A final cruise in November yielded a number of small prizes and one
large vessel most opportunely loaded with provisions. This removed the
last obstacle to a homeward passage. Five days were spent in the Dutch
harbour of St. Eustatius taking in fresh water and other necessaries.
Another five days in Cavaliers Harbour and they were ready for sea. On
December 12th, 1652, Rupert in the *Swallow* accompanied by four
prizes under the command of Robert Holmes[17] set sail for Europe. On
January 16th they anchored at the island of Fayal in the Azores, but found
the Governor a great deal less accommodating then he had been the year
before. In fact he fired on the *Swallow*, scoring a direct hit on her bows, and
refused to allow a boat to land. Similar treatment at the other islands
showed that Portugal was signing no more blank cheques for the Stuart
cause. Rupert held on his course for the mouth of the Loire.

On March 3rd the look-out sighted Belleisle dead ahead at nine in the
evening. To keep clear of so dangerous a coast during darkness they stood
out to sea. Next morning they entered the river and dropped anchor off
St. Nazaire. The guns of the castle and of a Dutch squadron in the port
fired salutes which the *Swallow* returned. She was nineteen years old and
had been two years in the tropics without docking.

To take her higher up the river to Paimboeuf (further up the estuary
than St. Nazaire and at that time a port of some consequence) Rupert had
to employ a Loire pilot who ran her aground on a steep bank in the middle
of the river. Thanks to Rupert's bold seamanship in trimming her, first by
hauling all the guns to one side and then as the flood tide took her shifting
them back she was righted and brought safely off at high water. Like the
Constant Reformation she was freighted with all the most valuable loot.
Having seen her safe to her anchorage Rupert set out for Paris, leaving
Holmes in charge of her and of all the prizes and prize goods.

V

Temporary Retirement

ALL THROUGH THE SPRING and the summer of 1653 Holmes was busy winding up the affairs of the expedition. This was a complex task involving the safekeeping and transport of valuable cargoes, the paying off of men, the settling of debts, the care and maintenance of the ships and of their rigging and armament which in turn involved the hiring of local labour and dealing with various officials and merchants. It involved also making arrangements for the sale of the ships and of their equipment. It meant firm but tactful handling of senior officers—Captain Fearns, Rupert's flag-captain in the *Swallow* and earlier in the *Constant Reformation* was an older man with a much longer experience of command. The twin problems of Stuart administration with which Pepys's *Diary* has made the world familiar—how to frustrate the dishonest practices of one's colleagues or superiors and how to get a quart out of a pint pot—ran through every day's business. Rupert himself took an interest in all these matters but it was hardly possible for him to superintend them in person. He was in poor health; and Charles II's commands as well as the settling of his own affairs required his presence in Paris.

A number of Holmes's letters to Rupert written during these months have been preserved. On April 14th he dated a letter from aboard H.M.S. *Hopewell* at Paimboeuf to the Prince 'att Palles Royale'. The senior officers had been taking advantage of Rupert's absence to throw their weight about:

> On Friday last Captain Fearmes [Fearns] and Mr. Pyne went aboard of an English shipp (notwithstanding your Highness's orders obeyed by me) and borrowed a long boat, myne ridinge by the shipp not imployd though as well, if not better, able to doe that service. I gave Captain Fearmes a small hint of it.

The mallie [mêlée] between Captain Fortescue and him is drownd and a new love highly begun.[1]

The tone of this passage shows the ease and confidence of a subordinate officer who knows that his judgment will be trusted and his decisions backed up by his Commander-in-Chief. The faint irony with which he evokes the sillinesses of two huffy and bibulous old codgers suggests that Rupert had chosen well. The rest of the letter is, like so much of Rupert's own correspondence, detailed and practical. He reports that he is stripping the frigate of guns, topmasts and yards. Most of the ship's companies had already dispersed; 'we have scarce men left in all the ships to way [sic] the Admiral's* anchors'. A fortnight later trouble has arisen through Fearns's failure to keep an accurate and thorough record:

> The great chest of Indigo your Highness commanded you out of the *Hopewell* is not mentioned at all by Captain Fearmes . . . though a barrell of Indigo be stolen out of the Admiral's [hold as] Captain Fearmes affirmes whose diurnall I have sent your Highness.[2]

Holmes goes on to explain his arrangements to sell the goods and stores 'at the dearest penny' and promises to send 'the little Neger† and the chest of Jacoletto'.

His next report written from Nantes on May 17th[3] shows him in the the thick of things. He has just received Rupert's order for 'two eliphants teeth and a barr of steel' which he will furnish as soon as possible though the steel is at 'Penbeef' (Paimboeuf) whence he has only that morning returned from putting down 'a very great mutiny' among the French, 'which I endeavoured to passifye with as much gentle mildness as possible could be, though they came with their swords in their hands against me ready drawn.' As the dismantling of the ships and the disposal of the cargoes went on apace the workmen naturally became anxious to have their wages paid. The same effect was produced in the few remaining members of the crew: 'as soone as they were here informed of your Highness's order

---

* I.e. the *Swallow*'s. Down to the eighteenth century the Admiral nearly always means the senior ship of a fleet, not the officer who flew his flag in her.

† Probably the child captured at Cape Blanco (see p. 42).

for the removall of the shipps the seamen and souldiers aboard the Admirall in general mutinied for money.'

Difficulties and disobedience were not confined to the seamen and the dockyard workmen. Captain Fearns still refused to produce any accounts 'although I have importund him'. He and his two cronies, Captain Fortescue and Captain Michell, have been living aboard the ships at Paimboeuf in spite of Rupert's strict orders to the contrary—Holmes told them to go ashore. Michell disputed his authority and his reasons and announced his intention of leaving for Paris 'being assured by Captain Fearmes that I am his chief adversary in this business'.

In spite of all this—and of the unexplained suicide of Rupert's sergeant—matters are being reduced to order. The gunners' accounts have already been sent to Paris; the stores accounts will be forwarded in a day or two. The powder and the guns are to be safely lodged in the French magazine. Even the ballast is to be scrutinised:

> I am informed by a soldier that there are some eliphant's teeth which lay hid in the ballast, being of that informed by the Master's Mate who is long since gone from hence . . . I hope that your Highness will be pleased to harbour no ill opinion of mee of any neglect of your businesse: here are marchants who desire to buy the flyboat,* gunns and iron . . . I doubt not your Highness receaved the samples of the sugar† which I sent along with the little Neger and some part of the Jocoletto. If your Highness please to have the rest I shall desire your orders.

Apparently this confidence was ill-founded. Although the Neger and the Jacoletto arrived at Paris in good order the sugar seems to have disappeared on the way.[4]

A week later the end of the job is in sight. Full particulars of the sugar and ivory so far discharged have already been sent. There remain still to dispose of four and a half hogsheads of indigo, two hogsheads of sugar, '4 or 5 tunns of Ginger without baggs and 2 skins of synamont' [cinnamon], twenty-four elephant's teeth and one chest of copper bars.[5] A Spanish merchant wants to buy the flyboat and is thought likely to make a

* A small merchantman.
† Still in the mid-seventeenth century an expensive luxury.

good offer. The powder and cannon are on their way to the magazine whose keeper 'was pleased with very high expressions of affection to promise your Highness the choice of his rooms for putting your powder, stores and guns'.[6]

An interesting interruption to these labours was provided by the arrival at Nantes of Captain Craven who had not been heard of since his ship the *Honest Seaman* had disappeared with the others in the hurricane off Sombrero. On June 2nd he wrote to Rupert to apologise for losing his ship and for failing to keep the rendezvous. Four days later Holmes wrote[7] from Port Louis, further up the coast near Lorient: 'Captain Craven and his cousin are come hither poore and much destitute of money: pray be pleased to acquaint his Highness with it and what care shall be taken of them. I have no moneyes left to supply my own present want more than what I borrow.' After tidying up the last details about the disposal of the rigging and the guns from the frigate and the flyboat he concludes: 'Sir, the small remnant of people left here are in much disorder cryinge out for money. Unless some course be taken very speedily I believe they will all be gone.'[8]

What was Holmes doing at Port Louis, half way from Nantes to Brest? Perhaps he was investigating the possibilities of employment as an officer aboard a privateer. After three years in the game he possessed a useful stock of information and experience. Five years later when Cromwell had reversed British foreign policy to ally himself with France against Spain his intelligence service reported:

'There is captain Holmes and captain Golden have gotten commissions, one from the King of Spain, and another from Charles Stuart, for each of them to set out a man of war to take prizes; and they are suddenly to go away to St. Sebastian to that purpose.'[9]

Whether this report was accurate, or, if so, whether Holmes ever commanded a Spanish privateer, are questions which the total absence of evidence makes it impossible to answer for certain. But if Holmes had actually put to sea in this capacity it seems almost inconceivable that someone somewhere, either friend or enemy, would not have mentioned the fact. If Thurloe's agents thought it worth reporting the granting of a commission they would, rightly, have thought it even more worthwhile if they had heard of him in an enemy port, arming a vessel for attacks on English ships. But whatever plans he may have had in 1658 there is no evidence that this was the motive of his journey up the Brittany coast in the summer of 1653. More probably if less romantically he was acting as a commercial traveller trying to hawk Rupert's old flagship the *Swallow*. Rupert himself evidently thought that the market for her would be better on the coast than in the estuary since he insisted on her leaving her moorings at Paimboeuf for the port of Le Croisic, a projected voyage that caused Holmes a deal of trouble. 'I purpose on Monday next to be very timely att Penbeefe to hasten away the Admirall for Crosswicke' he wrote on May 17th.[10] That his efforts were unsuccessful is clear from his letter of May 24th.[11] 'This morning we waited on the Marshall desiring his order to Captain de Lane whose shipp is at St. Nazares ready to sett sail that he might attend the *Swallow* to Crosswicke whereof there is need.' After all she had been through, including her recent grounding, she must have been an anxious craft to sail in. To add to the difficulties of the operation Captain Fearns was still her commanding officer and he was in a tricky mood, demanding money and refusing to clear his accounts. On June 6th Holmes wrote from Port Louis: 'Colonel Owen is gone to Penbeefe to invite Captain Fearmes once more to goe downe to Croswicke with the Admirall' and went on to complain that Fearns had already missed so many tides that now they were forced to hire men to go down with the Admiral. 'Go down with the Admiral' indeed they might have done. She sank at her moorings later in the year.

The affairs of the fleet wound up, Holmes disappears from history until the Restoration. There is nothing mysterious or even surprising in this. He held no official position so that nobody felt obliged to file his correspondence. A political émigré he would leave no mark in the countries of his exile. Apart from the intelligence report of 1658 already quoted there are only two or three clues to his activities. One day in the spring of 1654 an attempt was made on the life of Prince Rupert when he was returning to

Paris 'from hunting at Cam de la Reyne, with an Irishman called Holmes, a captain'.[12] The incident, which arose from Rupert's amours and had no political significance, shows that Holmes was still closely attached to him as a member of his entourage. Relations between Rupert and Charles II were at that point severely strained over the division of the proceeds from the sale of the ships and cargoes. Charles had built golden hopes on them; Rupert was determined to settle the debts incurred during the fleet's stay in French ports two years earlier and to pay his seamen their wages. As the cream of the loot had gone to the bottom with the *Constant Reformation*. there was in the end hardly enough to meet these liabilities. Charles, in a childish fury at losing the treats he had promised himself, claimed that at least he was entitled to the money paid for the *Swallow*'s guns which were Crown property. Rupert besides risking his life and injuring his health had spent a great deal of his own money on equipping the fleet. Naturally he found such a demand intolerable and counterclaimed by presenting his own accounts. There were plenty of people interested in inflaming the quarrel which soon came to an open breach. In June 1654 Rupert left Paris.[13]

'Sunday last Prince Rupert came on here from Paris with twenty-six persons, among whom are three Blackamoors and an African lad of five years old, which is part of the prey he brought over seas from those parts. He is going for Heidelberg and from thence to Vienna',[14] so wrote an English intelligence agent from Strasbourg on June 28th, 1654. It would seem probable that Holmes was one of the party but how long he followed Rupert or what exactly Rupert did for the next five or six years cannot be established. Everyone agrees that Rupert was well received by the Emperor at Vienna, that he shook the dust of the Palatinate off his feet forever after his brother the Elector had behaved disgracefully towards him, and that he spent a good deal of time in artistic and scientific experiment both at Mainz and at Vienna. Not the sort of thing that would appeal to Holmes. On the other hand there are reports, none of them very convincing, of his having taken service in the Imperial Army at different times in Hungary and North Germany. Did Holmes perhaps, like so

many Royalist, and in particular Irish, exiles, enter the Austrian service?
The inscription on his monument at Yarmouth*specifies France, Flanders
and Germany as scenes of his military exploits. France and Flanders are
accounted for by the campaign in which, as Rupert's page, he was severely
wounded, although, strangely, in the inscription they are made to follow,
not precede, his service in the Royalist fleet. It is at least clear that he was
no longer a member of Rupert's household by the time of the Restoration
in May 1660. Rupert was then in Vienna and did not return to England
until the autumn. Holmes had certainly been over in England just before
the Restoration, probably as a courier in the secret correspondence between
Charles II and Sandwich.† Why else should Sandwich note in his *Journal*
for May 2nd, 1660: 'Mr. Holmes went over to Ostend in the *Wakefield*'?
And why else should Holmes have been appointed to his first command in
the Navy, the Medway guardship *Bramble*, by the Earl of Sandwich's
commission?[15]

* Printed in Appendix II.
† Edward Mountagu, the Cromwellian General-at-Sea, Pepys's cousin and patron, who
was created Earl of Sandwich for his part in bringing about the Restoration.

VI

The Restoration Navy and the
Royal African Company

B Y THE TIME of Charles II's Restoration in 1660 the Navy begins
to rank with Parliament as one of the great formative institutions
of the nation. They were the rising stars in a historical sky from
which the twin luminaries of Church and Council were beginning to
decline. Both were on the verge of establishing that formal continuity
which had proved the foundation of ecclesiastical and royal power and
without which no real political or social pressure could be exerted or any
lasting effect be achieved. In the Middle Ages, even under the Tudors,
Parliaments were called and the Navy officered and manned only at
moments of mounting tension.

The explanation of this, to us, strange phenomenon is that both these
institutions were for centuries thought of as ultimate remedies in extreme
difficulty or danger. If Parliament was sitting or the Navy was at sea it
meant that something was up. The gradual acceptance of emergency as a
normal condition of life is the mark of political sophistication, distinguishing us from our rough and simple-minded forebears. All of us in the mid-
twentieth-century know that when a government qualifies its acts or
powers with the noun 'emergency' it means to persist in them for a very
long time. No false assumption about the past is more natural than to take
for granted that the same word or the same title means the same in one
century as it does in another. Old institutions mislead us by keeping so
many appearances unchanged.

Sir Robert Holmes became in the course of Charles II's reign both a
member of Parliament and a naval officer. We may without much effort

recollect that the House of Commons in his time was a very different place from that of Churchill, or of Gladstone or even of Fox: that its sessions only occupied a few weeks, and sometimes only a few days: that years might go by without it meeting at all: that a member probably never thought of himself as or saw himself referred to by the designation of M.P. But the words 'naval officer'; they have a comforting ring. We know where we are there, surely. The uniformed figure treading the quarterdeck alone, his telescope under his arm: the smart, clean, efficient, orderly life on shipboard: the distant stirring of 'Hearts of Oak': the stoic acceptance of unfair censure or disappointment over promotion: we see it all. But what we are really seeing is an archetype, inspired by naval officers many of us have known, tricked out with a few half-remembered details from some-one's life of Nelson, from Collingwood's letters, from Jane Austen's novels, from Captain Marryat or C. S. Forester. Sir Robert Holmes was not that sort of man at all: and the Navy he knew was not that sort of service.

To take a small point first, Holmes would have described himself as a sea-officer, not a naval officer, a term which applied only to permanent officials of the Navy Board like Pepys. He would not have worn uniform which was only introduced in the middle of the next century, about ten years before David Garrick wrote 'Hearts of Oak'. Consciousness of the Navy as an entity distinct from his country, his ship, or himself came to him, if it came at all, fitfully and by degrees. Obedience he rendered to his superior officers as he expected it from his juniors. It was the natural expression of the loyalty that is at the heart of military courage. But the loyalty of cold blood was beyond him so that he could not accept without rancour the promotion of someone else whose professional abilities he thought less than his own. Refused the post of Rear-Admiral of the White which he considered his due after the battle off Lowestoft he tore up his commission and left his ship. In the same way he recognised no general obligation to conceal any misgivings about the competence or personal courage of a brother officer. He was to cause a scandal by fighting a duel with one of his fellow flag-officers after publicly accusing him of cowardice; and it was his bitter animosity towards another that in the end undid him.

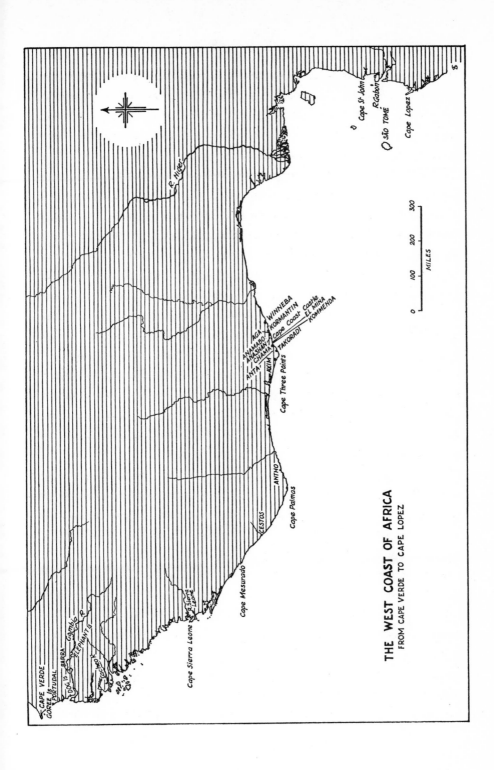

THE WEST COAST OF AFRICA
FROM CAPE VERDE TO CAPE LOPEZ

MILES
0   100   200   300

CAPE VERDE
GOREE IS.
PORTUDAL
BARRA
Gambia R.
DOG IS.
ELEPHANTS R.
CACHEO
Sierra Leone R.
Cape Sierra Leone
Cape Mesurado
CESTOS
Cape Palmas
ANTHO
Cape Three Points
ANTA
AXIM
CHAMA
ANASHAN
ANAMABO
AGA
WINNEBA
KORMANTIN
Cape Coast Castle
EL MINA
KOMMENDA
TAKORADI
R. Niger
Cape St John
R. Gabon
SÃO TOMÉ
Cape Lopez

These affairs will be dealt with in their proper place but they are instanced now to clarify certain points about the character of the Navy and the attitude of Sir Robert Holmes. His career was that of a professional officer; and incidents that might strike us as the excesses of vanity and amateurishness must be related to the context of a profession that, like Parliament, only occupied a part of life. Like Parliament too, it was not professionally exclusive. Throughout his naval service Holmes also held a commission in the land forces maintained for the defence of the Isle of Wight and even for a brief period appears to have been a Captain in the Coldstream Guards.[1] And lastly the Navy was, so to speak, the reverse of the Parliamentary coin. Parliament's growing importance in English history was founded on its power to raise money: the Navy's on its need to spend it. No other Department of State or administrative agency came near the size of its budget. There was only a tiny standing Army once Cromwell's redcoats had been paid off; there was no regular foreign service; all the great spending departments, Education, Health, Transport, Housing, Pensions, were then undreamt of. The ordinary charge of the peace-time Navy at the Restoration was estimated at £400,000 per annum. By 1670 this cost had risen to £500,000.[2] These were enormous figures by the standards of seventeenth-century public finance.

But glorious as the future of the service was to be and glittering the prizes it was to offer, Holmes was in May 1660, still in a somewhat inconspicuous position as Captain of the *Bramble*. All the same he had his foothold on the ladder. A few weeks later he exchanged her for the command of second guardship for which he received his commission from the Lord High Admiral, the Duke of York himself. He moved from her to yet another guardship and then in the autumn received the appointment through which he was to achieve prominence, the command of the *Henrietta* and of a squadron bound for West Africa with the right to fly the Union flag at the main top while out of the channel.[3] This was the long awaited reward for service on that coast with Rupert's fleet: and it is impossible not to connect it with Rupert's own return to England after an absence of fourteen years. At the same time Holmes received the first of his useful and lucrative appointments in the Isle of Wight, that of Captain and Commander of Sandown Castle.[4]

Rupert had, it seems, fired other members of the Royal Family with his vision of a mountain of pure gold. Pepys recorded in his *Diary* for October 3rd:

> This day I heard the Duke [of York] speak of a great design that he and my Lord of Pembroke have, and a great many others, of sending a venture to some parts of Africa to dig for gold ore there. They intend to admit as many as will venture their money, and so make themselves a company. 250 is the lowest share for every man. But I do not find that my Lord [Sandwich] do much like it.[5]

In spite of the sagacious reservations expressed by Sandwich plans went on apace. Besides the *Henrietta*, four other naval vessels the *Sophia, Amity, Griffin* and *Kinsale* were provided in exchange for a promise embodied in the Company's charter that the King should receive two thirds 'of all the gold mines which shall be seized, possessed and wrought in the parts and places aforesaid',[6] and should be allowed to take up a proportion of the shares if the speculation turned out well. The affairs of the company were to be managed by a committee of six which included William Coventry, who drafted Holmes's instructions, and John Vermuyden who was to accompany the expedition as its surveyor and engineer. In this function he was to be reinforced by a Frenchman, M. La Prairie, who was also to advise and report on all questions to do with gold-mining.[7]

Holmes's general instructions were simple enough: he was to afford the company's factors every assistance in promoting their trade: he was to include them as well as the commander of the troops (' the Captain of the Landsmen') in any council of war: the safe delivery of the company's cargoes and above all the materials for building a fort was to be his prime object. In this matter particular respect was to be paid to 'the opinion of Mounsr. la Prairie sent for his abilities in designing and fortifying'. Although the smaller vessels of the factors were to 'go so far up the river as occasion shall require' the *Henrietta* was 'to continue about the mouth of the river and not venture further up than may be with perfect security to His Majesty's Ship'.[8]

Besides these Holmes also received 'Private Instructions for them that goe up to the Myne in Gambia' and a copy of the Instructions for the Factors who were to take passage with him. The Private Instructions begin promisingly: 'At your arrival in the River Gambia you are to prepare with all diligence for your going up with the barges to the places directed you by the paper inclosed and take some with you (if possible) that are acquainted with the Language.' Empty casks and bags are to be filled with samples of the sand to be sent to England at the first opportunity; M. La Prairie is to make an exact map 'of the places where you take the sand and in what degree'; a detailed journal is to be kept and extracts, in duplicate, sent home with every ship; and the boats are to be brought down 'full of Gold or the richest sands'.

The Instructions for the Factors disclose the same systematic concern for general economic intelligence. Markets, prices, exchange rates, barter rates, political affiliations, all are to be recorded. The unfamiliarity of the trade is evident from the discretion left to the men on the spot: 'You are to endeavour . . . to provide such negroes, Hydes, and other goods as possibly you can to freight the *Sophia* and *Griffin* and, if you find any of the goods of that country profitable, to ballast them therewith, and if to your judgment they should not seem profitable to ballast them therewith, yet send some for trial . . .' The negroes who are mentioned in so matter-of-fact a tone were to be sold in the Canaries on the way home; if there were no market for them there they could always be sold at Cadiz or Lisbon. The vast profits of the slave trade were as yet but dimly discerned. But the Company, like their successors, were not troubled by any inconsistency between this instruction and their final injunction to Holmes and his fellow captains: '. . . they are to express in all their demeanure and conversation the benignity and candure of the English nation.'

The claim to monopoly, so characteristic of the Chartered Companies and so closely involved with the Royal prerogative,[9] reveals itself in the instructions to the Factors 'to stop all Goods aboard any of the ships and not suffer them to be sold until all the Company's are sold'. Holmes indeed proposed to William Coventry that they should take advantage of the letter of the law and seize all the goods of individual members of the expedition who were bent on doing a little trade on their own account. In a letter dated October 24th, 1660, Coventry approved the idea if the goods were to be confiscated and landed before the ships sailed but doubted the sense of waiting, as Holmes had suggested, till the expedition arrived on the coast of Africa. It does not appear that Holmes acted on this. Perhaps it would hardly have made for a harmonious and contented spirit among his shipmates to snatch away the hope of profit at the very outset of the expedition.

On November 2nd the *Henrietta* weighed in the Chatham river and Holmes made his first entry in the journal of the voyage. He spent four or five weeks at anchor off Gravesend taking in stores, and dismounting some of the *Henrietta*'s guns. Fierce westerly gales prevented him from clearing the river for another fortnight. At last on Christmas Eve, in company with the *Sophia* and the *Griffin*, he set sail. The foul weather persisted in the Channel, repeatedly forcing them to heave to and to strike yards and top-masts. On the 29th the *Griffin* had to put into Portsmouth for repairs to her rudder. On the 31st they were joined by the *Kinsale*, and the Factors who were to take passage came on board. They were ready to go, when the elements would let them. Dirty weather was followed by thick fog which gave way to dirty weather. As they rode at anchor at Spithead or off Yar-mouth, Isle of Wight, the only relief was to fire at an outward bound Dutch convoy on its way to shelter in Cowes Roads so as to make them strike their flag or to spend a few hours ashore at Portsmouth taking part in the junketings that greeted the return of the Queen from France.

At last on January 25th the weather cleared. Next day the whole fleet that had been berthed in Portsmouth or its adjacent anchorages put to sea. 'We ran out with them till Culver cliff bore N.W. by W. At half-past two we took our leave with firing of seventeen guns which were answered by the Vice-Admiral with fifteen guns.' Holmes was at sea in command of his own squadron.

Twelve days later he was joined by the last of his ships the *Amity*. They were making for Madeira where they were to take on water and beverage wine—an essential when the water was apt to become unpalatable and foul-smelling from the casks in which it was kept. They arrived at Funchal on February 11th and spent two days taking in wine and water (twenty-seven butts of beverage wine and two boat's lading of water was the *Henrietta*'s score for the first day). Just before they sailed Holmes had his first trouble over discipline: 'there happening last night some disturbance between the seamen and the soldiers I sent Captain Kirby [Captain of the landsmen] on board who brought some of the mutineers on board whereof one was this day soundly whippt by order of a Court-Martiall'.[10]

On the 17th the peak of Teneriffe was sighted. On the 19th Captain Middleton of the *Kinsale*, which had, as at Funchal, been sent on ahead to buy beverage wine, came on board to report that he had been discourteously treated by the Spanish authorities. Holmes, no doubt remembering his old grudges against the Spaniards from his days with Rupert, at once ordered the squadron to stand off 'resolving to have no dealings with the Spaniards there'. Almost immediately it came on to blow very hard so that the comfort of a sheltered anchorage together with the last opportunity of taking in wine must have presented attractions that only the sternest sense of injured dignity could resist. Fortunately the English merchants of the town sent off a boat with the welcome news that the Governor had apologised. He had been misinformed—no doubt maliciously—by a Dutch merchant that the *Kinsale* was a picaroon.* In view of what was to happen on the coast of Africa the Dutchman might have pleaded fair comment.

On March 1st they sighted Cape Verde and anchored for a few hours in the bay. There were about eight other ships in the roadstead including one Hollander and one Frenchman from Dieppe. To reach the Gambia they sailed along the coast 'till we saw a great Bank of Sand dry and the sea break upon both ends of it'. Then they steered on down the bar till they saw a breach in it and anchored in six or seven fathoms. It was Monday, March 4th.

The anchorage was protected by an island in the mouth of the river hitherto known as Dog Island, which Holmes within three days of his

* Pirate.

arrival renamed Charles Island. On the first day Holmes saw to the mounting of ten guns in the *Henrietta* which had been dismounted for the voyage. He then called a general meeting of all the commanders and factors to consult what was to be done and rounded off the proceedings by taking them all ashore to view Dog Island. That done he sent the *Griffin* up the river to Jillifri, then the chief town of the estuary, to obtain intelligence and, if possible, interpreters. She came back next day bringing some Portuguese-speaking natives.

The survey of Dog Island had revealed a suitable site for the fort. Captain Kirby and his soldiers were put ashore with their tools and materials first thing the next morning, to be joined a day later by twenty-four sailors from the *Henrietta*. In the evening Holmes received an embassy from the King of Barra. His journal for the next three or four days is full of his diplomatic treatment of them and other native visitors: 'the Blacks daily amongst us whom I caressed and entertained very civilly to gain their friendship for our People and interest'. A few days later he decided to accept the hospitality of one of these local rulers. Since his journal tells us, as a rule, little about his impressions of other people the entry in which he described this is unusually full.

> Wednesday, March 13th. This day I went ashore with Captain Stokes [of the *Amity*] and divers others to see the watering place at Combo and to visit the King of that place with 2 boats of armed men along with us for our Guard in case the Blacks should prove false to us. The King living ten miles up in the country we walked up thither where I was very civilly received by that King after their manner.
>
> It was a very hot day, no breath of wind stirring. The King accommodated me with the only horse that was there to be had, but being young and strong and Captain Stokes old, fat and burly, I let him ride and I walked, which was one of the hardest tasks that ever I undertook, the sun shining so very hot, and all our way upon dry sand it was so very hot that our Chirurgeon's mate (whom I took along with me for fear of any accident) not able to walk and keep us company fell down dead upon the way, and so did a greyhound I had with me; nay, one Mr. Fowler, a Factor, walking along with me carrying a gun upon his shoulder the excessive heat of the sun fired it off upon his shoulder, which I would not have believed if I had not taken the gun in my hand and felt the heat of it and found the cock stand at the half bent.

When I went ashore I gave orders to all the officers of the ships that they should fire no guns, except they saw some ships coming into the river; then to fire several guns to give me notice that I might make the more haste on board. After my tedious hot march in the morning I was not sat above one quarter of an hour by his Majesty who had sent for some palm wine for me and my company to drink, but the guns began to fire on board the ships, which when I heard I scarce took leave of his Majestie but flung out of his doors and marched towards my boats as hard as I could go, leaving my horse with Captain Stokes. It was in the very heat of the day that I began to march with five or six and twenty men with me. The rest came with Captain Stokes who could not endure the heat but put himself in the wood under the shadow of the trees till the cool of the evening. And my Cockswaine fell down 2 or 3 times, but the poor fellow having a great kindness for me did endeavour to get to the boats so soon as I did. All the rest of my company left upon the ground gasping for breath, when I got to the boats I ordered my pinnace to row me on board, and the rest of the boats to stay for those that were left behind.

I got on board early that afternoon. Presently at my arrival on board I called the officers of the ship to know the reason of the firing of the guns. They told me they could not tell; that they were fired on board Captain Stokes's ship. I ordered the Gunner of that ship to be sent for. When come on board I asked him whether he had not orders from his Captain not to fire any guns unless they saw a Fleet of Ships coming into the river. [He answered] that his Captain had said nothing and the occasion of his firing was that they had struck 10 or 11 of their guns at Gravesend which they hoysed up and mounted yesterday and seated them this day. Now I did heartily repent me of letting Stokes have the horse for I was so angry with him that I would have been well contented to have seen him hanged. I was 3 or 4 days so dazed in my head that I thought I should never have recovered.

If relations with the Africans were so far satisfactory grounds for conflict with the Dutch had already been given. According to them, Holmes had taken the opportunity when he touched at Cape Verde of informing the Dutch Governor that the King of England claimed the exclusive right of trade and navigation from Cape Verde to the Cape of Good Hope; by virtue of this right all Dutch forts and trading posts along the coast were to be evacuated within a few months.[11] Whether or no the commander of four very small ships would have held such high language towards the representative of the richest, strongest and best established commercial power in Africa may reasonably be questioned but cannot, since Holmes

was the man concerned, be confidently denied. What is quite certain is
that shortly after he arrived in the Gambia he took direct military action
against a small, tumbledown fort which the Dutch claimed, and Holmes
half-admitted, to be one of their garrisons.

This trivial incident was to provide matter for every Anglo-Dutch
diplomatic negotiation over the next decade.[12] The entry in Holmes's
journal for Saturday, March 16th provides an illuminating introduction
to it:

> There being a small island up the river near Julyfree [Jillifri] called St. Andreas
> inhabited by some Dutchmen pretending to be the Duke of Courland's subjects
> who had a small fort thereon and a little factory, conceiving its vicinity to be
> prejudicial to the Royal Company's trading in that river, and that it would
> prove of worse consequence if the Hollanders should get it into their hands, it
> was resolved in a Council of officers and factors that I should get possession of
> it for the Royal Company by fair or foul means. Especially the Blacks being
> desirous the English should have it; whereupon I sent my master in the
> *Griffin* to sound as near the island as he could; and in case he should be inter-
> rupted by the Courlanders immediately to desist. Which he accordingly per-
> formed without any obstruction, and that day returned with a good account of
> his proceedings.

Connoisseurs of Imperial apologetics will savour the effortless transition
from candid, unabashed rascality to the solicitude expressed for the prefer-
ences of the native population. Fortunately Holmes had a pretext for
action. A week earlier the Governor had fired at one of the frigates and
would not let her water at the island.[13] Accordingly on Monday, March
18th, the *Henrietta*, accompanied by the *Amity* and the *Kinsale* anchored
'within half shot of the fort' and demanded its surrender. This the
Governor prudently conceded in exchange for a safe-conduct for himself
and his people and their possessions 'being 7 white men and white women,
the rest Blacks'.[14] Twelve years later when the international repercussions
of this remote skirmish were again ruffling the in-trays of Whitehall
Holmes with pardonable irritation described it as 'a little fort that had two
men and a boy in it',[15] one of the earliest instances of that phrase. Militarily this conquest achieved nothing since the fort, already in decay, was

accidentally destroyed by fire a few months later. But the diplomatic cats-cradle woven by the activities of the Duke of Courland, his agent, the Dutch West India Company and Sir Robert Holmes was to keep a number of persons happily and pointlessly occupied for many years.[16]

It was high time to be getting on with the main object of the expedi-tion, the discovery of the gold-mines. As early as March 7th, his third day in the Gambia, Holmes had held a conference of commanders and factors aboard the *Henrietta* to plan the sending of boats up the river. It was decided to send three barges and two wherries which were to carry pro-visions for a month and two quarter casks of brandy.[17] On March 19th Holmes recorded in his journal 'I sent the *Kinsale* with Mr. Vermodden and Captain Cushing up the river with the barges so appointed for them to prosecute their design of Goldfinding.'

Colonel John Vermuyden who was Chief Engineer to Prince Rupert has left a brief summary of this voyage up the Gambia.[18] There were thirty-six men in all, distributed between three barges and one wherry which was all that they could muster. Besides Cushing and another Captain there were two factors and, of course, the two experts, Vermuyden and La Prairie. Apart from picking up any gold they happened to come across they were to survey Elephant Island and report on its possibilities as a site for a royal fort. 'On the 21st', wrote Vermuyden, 'we viewed Elephant Island, the which is seated commodiously as to command of the river, being from the mouth thereof forty-five leagues; however it is not habitable, for that it flows every tide a foot above the island, it being wholly a wood of man-groves, so thick that it is not passable without much difficulty. According to my opinion, the only seat in this river is Charles Island, being a healthy air, and in the main, commodious ground for plantation.' Once planted with the crops he recommends, sugar, tobacco, wines, indigo, oranges, lemons, cotton and pepper, he estimates that the trade of the river would employ thirty ships.

This was all very well; but the approach of the rainy season meant that any further 'goldfinding' would have to be postponed for a long time. Holmes decided to concentrate his men and resources on finishing the new fort on Charles Island, sparing what he could for refurbishing the captured fort on St. Andreas now renamed James Island. Meanwhile the barges and small frigates were employed in fetching water both for the fort and for the ships and in taking the factors and their goods to such places as they had chosen for factories. Towards the end of April these tasks were within sight of completion. Holmes called a council of officers and factors on board the *Henrietta* and announced his intention of sailing for England as soon as he had careened his ship, 'leaving the *Amity*, *Sophia* and *Kinsale* to attend them so long as it should be needful' and sending the *Griffin* along to Sierra Leone and the Gold Coast.

At the beginning of May Holmes sailed from the Gambia in company with the *Griffin*. Everything was in order on Charles and James Islands. The factors had given him their letters for London. The commanders had sent in their journals. For some reason, probably simple curiosity, Holmes had decided to go and have a look at Sierra Leone for himself. The voyage was uneventful except that on May 9th, the day before they sighted Cape Sierra Leone, he records laconically: 'we had a Turnado which was the first we met up with upon the coast'. To one who had lived through the hurricane that had smashed Rupert's fleet in the West Indies it called for no comment or description. On May 11th they steered in for the river and anchored in Dorothy Bay.

Like Cape Verde, Sierra Leone was a common port of call for vessels trading along the coast because of the excellence of its water supply and the abundance of very good fish of which Holmes claims to have caught a number himself. During the week he was there three other ships came in: an English pink, a Hamburger flying Danish colours and a Dutchman. On the 19th he sailed for England, parting company with the *Griffin* who was bound further along the coast. Once clear of the African coast he sighted no land and no sail for five weeks. On June 25th they made out the peak of Fayal in the Azores far to the north and on the 27th they anchored off Terceira.

They spent a busy week there, taking in water and beverage wine, hauling the guns aft to bring the bows up for a leak to be stopped, gathering news of the international situation and the movements of shipping. As soon as they had dropped anchor in the roadstead at Angra the master of a French ship that had just come in came on board to tell them that England had declared war on Spain and that a fleet of fifty-two ships had been sent out to bring the Infanta of Portugal over to England. Holmes at once sent his Purser and his Lieutenant ashore to inform the authorities of his arrival and to fetch the English Consul. No doubt he learned from him that the Frenchman's report was somewhat exaggerated: England was not at war with Spain and nearly a year was to pass before the English fleet was to sail into the Tagus to bring Catherine of Braganza over to her wedding. But the publication of the marriage treaty ensured a visiting English warship every civility from the Portuguese Governor, even to the extent of a small present to her Captain. By July 4th Holmes was ready to sail but hearing that 'there were two considerable English ships waiting for a convoy for England' off the island of Fayal he cruised in the offing until he sighted them on the 7th. They set course for the mouth of the Channel, were in soundings on the 22nd and sighted the Lizard on the 26th. About 1 p.m. on July 28th they arrived in the Downs.

What were the results of Holmes's first voyage to West Africa? As a financial speculation there can be no question that Sandwich had shewn his usual shrewd judgment in keeping his money out of it. When the Company struck its balance the sale of ivory, wax and hides, mostly brought back in the *Amity*, amounted to £1,567 8s. against a total expenditure of more than £4,000.[19] Even Holmes himself seems, on paper at least, not to have done at all well out of it since, as a punishment for exceeding the complement authorised for the expedition, he was deprived of his pay.[20] And yet . . . and yet . . . for a man of no private fortune he seems to have been able to live a fashionable life without embarrassment. And so practical a man would hardly have bothered to bring back an exotic animal if he had not already found room for a more negotiable cargo:

> By and by we are called to Sir W. Batten's to see the strange creature that Captain Holmes hath brought with him from Guiny; it is a great baboon, but so much like a man in most things, that though they say there is a species of

them, yet I cannot believe but that it is a monster got of a man and a she-baboon. I do believe that it already understands much English, and I am of the mind it might be taught to speak or make signs.[21]

Indeed, as has been mentioned earlier, Pepys found Holmes's magnificence positively disturbing:

My wife and I to church and there in the pew, with the rest of the company, was Captain Holmes, in his gold-laced suit, at which I was troubled because of the old business which he attempted upon my wife.[22]

Diplomatically, as we have seen, the immediate consequence of the expedition was a vigorous protest from the States-General in Holland supported by retaliatory action against English ships trading along the West African coast.[23] Both the King in London and Sir George Downing, our ambassador at The Hague, disavowed the high claims that Holmes was alleged to have advanced to the Governor of Cape Verde and promised to examine him stringently on his actions over the island of St. Andras (which Holmes had now re-named James Island). No real attempt was made to do so; or, if it was, Holmes's version of the affair must have been unofficially accepted.

For Holmes himself the voyage was the turning-point of his career. Before it he was an unknown ex-Cavalier, said to be a good man in a tight corner, whose abilities Rupert was known to value. He returned a commander of proved abilities. The expedition may not have yielded a profit but when one considers the haziness of its objectives, the weakness of the English on the African coast and their inexperience of the trade, the remarkable thing is that it did not end in disaster. The difficulties with which Holmes had to contend were intensified by the notorious hazards to health of a coast that even in Victorian times was feared and avoided by seamen. On this occasion no less than thirty-eight of the crew of the *Amity* (probably about half her complement) had died before she cleared the Gambia and sailed for home.[24] Alike in his dealings with the Dutch, the Africans, the Factors of the Royal Company and the officers and men under his command Holmes had shewn himself competent to every occasion. When any further expedition should be sent his knowledge and

conduct would make him the obvious choice to command it. And the
dismal trading returns of the Royal Adventurers did nothing to diminish
the general belief that the West African coast held the key to vast undis-
covered treasure. Even a decade later Marvell was to summarise the world's
wealth thus:

> Furrs from the *North*, and Silver from the *West*,
> From the *South* Perfumes, Spices from the *East*
> From *Gambo* Gold, and from the *Ganges* Gems.[25]

VII

The Clash with Pepys

A MONTH OR TWO after Holmes's return from the Gambia Pepys was spending a Sunday at home of a type familiar to the busy civil servant of three centuries later. He had woken after a night of heavy rain to find that the gutters were blocked and water was coming through the roof. He was just in time to save his ceilings and when he had cleared up the mess it was time for church. He returned with his wife to their Sunday dinner after which he dropped in on his neighbour and colleague Sir William Batten. There he found another colleague Sir William Penn, like Batten an admiral as well as a civilian official, and the newly returned Captain Holmes.* They spent the afternoon pulling Sir William Penn's leg about the supposed theft of his tankard which was in fact a hoax contrived by Batten and Pepys. At last Holmes and Pepys took their leave and shared a coach to Whitehall. Pepys' record of their conversation is the more valuable because they had not yet fallen foul of each other:

> I found him by discourse to be a great friend of my Lord's, and he told me there were many did seek to remove him; but they were old seamen, such as Sir J. Mennes† (but he would name no more, though I do believe Sir W. Batten is one of them that do envy him), but he says he knows that the King do so love him, and the Duke of York too, that there is no fear of him. He seems to be very well acquainted with the King's mind, and with all the several

---

* Holmes's prefix is a sensitive indicator of the almost imperceptible, wholly unconscious progression of naval ranks, and the Navy itself, from occasional to permanent institutions. Hitherto he has generally been referred to by Pepys and others as Major Holmes. From this point on Captain is used about as often as Major until a knighthood put an end to the question. It is noticeable, however, that when the rank alone is used it is nearly always 'the Major', rarely 'the Captain'.

† See p. 31.

factions at Court, and spoke all with so much frankness that I do take him to be my Lord's good friend, and one able to do him great service, being a cunning fellow, and one (by his own confession to me) that can put on two several faces, and look his enemies in the face with as much love as his friends. But, good God! what an age is this, and what a world is this! that a man cannot live without playing the knave and dissimulation.[1]

It was, it is, a solemn thought: but not less interesting is the contempt that Holmes reveals for his fellow Royalist Sir John Mennes (on another occasion[2] he told Pepys and Sir William Penn 'that he was a knave, rogue, coward, and that he will kick him and pull him by the ears') contrasted with the friendship and respect that he professed for Sandwich, the ex-Cromwellian. Holmes, like his old commander Prince Rupert, had more of the professional in him than the partisan.

No doubt it was owing to his familiarity with the King that he was appointed Captain of the *Royal Charles,* the flagship that had carried the King to England and was now to fetch Catherine of Braganza from Lisbon. As Sandwich, then serving as Commander-in-Chief in the Mediterranean, was to join the ship in Lisbon Holmes was probably to serve as a kind of second-Captain or understudy:[3] but even if it was not quite so dizzying an ascent for an officer who had so far commanded nothing larger than a middling-sized frigate it was still impressive. Its immediate results were, however, unfortunate. At the beginning of November Holmes was taking the *Royal Charles* down the Thames when he met the Swedish ambassador coming up in the *Drake,* a 66-gun ship, and failed to make him strike his sails. The importance attached to this formal acknowledgement of sovereignty seems to us, as it seemed to our maritime neighbours in the seventeenth century, excessive. Pepys noted in his *Diary* for November 12th: 'This day Holmes come to town: and we do expect hourly to hear what usage he hath from the Duke and the King about this late business of letting the Swedish Ambassador go by him without striking his flag.' According to a contemporary newsletter:[4]

> . . . Captain Homes, formerly Admirall of the ships in Guinea, did his endeavour to make the Swedish ship strike her sailes and did fyer 2 gunnes at her but at last he was persuaded by the said Ambassador that the King had

given him leave to proceede his journey without stryking sails to any ship.

This was taken by His Majesty soe haynous that he did immediately casshiere the said Captain Homes and did declare him not worthy of further employment and doth yet more threaten him with further punishment.

It is certainly true that Holmes was dismissed his ship; a successor was appointed and reported on board her in the Downs on November 17th.[5] A fortnight later the Duke of York as Lord High Admiral asked William Coventry and Pepys what the form was about striking the flag. Neither of them knew but Pepys, rather than admit to ignorance, invented a plausible piece of moonshine: 'that I had heard Mr. Selden [probably the most learned lawyer of the century] often say, that he could prove that in Henry the 7th's time, he did give commission to his captains to make the King of Denmark's ships to strike to him in the Baltique.'[6] A few days later, looking in on Sir William Penn, 'with him I found Captain Holmes, who had wrote his case, and gives me a copy, as he hath many among his friends, and presented the same to the King and Council. Which I shall make use of in my attempt of writing something concerning the business of striking sail which I am now about.'[7] Evidently it served its purpose since there is no record of any further action[8] against Holmes: indeed he was given another command a few months later. Meanwhile he continued to live in an elegant not to say luxurious style in his lodgings in Trinity House, alarming Pepys, as we have seen,* by a display of gold lace that might excite feminine susceptibilities and gratifying masculine ones by the excellence of the lobsters at his supper-parties.[9]

In the spring Holmes received two marks of royal favour that shewed the incident over the flag to have been no more than a minor check. In April the King gave orders that he should be paid £800 out of the cash balance that had not been accounted for when Cromwell's army was paid off;[10] and at about the same time he was appointed Captain of H.M.S. *Reserve*.

The exact date of the appointment is not known: but the *Reserve* was only launched at Chatham on February 24th[11] and she was still being victualled and manned there in July and August.[12] It was at this point that

* p. 73.

Pepys took a step that was, not surprisingly, to involve him in a fierce personal quarrel with Holmes. Pepys like every other official of his time took it for granted that his position entitled him to provide for his relations, dependants and friends by appointing them to any vacancy from which they were not in set terms disqualified. In making his old mathematics teacher, Richard Cooper, master* of the *Reserve* he was thus acting in accordance with the general practice and custom. Indeed, it appeared on paper a perfectly suitable appointment since Cooper had not only the necessary facility as a mathematician for computing the ship's position but had actually served as a master in another ship. At least this seems the inescapable inference from the querulous letter he wrote to Pepys within three weeks of his appointment, complaining that he was not allowed 'the two servants as he had been accustomed'.[13] It would further appear from this letter that the Captain had not yet joined the ship as there are protests about undermanning and the consequent impossibility of working the ship, which would hardly have come from the master if the Captain had been there. However, less than a month later they were at sea, on the point of leaving home waters for the Straits and Tangier.[14]

The voyage was, so far as we know, uneventful. On February 3rd the ship was in Lisbon homeward bound[15] and she was back in Chatham by March 2nd.[16] A few days later Pepys ran into Holmes at Sir William Batten's:

> . . . where Major Holmes . . . lately come from the Streights . . . do tell me strange stories of the faults of Cooper his master, put in by me, which I do not believe but am sorry to hear and must take some course to have him removed, though I believe that the Captain is proud and the fellow is not supple enough to him.

Pepys was sufficiently aware that he might have prejudices in the matter to sound out his colleague the Commissioner at Chatham, Peter Pett, one of that great dynasty who passed from generation to generation the secrets

* From the Middle Ages to the nineteenth century the master was the officer responsible for the navigation and pilotage of the ship, essentially a civil rather than a military function. The Captain told him where to take her and was responsible for fighting her. See on this Michael Lewis *England's Sea Officers* and his *The Navy of Britain*.

of naval architecture and of successful embezzlement. Pett thoroughly understood the importance of presenting an unbroken official front. He expressed himself anxious to continue the master of the *Reserve*, although of a weak brain and 'sometime disguised with drink', and thought that it might be managed, provided that he chose a competent master's mate.[17] Fortified by this opinion Pepys prepared to stand up to Holmes before a full meeting of the Navy Board on March 21st. If the *Diary* is anything to go by the spectators certainly got value for money:

> Captain Holmes being called in he began his high complaint against his Master Cooper, and would have him forthwith discharged. Which I opposed, not in his defence but for the justice of proceeding not to condemn a man unheard, upon [which] we fell from one word to another that we came to very high terms, such as troubled me, though all and the worst that I ever said was that that was insolently or ill mannerly spoken. *When he told me that it was well it was here that I said it.** But all the officers, Sir G. Carteret, Sir J. Minnes, Sir W. Batten and Sir W. Pen cried shame of it. At last he parted and we resolved to bring the dispute between him and his Master to a trial next week, wherein I shall not at all concern myself in defence of anything that is unhandsome on the Master's part nor willingly suffer him to have any wrong. So we rose and I to my office, troubled though sensible that all the officers are of opinion that he has carried himself very much unbecoming him.[18]

The next day was a Sunday. Pepys spent it agreeably, taking his wife by coach to Westminster and then to Chelsea for some country air. He had some interesting talk with his patron, Lord Sandwich, about the situation in Ireland and about the Government's policy on the question of religious toleration. He rounded off the day by going to a particularly enjoyable evening party, where there were many fine ladies, a handsome house and plenty of good food and drink. But when he had gone home and said his prayers and got into bed he records:

> This day though I was merry enough yet I could not get yesterday's quarrel out of my mind, and a natural fear of being challenged by Holmes for the words I did give him, though nothing but what did become me as a principal officer.[19]

* My italics. Holmes certainly meant that if Pepys had spoken to him in this way outside the protection of an official, quasi-judicial meeting he would have challenged him to a duel.

Natural indeed his fear was. Holmes did not wear a sword for show, and his temper was neither mild nor forgiving. Pepys's agitation increased the next day when he had to go to Whitehall to see the Duke of York about naval business and to attend the Tangier Committee 'being fearful almost, so poor a spirit I have, of meeting Major Holmes'. He was not too frightened to take an interest in what was discussed and left with his head full of business:

> Thence to see my Lord Sandwich, and who should I meet at the door but Major Holmes. He would have gone away, but I told him I would not spoil his visit, and would have gone, but however we fell to discourse and he did as good as desire excuse for the high words that did pass in his heat the other day which I was willing enough to close with, and after telling him my mind we parted.[20]

Pepys says nothing of the relief and exhilaration he must have felt at the sudden lifting of so dark a cloud. But the next day's entry in which he concludes his account of the business has an airy off-hand tone that reveals much:

> . . . and so to my office, where we sat anon, and among other things had Cooper's business tried against Captain Holmes, but I find Cooper a fuddling, troublesome fellow, though a good artist, and so am contented to have him turned out of his place, nor did I see reason to say one word against it though I know what they did against him was with great envy and pride.[21]

Holmes, it will be noticed, has almost disappeared from the picture, as have the great principles of justice and the simple question of fact: were the allegations of professional incompetence made against Cooper true or false? In their place we recognise the familiar authors of all ill, Pepys's colleagues, Batten, Penn, Mennes and Carteret. It seems a disappointingly tame conclusion to draw from so dramatic an affair.

Pepys, of course, is throwing dust in our eyes. He was glad enough of any settlement that obliterated the terrifying prospect of a duel with Holmes. But the rancour, the resentment he still felt towards him was not lessened by the need to conceal it. It coloured his private opinion of Holmes for the rest of his life and may well have contributed to the refusal of his services in the later stages of the Third Dutch War.* This opinion he freely disclosed to anyone of importance whom he trusted not to repeat it to Holmes. whom he treated thereafter with a wary courtesy.[22] It has, together with the opinion of Sir William Coventry (Pepys's great friend and closest colleague), been crucial to the view of Holmes that is to be found, when one is found at all, in the history books. Take for instance this passage from the work of a distinguished modern scholar Professor Charles Wilson:

> Swaggering, roystering and corrupt, Holmes was exactly the kind of courtier-officer whose indiscipline was to be the curse of the Restoration Navy . . . [and goes on to identify Holmes as the professional equal of courtier-politicians like Clifford and Buckingham].[23]

The point is made again in the telling comparison between Coventry and Holmes:

> It was indeed thanks to Coventry that the Navy had any officers at all, for in complete disregard of his own popularity he had fought for and secured the King's agreement that the old sea commanders of the Interregnum should be re-employed. He had supported and promoted professional sailors like Sir Christopher Mings,[24] who were despised by the 'gentleman officers' as being of humble birth, and he shrewdly calculated the risk of employing a man like Robert Holmes, who, though dashingly courageous, was hopelessly irresponsible.

No one who has read an instruction or a minute or a note drafted by William Coventry can ever quite escape the fascination of that brilliant intelligence, that incisiveness of expression and that handwriting, at once exquisite and unaffected, in which they are recorded. Never obscure, never crabbed, never irrational, he seems to personify civilisation and efficiency. That he and Pepys deserve the credit everywhere accorded them as creative naval adminstrators of incomparable quality is not here contested. But we should none the less beware of attributing to them virtues which they would not have claimed and which the evidence does not support. To describe Holmes, for instance, as corrupt and by implication to contrast

* See pp. 184–5.

F

him with Coventry and Pepys is to forget what standards we are judging
by. No reader of the *Diary*, no student of their papers could possibly acquit
them of such a charge. By the same token before we accept the view of
Holmes that I have quoted we should remember that it is strongly
influenced by, if not based largely on, the writings, eloquent, witty and
well-informed, of the same pair of sirens.

And what, if we consider the two points at which Holmes and Pepys
ran across each other professionally in these first years after the Restoration,
what was the record? When Holmes is in trouble over the salute to the
flag, Pepys, to cover his own ignorance, deliberately fakes a piece of pano-
plied legalism which makes Holmes's action appear less excusable. When
Holmes, quite rightly, tries to get rid of a drunken and incompetent
master, Pepys takes his action as a personal and professional insult
because the man was his nominee. It is, no doubt, only natural, only
human, that he should do so. But Holmes was human too. As he saw it, the
safety of his ship, the lives of his men, above all his own career were not to
be jeopardised simply to save the face of a jumped-up young clerk who was
some sort of cousin to Lord Sandwich. We know what Pepys thought of
Holmes: but what did Holmes think of Pepys? A University-bred young
fellow with a pretty wife moving easily in rich and fashionable society he
seemed to have arrived almost without effort at a position that Holmes had
won for himself through hazard huge. It was not to be expected that an
older man who had seen long and arduous service, much of it as a junior
officer, and who had suffered the humiliating poverty of exile would take
kindly to correction from such a fair-weather spark.

Why then did Holmes not challenge Pepys to a duel? It would have
been entirely in character for him to do so. He had (as Pepys's fears attest)
received what would have then been considered perfectly adequate grounds.
He would, no question, have made short work of his opponent. Yet on
Pepys own evidence it was Holmes who made overtures of friendship
when they met on Sandwich's doorstep. On the Pepys–Coventry hypothesis
that Holmes was simply a sly, ruthless thug this makes no sense. But if one
substitutes a reading of his character based on the opinions of those who

served with him, Prince Rupert, for instance or Richard Atkyns, his troop commander when he was a young cornet of horse in 1643, it does. Holmes was a serious professional officer, not a courtier dilettante. As such he may well have recognised a kindred spirit in the young Clerk of the Acts. As such he may have calculated that his own prospects of future employment might be prejudiced if he were to give this promising administrator his quietus. And was there not a good deal to be said for having such a man, efficient, intelligent and ambitious, among the crusty veterans at the Navy Board? As private persons Pepys and Holmes had little in common: professionally they had a great deal.

This conflict with Pepys was so far as we know the only hostile encounter during Holmes's commission as Captain of the *Reserve*. Towards the end of April she sailed again for Lisbon and the Straits. On May 7th she was in the Tagus and on June 3rd Holmes was back in Lisbon, having made a voyage to Tangier in the interval.[25] He reappears in Lisbon yet again towards the end of July, this time in company with Colonel Norwood, the newly-appointed Deputy Governor of Tangier. Holmes was on very good terms with our ambassador in Lisbon, Sir Richard Fanshaw, an old Royalist whose charm and good-nature were not complemented by any marked capacity for diplomacy.[26] Out of friendship for Holmes and as a courtesy to Colonel Norwood, Fanshaw arranged for them to be shewn the King's bulls. What happened on the visit is not clear except that some deep offence was given and Holmes and Norwood were bundled out of the royal bull-stables. Their official standing raised such treatment to the level of a diplomatic incident. The English consul was summoned by the Conde de Castelmelhor who accused him 'in a very high voice' of endeavouring to make a breach between the two crowns. The consul was firm but tactful and a new invitation was extended by the King to the two officers who were to be accompanied by the ambassador.[27] Soon after this Holmes conveyed Norwood to Tangier. On September 4th he arrived in the Downs[28] and on September 15th the *Reserve*'s commission ended.[29]

This uneventful voyage provides an early, perhaps the earliest, example of those many and considerable services that the Royal Navy has rendered to the learned world. Christiaan Huygens, the great scientist and mathe-matician, had for some years been experimenting with a pendulum watch as a means for determining longitude at sea. In this work as in some of his other projects he had been assisted by two highly gifted Scottish Royalist émigrés, Alexander Bruce, Earl of Kincardine, and Sir Robert Moray, the moving spirit of the Royal Society. They had, after the Restoration, easily succeeded in arousing the interest of the King and Prince Rupert, both keen amateurs of science and both quick to see the importance of such an advance to the science of navigation. An offer to test the watches at sea in a ship of the Royal Navy was accepted; and the *Reserve* was chosen, perhaps because Rupert knew that he could rely on her Captain to do a thorough job. On his return, Holmes duly submitted 'An Account of the Going of two watches at sea from 28th April to 4th September 1663' to Sir Robert Moray who presented the report to the Royal Society on October 21st.

From the copy preserved in Huygens's papers,[30] the results seem to have been encouraging. Holmes checked the watches against the sun at noon on such days as it was visible and recorded errors that were generally of about half an hour. Huygens, though pleased with their performance, was not so satisfied with Holmes's. Why had he not kept a check on the outward voyage? And why did he discontinue his observations as soon as the ship was in English coastal waters? Sir Robert Moray did not, it seems, share Huygens's reservations. On November 19th, he wrote to tell him that 'the two watches A and B are to be sent with the same captain to Guinea and from there they will go to Jamaica . . .'[31] Within two days of this letter Holmes had left London to assume command of a second and much more important expedition to Africa.

VIII

The Guinea Expedition

W
HAT WAS THE OBJECT of the Guinea Expedition of 1664?
The best person to ask would be William Coventry who had a
larger share than any man in the planning, direction and subsequent assessment of the operation. After it was all over, and the Dutch
War to which it led was over too, he sat down to disentangle the causes of
the war and to summarise the lessons to be learned. It is a characteristically
brilliant analysis, running to some ten pages of manuscript.[1] He dismisses
any idea of Machiavellian policy:

> The truth is the Dutch warre arose by strange accidensall things concurring
> from severall parts and parties without any interest to helpe each other.[2]

Among these he notes the forward policies and provocative dispatches of our
ambassador at The Hague, Sir George Downing; but the importance he
attaches to the Guinea Expedition leads him to give the following account
of its origins and conduct:

> At the same time the Guinney Company, of which his Royal Highness [The
> Duke of York, to whom Coventry was secretary] was governour (and in pro-
> moting which he tooke great delight), the company being then much steered by
> Sir Richard Ford, Captain George Cocke and Mr. Gray of the Court party as
> they called it: the first (though underhand) governing the Merchants by the
> Dependance they had on him for trade and payment in the Navy, the latter, if
> Mr. Gray steered by the Merchants partly without perceiving it (being zealous
> for the Company) and partly out of a desire to maintain a popularity with the
> merchants as well as Court Party, that soe he might be chosen the next year
> Sub-Governour, of which he was ambitious, partly having nothing else to doe
> and partly for the opportunity it gave him to make his court to his Royal
> Highness, I say the Guinney Company in this condition and thus supported
> grew very violent in their Debates against the Dutch, and nothing would serve

but their sending ships of Force to the Coasts of Africa to support (they called it) their trade; but the intent was to take away the Dutch Forts or at least Cape Corse* which the Dutch possessed, but to which wee had some pretence.

For this, under the name of convoy, some of the King's ships were demanded and granted by the Councell. Upon this designe Captain Holmes (now Sr. Robert) was sent in the *Jersey*, a man of an understanding fitt to make a warre, and a courage to make it good; in the latter few goe beyond him; in the former few come short. This Captaine, being sent with instructions drawne according to the dictates of the R^{ll.} Company, my selfe having drawne them by notes receaved from Sr. Richard Ford (being soe commanded), though the instructions were pretty bold, yett they served not the Captain's turne, whoe not having patience to stay till he came to the Gold Coast (where it was intended by the Company the game should begin) meeting some Dutch ships outward bound at or near Cape de Verde, hee seized them and fell to shooting at the fort (on wch wee had noe claimmance) and by the Cowardice of those within it, it was surrendered to him . . .[3]

One of the Africa Company's Directors here mentioned, Captain George Cocke, impressed Pepys, shortly after Holmes had sailed, by his arguments in favour of a war with the Dutch: '. . . that is, that the trade of the world is too little for us two, therefore one must down.'[4] Pepys, notwithstanding, remained constant to his own instinct that a war would be a wild and reckless gamble. Coventry himself was generally recognised as one of the leaders of the war party.[5] But this, of course, was before its gigantic cost and disastrous unpopularity had come close to ruining his own public career.

Coventry's draft instructions[6] to Holmes differ in no significant way from those which the Duke of York signed on November 10th, 1663.[7] Holmes was to sail in H.M.S. *Jersey* for the Gambia where he was to enquire for the Africa Company's ship *Katherin* whose commander Captain Ladd he was to assist in 'protecting and promoting the Interests of the R^{ll.} Company, which is the sole end of your present voyage'. In general he was to maintain the right of the Company to trade where it pleased on the African coast and he was specifically empowered 'to kill, take, sink or destroy such as shall oppose you and to send home such

* Cape Coast Castle.

shipps as you shall soe take'. Finally he was to do his best to seize and send home the *Goulden Lyon* of Flushing commanded by 'one James Johnson a Scotchman (by birth) but employed by the Dutch West India Company in those parts' as also a sister ship the *Christiana* with both of which the Royal Company had a long score to settle.

Holmes went on board the *Jersey* at Queenborough on November 21st. The keynote of the expedition was struck that very day. Going down river the *Jersey* was forced to anchor by thick fog. A Dutch pink, groping her way up, passed close by without striking her flag. Holmes at once fired at her and had her master brought on board. In such conditions the formality of the salute might have been waived: but the Dutch were not to be allowed the benefit of any doubt. And in any case the salute was a sensitive matter for Holmes. Ten days later, having taken in ballast and provisions, the *Jersey*, standing down Channel came up with a large Dutch East Indiaman outward bound. She too failed to strike, so Holmes fired a gun at her. She took no notice so he fired again and carried away the head of her mizzen topmast. She still declined at which he opened up with two guns. She struck both her topsails, but Holmes demanded boats to be put out for a boarding party. She refused. Holmes fired. She gave way. She proved to be a vessel of eight hundred tons with a complement of two hundred and eighty men. As a final insult Holmes exacted payment for the shots expended.

Amongst the papers that Holmes was carrying with him was a letter from the African Company to Captain Ladd, urging at least as provocative an attitude to the Dutch in the matter of searching their vessels and demanding the salute as Holmes had evinced in home waters. This was part of Coventry's policy, as outlined in the retrospect already quoted: '. . . the Gold Coast, where it was intended by the Company the game should begin'. That Coventry thought it a promising game is evidenced by a letter he wrote recommending a friend's son, asking Holmes to 'afford him not only accommodation and protection but that you should give him such advice as he shall need. Perhaps it may not be amiss for you to practise the Father's part in Education being soe perfect as you are in the rest, for I believe when you have brought home the Goulden mountaines the common contagion of the rich (marriage) will seize you.'

A steady following gale brought the *Jersey* off Funchal by December 14th. Standing in to the roads to take on beverage wine Holmes saw a small frigate bearing away before the wind under all the sail she could make. He at once altered course to give chase. After fifteen miles they found they were not gaining on her and gave up. But the fifteen miles they had run before the wind would cost them a lot of time if they were to beat up to windward of Funchal. They had learned from the East Indiaman they had boarded in the Channel that a Dutch frigate and some other vessels were already at sea bound for Cape Verde. The beverage wine had regretfully to be abandoned and course was set for the Cape.

A week later, on December 22nd,

. . . in the morning one of the master's mates came down into my cabbin and told me that they did believe wee were bewitcht. Whereupon I ask'd him what the matter was, he told me that all our Sayles were coloured red. I bid him goe up and not to meddle with any of the sayles till I came upon deck. I did ghesse what it was soe soone as he told me for I did find of it the day before but was laught at for speaking of it, because we did reckon ourselves above 50 Leagues off the shore; soe soone as I came upon the Deck I did order the master to putt the shipp about which he presently went about to doe. As soone as the sayles fluttered in the wind all the sand and stuff that was in the sayles shook out, and the ropes left a print on the sayles like as if there were flower or sand upon a table and that you may draw a stick or your finger thorow it.

On Christmas Day they sighted Cape Verde at two in the afternoon. Darkness was falling as they approached so that Holmes thought it wiser to stand off until he could see what ships were in the roadstead. During the night a fresh north-easterly gale sprang up which prevented him from closing the Cape all the next day. Early in the morning of the 27th the wind backed to north-west: the *Jersey* could now steal round the eastern bluff of Cape Verde and see what ships the Dutch had lying at anchor in the harbour of Goree. But before Holmes had given the necessary orders a sail was reported to the northward, rounding the Cape. An hour or so later she was clear of the breakers, a fine Dutch West Indiaman of about three hundred tons, her colours at her main. The *Jersey* cleared for action and weighed anchor. She was about a mile to leeward of the Dutchman who was hugging the coast. Holmes tacked towards her and fired a gun. She struck her flag but not her topsails. 'Upon which', he records, 'wee fired severall guns at her untill she struck and bore away right with us.' The prize proved to be the *Brill* an 8-gun West Indiaman carrying cargo of lime, iron and brandy for Goree Island and twenty-seven passengers for the West Indies. Holmes took the master and most of the seamen aboard the *Jersey* and manned the *Brill* with his own men, appointing Charles Talbot, one of his own officers, to command her.

To take a Dutch ship within a few miles of a Dutch base on the pretext that she had not acknowledged the suzerainty of the King of England over the whole African littoral from Mauretania to the Cape of Good Hope was certainly a bold stroke. And the dilution of strength consequent on the manning of two vessels and the supervising of a large body of prisoners left Holmes vulnerable to counter-attack. He therefore decided to postpone his reconnaissance of the anchorage at Goree and to sail straight for the Gambia, where he could land his prisoners, sell his prize goods and, very likely, recruit some seamen from the ships of the Royal Company. The low-lying, shoaling, featureless coast along which their course lay was familiar to Holmes. On the 28th he noted in the margin of his journal against the name of a small town on the coast:

> At this Portodally [Portudal] if it had not been by God's providence I had been murthered by some of the Blacks of the Countrey on shore. When Prince Rupert and Prince Maurice were there with part of the revolted Fleet.*

Two days later they anchored in the Gambia.

The next fortnight was given up to every kind of warlike preparation: political, psychological, diplomatic, naval and military. Politically attention was concentrated on producing, or at least outlining, the principal *pièces justificatives* which would pin the blame for the war on the Dutch. Stephen Ustick, the Governor of James Island, provided some most useful

* See pp. 44–6.

material.[8] According to him, among the worst of 'the great violences and spoils committed against our Trade and Traders in these parts' were the intolerable acts of the Dutch West India Company's Factor and Agent, Peter Justobaque (occasionally styled by the more probable form of the name Joost Bacqur). Only recently Justobaque had been on the coast in his ship the *Black Eagle*, stirring up the King of Barra to make war against the English. Indeed, by the time of his examination in the Tower in March 1665 Holmes was apparently able to produce the narrative of the King of Barra 'which appears to have been made by that King in good forme and to be attested by severall . . . present', together with the reported evidence of 'a Duke of that country called Tambo', Twice in the previous year Justobaque had defied Ustick by taking ships up the Gambia to trade: worse, he had even endeavoured to suborn the officers of the garrison by bribes and had compounded the offence by forging a pass for himself over Charles II's signature. Ustick, perhaps apprehensive of the effect of such offers on the less than Roman virtue of his subordinates, had opened fire on the ships as they came up past the fort on the second occasion and they had returned it with interest. On arriving at a trading station further up the river Justobaque told the Portuguese merchants there that he would cool the young fellow's courage and that he had now more than a hundred men on board with which they would do his business. At midnight ten days later the *Black Eagle* and her consort were silently approaching James Fort when Ustick, warned by his Portuguese friends to keep his defence manned, 'espying them by the serenity of the night', opened fire on the leading vessel and luckily brought down her foretopmast. Justobaque, discomfited, retired from the river. But he contrived, according to Holmes and his informants, to practise such villainies as offering the natives a bendy of gold for the head of every Englishman and a much larger sum for that of Holmes.

Psychologically the great obstacle in the way of any aggressive policy was the demoralised, quarrelsome and petulant condition of the Company's servants. 'The Company's affairs stood very ticklish before we arrived on the coast', wrote Holmes to Coventry a few months later, 'I find but few of those you employ fitt for anything unless it be Mr. Selwyn.'[9] Selwyn, the Company's Chief Factor, was at the time of Holmes's arrival embroiled in a furious row with one of his subordinates who had charged him with every kind of corruption and incompetence. He was in any case based on the Gold Coast some hundreds of miles further to the east. In the Gambia itself things had certainly stood very ticklish indeed. On January 25th, 1662, Charles Fort—one of the two that Holmes had built on his first expedition the year before—was abandoned and all forces and supplies concentrated in James Fort.[10] The various minutes of the factors and officers who reached this decision betray an unmistakable undertone of panic. Perhaps things had improved under the fire-eating Ustick but they still left much to be desired.

The diplomacy that Holmes employed was simple: to encourage any-one, Portuguese or Danish trading companies, local African rulers, even Dutch merchants or officers who might have grudges against the senior officials of the West India Company, to undermine its power. It was indeed from a Portuguese merchant that Holmes received his first impor-tant intelligence.

On January 11th Manoel Alvis, a Portuguese trader resident in the Gambia, returned from a voyage along the coast down which the *Jersey* had sailed a fortnight before. He reported that the Dutch factor at Joal, a small post about midway between Cape Verde and the Gambia, had received express news of the arrival at Cape Verde of a Dutch ship of 36 guns with a crew of a hundred and sixty men.[11] Holmes at once called a conference of commanders aboard the *Jersey* at which it was unanimously agreed 'that the only way to secure both the Forts, Goods and the ship *Katherin* likely to be left behind the *Jersey* at Sierra Leone, is to go with all three of the ships here present with all the expedition that may be up to the Cape, there either to take, sink, burn or drive her away to the southward before us.'[12] From first to last Holmes was a pre-emptive strategist. He knew, and his conference agreed, that the Dutch were not going to take the capture of the *Brill* lying down. He had, for the moment, a local preponderance of strength but there were other Dutch ships—how many?—bound for the coast. Not much was needed to turn the scales.

The three ships with which he proposed to attack were the *Jersey*, her prize the *Brill* and the Company's ship *Katherin*[13] which he had found at James Island on his arrival in the Gambia. In the event neither of them* took any part in operations though the *Katherin* probably and the *Brill* possibly left the river in company with the *Jersey* when she set sail for Cape Verde on the 15th. No doubt Holmes preferred one ship well-found and manned to three doubtful quantities. The principle of concentration of force would have been strengthened by the fact that sailing ships were seldom capable of maintaining a uniform speed. The *Jersey* made a swift and uneventful passage. Apart from a small frigate of the Royal Company's, aptly named the *Coaster* which was inward bound to the Gambia from the Cacheo and Rio Grande, they sighted no ships. At eight o'clock on the 18th they saw far away to the north-west the high hills of the Cape Verde Islands. Forty-eight hours later they were in sight of Goree Island. Sure enough there were three or four vessels riding at anchor and a small frigate plying to windward. As if this was not enough, another sail was sighted in the offing. Holmes at once stood out 'to speak with her, which proved to be a Dutch Pink which we spoke withall in the channel bound in for Goree Island which we took and towed in near the road and anchored about 4 miles off at 5 in the afternoon.'

This laconic entry in the journal, transcribed in its entirety, wastes no time on justification. The real business was about to begin. Next day's, though longer, is equally concise:

> This morning at 4 of the clock wee weighed with the wind at N.N.E. a fresh gale, and stood in close under the island within half Canon shott of the Lower Fort. I anchored, and presuming more upon the dissensions I understood to be among the Flemings ashore and their want of Provisions than any other hope I had of taking so strong a place with one ship, I sent ashore to demand that Island. Whilst my messenger was on shore I warped in close within less than musquett shott of the Fort, resolving in case they would not deliver it, to exchange some shott to try what might be done that way. Having received a

---

* Perhaps their function was to act as lifeboats or despatch vessels in case the *Jersey* was sunk or disabled.

slight answer (as they might very well have given me considering both our conditions) wee began to fire at one another which continued almost 6 houres, being so long as we could see to shoot.

My mast and rigging being much shattered I was forced to hale off out of shott to repair them. At the same time I sent my boats to bring off or burn the vessels that were haled in close under the Fort. They brought off a Galliot and a small Pink. Another was so battered with our shott that she was not fitt to be taken paines with. One of those brought off within 3 houres sunk, finding no way to salve her, by reason of so many shott she had received between wind and water.

What the issue would have been if the 36-gun ship had been there to add the weight of her broadsides to the argument is a matter for speculation. Holmes had hit the Dutch hard; two ships sunk, two made prize; but blazing away for six hours had made serious inroads on his supply of ammunition. And with his powers of manœuvre impaired by the damage to his masts and rigging he would have been easy meat for the *Goulden Lyon* if she had chosen that moment to come up over the horizon. But his luck was in. To his astonishment as he lay off repairing his mast he saw a white flag hoisted ashore. A few minutes later he made out a boat, on which it was flying, coming towards him. A Dutch officer was bringing terms of surrender.

The next day, January 23rd, Holmes took formal possession in the name of the Royal Company. He garrisoned the Upper Fort with eighteen men, filled their cisterns with water and provisioned it for ten months. The Dutch were allowed a few days grace to settle their affairs but all the merchandise belonging to the West India Company, including '400 kentalls [quintals] of wax and teeth'[14] were forfeit to the Royal Company. On the advice of Captain Ladd, whose presence suggests that the *Katherin* had perhaps been covering operations at a discreet distance, Captain Morgan Facy, an officer in the Company's service, was appointed to command the place. On February 8th Holmes wrote a long letter to Coventry giving him a full account of all his actions since his first sighting of Cape Verde on Christmas Day.[15] He concluded his relation of his recent triumph with the words:

You have now all the trade in your owne hands from Cape de Verd to the Gould Coast . . . being the most considerable trade in Christendome. I hope you will take a resolution to keepe it.

But even this ambition would be inadequate. He told Coventry that he was sailing for Sierra Leone and expected to make himself master of the whole coast, adding 'if I goe beyond my instructions I hope you and the rest of the royall Company will mediate for mee'. Holmes, like Pepys's friend Captain Cocke, thought the trade of the world too little for two. He might not dispose of great forces—one 40-gun ship and such other vessels as he could capture and man: but he had, as Coventry wrote of him in the passage quoted at the beginning of this chapter, 'an understanding fitt to make a warre'. His grasp of military principles, of strategy, tactics, logistics and propaganda, of the relations between them and of the limits set and the chances offered by economic necessity, is modern and professional. He knew what he was up to; perhaps better than some of those who employed him. He ends his letter by providing Coventry and the war party with ammunition at the same time as he requests a replenishment of his own. After asking that some powder and shot be sent to meet him at the Canaries he writes:

> I am credibly informed by the late Governor of this Island [Goree] that since the last tyme that I was upon this coast the Dutch have taken 18 saile of English shipps, and some lately.

To make quite sure of his points, Holmes had another two copies of the letter made and himself wrote a much briefer but equally strong letter to the Royal Company.[16] These were dispatched by two homeward bound Portuguese vessels. The Dutch pink, captured on the approach to Goree, was handed over to Captain Ladd for the Royal Company's use. She sailed on February 10th for the Gambia, in company with the *Jersey*, which in accordance with the instructions drafted by Coventry was bound for the harbour of Cestos, an anchorage on the coast of what is now Liberia, 'where his Majesty's ship *Expedition* and some ships of Force in the service of the Royall Company shall meet you'.[17]

IX

The Challenge to the Dutch

THE GENERAL SCOPE of Holmes's instructions has been discussed in the preceding chapter. Whether or not the taking of Goree came within them is an open question: but it hardly seems more than an exercise in casuistry to try to resolve it. The Royal Company and the politicians associated with it half, perhaps more than half, intended a war with the Dutch. Coventry as good as lets the cat out of the bag when he refers to the Gold Coast as the place 'where it was intended by the Company the game should begin.'* Games played against so thrusting and powerful an opponent as the Dutch West India Company were apt to be rough. As a Commander-in-Chief, Holmes had always to keep in mind three questions: What did his political masters really want him to do? How far had they, in set terms, committed themselves? How much, given the military facts of the situation, could be achieved? In the light of these considerations it is not hard to believe that he thought he was doing what he was sent out to do when he 'fell to shooting at the fort'. It is equally clear from his letter to Coventry that he understood that his action might be disavowed.

However that might be it was in direct pursuance of his instructions that he sailed on February 10th. Before making his rendezvous at Cestos he was to convoy Captain Ladd in the *Katherin* to Sierra Leone and to provide convoy for other ships of the Company between Sierra Leone and Cape Palmas. After meeting the other ships which were to be under his orders, he was to put himself and them at the disposal of the Company and to co-operate with the factors in every way even to the extent of discovering interlopers who were infringing the monopoly of trade. Finally when his

* Above p. 86.

remaining stock of victuals made a return to England necessary he was 'to turne up to the Fort Cormentine and there receave on board such Gold and Elephants teeth as the Companies Factors there shall putt on board you'.[1]

From Cape Verde to Cestos was a voyage of some seven hundred miles. Two days out, Holmes anchored off the mouth of the Gambia while Captain Ladd in the captured pink went in to find if there were any messages for Sierra Leone and the Gold Coast. There was a bank of red sand lying close to the ship which Holmes had noticed before:

> I attempted to goe on shore in my pinnace as I did in my first voyage in the *Henrietta* but could not compass it by reason of the great Breach [? breakers] and shoale water. This sand I guess to be a League in Length dry and a mile in breadth. It is perpetually covered (especially in the night) with a sort of Birds that the Portuguese call Soldadoes; it is a bird about the bigness of a Brand-goose; they smell verie sweet of musk and are good meate to eat. My desire of going ashore on this sand was to see to bring off some Cakes of their Dung, wch the Portuguese and natives say doth smell rather sweeter of ye musk than the birds themselves doe. Their perpetuall Roosting on this bank does make verie great and thick Cakes of their Dung, and I can attribute your Amber-greece to be noe other but this verie stuff, that upon great rages that the water washes over these Banks, doe wash away great Cakes of this Dung, wch lies driveing up and down as the wind and sea doe carry it. All the Coast of Africa (where I have been) have of these birds, more, or less, and upon all Bankes of the shore these birds roost, as they doe on this Bank short off the River of Gambia. The coast of America is alsoe full of the same Birds. It is to be taken notice of that between the heat of the sand and the heat of the sun, these cakes of Dung come to hardness, and severall foot in thickness as I have heard, but soe verie light that they always float upon the water when they are washed off the sand. I never heard any description come so near Ambergrease as this.[2]

I have printed this entry from Holmes's journal in full because it is one of the very few that gives one any idea of what he thought about when he was not occupied with military projects or navigation. Like so many of his more famous contemporaries, Wren, Evelyn, Pepys or Prince Rupert, he observes, he compares, and is not inhibited from offering an explanation of natural phenomena. His airy allusion to the coast of America presumably refers to his recollections of the West Indies.

The entries for the next twelve days are typical; a bare record of sightings, noon positions, the force and direction of the wind. On the 24th they sighted Cape Sierra Leone. The *Jersey* had two ships in company; the *Brill*, the Dutchman captured off Cape Verde on the way out to the Gambia; and the vessel cut out under the guns of Goree, described simply as 'the galliot'.[3] Darkness fell as they were approaching the Cape, in line astern of the *Brill* 'which carried the light'. Heaving the lead as they came in they found the water shoaling rapidly and anchored for the night. Next morning they saw two ships at anchor three miles off and recognised them as the *Katherin* under the command of Captain Fenn and the Dutch pink given to Captain Ladd which had arrived from the Gambia during the night. During the forenoon all the ships entered harbour where Holmes heard from Captain Peter Brathwait of the *Dover Merchant* that the reinforcing squadron had called in on its way to Cestos.

In spite of his anxiety to unite his forces Holmes found ten days hardly enough for all that needed doing at Sierra Leone. Goods had to be landed from the ships, the affairs of the Royal Company put into order and time and trouble spent in 'Caressing and presenting the natives whose friendship wee had almost lost by meanes of the Dutch'. Besides these commercial and diplomatic duties the ships had to be wooded and watered and repairs carried out to the bowsprit of the *Jersey* which had been damaged by a shot from Goree fort. Once again Holmes discloses his natural curiosity and faculty of observation:

> Here I went ashore to see what was become of a plantation of the Kernells of China Oranges I put in a fine plain field I mett withall the first voyage I was there in the *Henrietta*, about a mile above the watering place upon the side of a small Rivolet that makes the watering place, wch is one of the best watering places in the world. I went to the place where I made my plantation and found the River, but the fine plaine where I put my seed the voyage before I could not find in a good while, for all the whole plain was overrun with Briars, Bushes and weeds that it was almost Impossible to find it out. But by casting our way before us, at length looking verie narrowly and knowing myself certainlie to be in the verie place, I look'd up towards the Topps of some fine young straight trees I saw growing there. I had not the confidence to say they were orange trees by reason they were grown to that biggness and height, but at last wee all concluded that they were Orange trees and to confirme us in that opinion found

G

severall of ye stocks that wee sett the seed by in the ground, that we may see how to sett them straight in Rowes. The trees were at that time in their Blossomes, and did look the finest that ever I saw. I had on shore with me severall of those men that I had with me at the first planting of them.[4]

The concluding sentence of this entry is one among several pieces of evidence scattered up and down Holmes's life that he was an officer who inspired personal loyalty. No regular long-service engagement in the Royal Navy was open to seamen until the time of Queen Victoria. When the *Henrietta* paid off in 1661, her crew were free to take service in any ship they might choose, merchantman or man-of-war. That several of them should re-appear aboard the *Jersey* more than two years later can hardly have been coincidence.

There had been one violent tornado during their stay at Sierra Leone but when they sailed on March 8th the wind was light. The fleet consisted of the *Jersey, Brill, Galliot, Dover Merchant* and the captured pink which is henceforward known as the *Neptune*. Although Holmes had made a present of her to the Royal Company she seems to have reverted to his control. Perhaps she was not a very handy vessel. Certainly she had to be towed out of Sierra Leone. And no doubt the Company had as many ships as it could man already. Two days out two more of its coasters were sighted inward bound for Sierra Leone. This may well have prompted Holmes's decision to call a council of war next day aboard the *Jersey* at which it was agreed to get rid of their Dutch prisoners by giving them the *Neptune* and victualling her for a voyage to Europe. Eight of them including the commander at Goree had lived at Holmes's table. On the afternoon of Sunday the 13th the *Neptune* stood away on a south-westerly course while the English squadron sailed on south-south-east parallel with the coast.

On the 15th there was 'much Thunder and Lightening and a verie dark sky in the southerboard all night'. On the 18th they sighted land '. . . high; full of mountains in the Countrey and Hummocks by the Waterside' and on the 20th 'wee saw the long Hummock of trees over Cestos and 3 shipps at Anchor in the Roade'. Wisely Holmes decided to pause for a day before taking his ships through the treacherous approaches of this anchorage. A boat came off to inform him that the ships lying at anchor were the *Expedition*, *Welcome* and *Sophia*, all King's ships of about 30 guns, [5] and that Captain Merrett of the *James* had gone on ahead to the Gold Coast. Next day he piloted his ships in and called a Captains' conference for the following morning.

Here he heard for the first time of the marauding activities of a Dutch ship called the *Hendraught** lately arrived on the coast. After touching at Cape Verde she had called at every English factory or trading post and had tried to make trouble with the Africans. At Cestos itself where the King had refused to conspire against the English, the Captain of the *Hendraught* had seized all the local people who came on board to trade (including two of the King's cousins), put them in irons and carried them away for slaves. He crowned this outrage by hoisting English colours '. . . as their custome is in like insolencies upon that whole coast, to draw the greater odium upon the English nation'. Quite apart from the mischief the *Hendraught* might make with the natives, her very presence on the coast made it the more urgent that Holmes should put the Royal Company's stations along the Gold Coast in a position to defend themselves against any reprisal for Goree. He therefore stayed a bare two days in Cestos, watering the ships and landing materials for the building of a fort which the Company's factors were to complete 'upon a Rock on the starboard side of the River as you goe in'. At two o'clock in the morning of the 23rd they sailed on a fine north-easterly gale in the direction of Cape Palmas.

The coast down which they were now sailing was known by contemporaries as the Windward Coast, to distinguish it from the Gold Coast which began at Cape Three Points, nearly four hundred miles beyond 'the Cape of Palmes'. This distinction was reflected in the type of trade; along the Gold Coast it was castle-trade, conducted from a permanent and generally fortified base; along the Windward Coast ship-trade, conducted by means of canoes coming off to vessels anchored off shore. [6] Holmes's attempt to set up a permanent post at Cestos was exceptional. But in spite of the recent atrocities committed by the *Hendraught* the Africans do not seem to

* Probably the *Eendracht* (unity).

have been at all coy about trading. On the 24th two negroes, one of whom 'spake good Dutch', came on board: and three days later off Cape Palmas no less than three canoes put out to them. Contact with the local inhabitants was the more valuable because the coast was an extremely tricky one, bedevilled by strong inshore currents and studded with reefs rising sheer from deep water that are covered at all states of the tide. Like other dashing commanders Holmes was too professional a navigator to take unnecessary risks.

It was early on the morning of March 25th when Holmes was taking the *Jersey* out of an uncomfortable anchorage, 'a strong current setting in to the shore and a great sea setting home upon the shore, being distant from the rocks 4 miles', that he sighted a sail to the north-west and immediately gave chase on a light south-westerly wind. By two o'clock in the afternoon she was still nine miles off and keeping her distance. A slight change of wind forced Holmes to give up the chase for the time being and to direct the rest of his fleet on to a new course. In the evening:

> I sent to Captain Cubitt [H.M.S. *Welcome*] to let him know that I intended so soon as it was dark to clapp upon a wind all night to see if I could gett to windward of the sayle I chased, and that Captain Pyne [H.M.S. *Expedition*] should keep astern of the Fleet 3 or 4 Leagues and sayle as neere the shore as he could well venture for feare this shipp should slipp betwixt us and the shore.

The tension aboard the *Jersey* as she stood on and off the shore, tacking every half-hour or so, was matched by the weather.

> This night wee had a Turnado with a great deale of Raine and the most Lightning and Thunder that ever I saw.

Holmes stayed on deck all night. About two in the morning a tremendous thunderclap and lightning of unearthly brilliance—'as cleere as if it were noone day'—made him think at first that the ship had caught fire. For an instant the sea was held for several miles around in a dazzling incandescence. And in that very moment he saw her, a bare three miles off on his weather quarter, standing off on the same tack as himself. She had not, as he found out later, seen him. But when day came there was no sign either of the ship or of the coast.

Holmes at once bore up for the land which the lookout sighted from the topmast head about noon. He continued to close it for the next twenty-four hours, rejoining the fleet near Cape Palmas on the afternoon of the 27th. On the night of the 28th he ordered the ships to anchor as near the shore as possible,

> being afraid that the ship that was astern of us would give us the goe by in the night, as he had certainly don, if I had not lookt out verie yare for him.
>
> Being upon the Quarter Deck something after 12 of the clock I saw a shipp creeping alongst the shore. Presently I caus'd my pinnace to be mann'd and sent my Cockswaine on board the other shipps to tell them that I saw the shipp, and that they should take no notice of her, with directions to Captain Cubitt to weigh and stand alongst shore with the fleet, and ordered Captain Pyne in the *Expedition* to follow our shipp.

While his coxwain was away in the pinnace, Holmes stealthily got up his anchor, manned the yards and loosened the lashings of the sails so that the *Jersey* could be under way the minute that her quarry caught sight of her. In any case the wind and current were driving her towards the unknown vessel so that all the ships were very close before the stranger recognised his predicament. The reason was that the English ships were in the shadow of the moon and that the Captain took the *Welcome* and the *Expedition* to be part of the coast until he was almost on them. When he clapped on more sail Holmes was ready for him:

> I kept under his Lee quarter till about an houre before day, it growing then verie dark by the moone being downe, [I] lost sight of him. But the saylors had him on all sides of us. I had as good eyes as any of them but could not see him.

With his usual tactical flair Holmes declined the obvious choice of simply pressing on; instead he manœuvred so that, twist how he might, his enemy would have to reckon either with the *Jersey* or with the fleet cruising inshore. It paid off handsomely.

> . . . the first thing we saw when it was day was the shipp under our Lee bowe, about 2 miles from us. I thought the saylers would run madd for Joy: not a man

off the deck all night. About 8 of the clock wee got alongst his broadsides; He saluted us with a noise of Trumpetts; wee answered him in some Language which he did not like: wee called to them to strike which he refused to doe. He had not much time given him but had a shott betwixt his masts through his mainsaile.

Some more of the same treatment briskly administered quickly induced the captain to surrender. There had been, as Holmes proudly pointed out, no casualties on either side. With a less decisive commander or a less well disciplined ship it might have been a bloody business.

I sent my Lieut^t with some men to man her. The Gunner of her, being a Scotchman, when he saw my Lieut^t and the men coming on board to take possession of the shipp, runs and gathers some light[ed] matches and goes downe the Fore Hatch, and just stepping into the scuttle of the Powder Room with a resolution to blow up the shipp, my Cockswain got hold of his Leggs, and pull'd him upp, and the Cockswain and the Saylers did sufficiently drubb him and threw him into the Pinnace where he lay all day. At night I ordered good store of Iron about him and a watch upon him, and soe was kept till wee came into England. Had this villain succeeded wee had all bin lost for there were 400 Barrells of Powder in her and the shipps yard Arm to yard Arme.

This shipp proved to be the *Walker** formerly called the *Goulden Lyon* having 30 guns mounted and 74 men whereof was Commander Jacob Johnson a Scotchman by birth, bound for Castle de Mina,† being a shipp that by my Instructions I was particularly directed to secure together with the said Jacob Johnson for Injuries and violences by him committed in former voyages to this Coast to the great prejudice of the Royall Company . . .

No wonder Holmes felt pleased with himself: and no wonder the sailors were so cock-a-hoop. Not only was the *Goulden Lyon* a valuable prize in herself—she was taken into the Royal Navy as a fourth-rate and subsequently handed over to the Royal Company after the war[7]—but she was carrying, if her commander is to be believed, a various and expensive cargo. On his return to England in the following year Johnston‡ wrote to Sir William Coventry from a pub in Wapping called the Six Stars for his assistance in

* Probably a mistake for *Walcheren*: see Coventry's letter on p. 105 below.

† El Mina 'the Mine' the most strongly fortified base on the whole Guinea coast which the Dutch had captured from the Portuguese in 1638.

‡ So he signs himself.

obtaining redress for his losses. He attached to his letter[8] 'a particular of the goods belonging to James Johnstone, Commander of the *Wallagher** allias *Golden Lyone* taken by Major Holmes one the coast of Guynea'. It included 'Knyves, Beads, Carrabeins, Spanish foulling pieces, Musketts, pistolls, Brandy, Frensh wyne and Gravs Wyne, powder, two childrens hats with feathers, a curvall for a childe with bells and cheane'. The total value of this mixed cargo was estimated at about £7,000 of which Johnston claimed £2,828 9s. 2d. as his personal share. He substantiated what might be thought a generous estimate with the concluding assertion; '. . . wch Major Holmes sold one the coast of Guynea for more than the dubbell of this summe.' It is permissible to doubt if Captain Johnston was as truthful as he was enterprising. Holmes certainly doubted it when he noted in his journal a few weeks later:

> This Johnson that was Commander of the *Goulden Lyon* told me that he was once sayling under this Divell's hill† and hove his lead with Talow on it and the first cast brought up some Gould upon the Tallow. He heav'd the second time and brought up more; and the third time a much greater quantitie; and that he had taken short marks and long marks with the best notice he could how to find this place again, and made all the sayle he could to make the Generall of Castle De Mina acquainted with it. And that the Generall did send another shipp along with him with all necessaries to get up the Gould, but when he came there, could never hitt upon the same place again. Let those believe this fellow that have a mind to it, for I gave but little credit to him. [9]

This skilfully executed operation marks the professional *début* of another officer who was to share in all the hardest-fought battles of Holmes's career, who was, like him, to achieve flag-rank and a knighthood, and who was in the end to reach the great commands at sea that eluded the trusted friend of Prince Rupert. This was the Lieutenant of the *Jersey* who led the boarding party—Holmes's younger brother John.[10]

With each success Holmes inevitably intensified his principal logistic problem—manning. The capture of a ship or a fort might, usually did, mean more munitions: it could not in the nature of things mean more

---

* Probably a mistake for *Walcheren*.
† A prominent coastal feature six miles W. of Winneba.

men; indeed, unless the ship was broken up or the fort destroyed, it was bound to mean less. Six weeks later on the morrow of his most important victory, the storming of Cape Coast Castle, Holmes wrote to Coventry:

> If we had in all our shipps that are here but 200 men more, we may take De Mina and all the rest of their factorys from them. As for my own part I have not men to saile my shipps; I must be forced to make use of Dutchmen.[11]

And at sea the question was complicated by the presence of prisoners-of-war. Some of the seamen were no doubt ready enough to accept service in English ships. It was, as we have seen, the general practice in the seventeenth century. No disgrace attached to it, if only because no government made any provision for paying and maintaining soldiers or sailors who fell into enemy hands. But there were obvious dangers in diluting the loyalties of a crew, as Holmes would remember from his experiences with Rupert's fleet in the Azores.* For officers, except mercenaries, such a solution was dishonourable: they would require at least nominal guarding: and there was always the risk of cads or fanatics like the gunner of the *Goulden Lyon* who might be prepared to blow everyone to glory. For the time being Holmes transferred his prisoners to the *Expedition* and took some seamen out of her, the *Welcome* and the *Sophia* to man the prize.

The fleet now resumed its interrupted course. On April 4th off the Ivory Coast,

> 2 canoas came by our shipps side haveing Lymes and oranges and told us they had some gould and that they had some slaves ashore. But being afraid did not come on board.

As on his previous voyage Holmes noted the facts of the slave trade without evincing any interest in its profitability or any concern at its nature.

At five o'clock the following morning the *Sophia* hoisted her colours to show that she had sighted a sail. Just short of Cape Three Points the newcomer came up with them. She proved to be the Royal Company's ship the *Reliefe* six weeks out from England with this letter from Coventry.

* See above p. 47.

January the 28th 1663 [o.s.]

Captain Holmes

This comes to you by the *Relief* a shipp freighted by the Royall Company. The whole busyness of it is this to let you know that wee were verie well informed that there is a shipp gon from Zealand called the *Walcheren* wh. is the same shipp which was formerly called the *Goulden Lyon* which is now taken down out of the stern to disguise her. The commander is called Jacob Johnson wch is the same with James Johnson, soe that I conceive it is the same mentioned in your instructions. I wish good success and a happie return.

I am

yours &c

W.C.

If this gratifying communication showed how quickly intelligence could travel, another and more disquieting instance was afforded the next day by Captain Merrett of the *Loyal James*.* He reported that the Dutch prisoners who had been given the *Neptune* pink in which to return to Holland had arrived at El Mina and had given the alarm. He added that there were three ships in harbour there. Holmes's immediate resolve to press on for the Gold Coast was checked by the appearance on board at three o'clock in the morning of three Africans who offered to deliver the small Dutch castle of Axim that lay just to the west of Cape Three Points. In spite of the hour Holmes called all the other commanders on board for a conference, at which it was agreed to leave the *Expedition* and the *James* behind to encourage the natives (although the two ships were instructed to keep themselves out of range). At seven o'clock the rest of the fleet sailed for the Gold Coast.

Two days later they dropped anchor off Takoradi within sight of the Dutch fort at Anta. The English factor came off in a canoe to complain of Dutch insults to the Royal Company's flag. At a council of war held that afternoon it was decided

to take or destroy that Castle, for the securitie of the Royall Company's trade in those parts, and more especially to get into my hands one Captn Froome who was Governor there, being one that had don the R^ll Comp. great Injuries,

* The ship generally referred to as the *James* already mentioned on p. 99.

whom I was directed by my instructions particularly to seize where ever I should find him.

The *Galliot* and the *Jersey's* pinnace were at once sent close in shore to take soundings. The same afternoon thirty men were landed under Captain Brathwait of the *Dover Merchant* 'to endeavour the gaineing of the natives and to view and observe the place'.

Next morning, Sunday, April 10th, the *Expedition* and *James* arrived from Axim, where nothing had been effected. Holmes, no Sabbatarian, ordered the *Expedition* and *Welcome* to bombard the castle at short range and brought the *Jersey* close in to the shore. He was annoyed at hearing nothing from Brathwait, particularly as to 'whether or no the Blacks will undertake what is desired of them'. So:

> haveing ordered Captn Muschamp ashore with 40 men to Joyne Cap^n Brathwait and 35 men he had with him ashore and to storm the Castle (after I understood it might feazibly be don), seeing from my shipp that most of the *Expedition* and *Welcome's* shott hitt in the Cliff or went quite over the Castle, I got into my pinnace going [i.e. to go] on board the *Expedition* to remedie their ill fireing. The Castle fired severall shots at my boate, and wee rowing on board some of them came very neare, but did me no more hurt than beating the water in our faces.
>
> When I gott on board I found they were too neare in under the Cliff that they could not see the Castle, only the topp of their Flaggstaff, whereupon I caused to desist fireing and to weigh and to anchor further off.
>
> Soon after night came on [and] they could doe no more. Then I rowed ashore to the landing place to give directions . . . After I had given them their instructions how to proceed, I rowed towards the shipp, the Castle fireing at me whilst I was within reach of their Guns. The officers on shore took their time to pursue the directions I gave them soe that cutting down the outer Gate they stormed the Castle and gained it by 12 at night with the loss of one man and 2 or 3 wounded.

Next morning Holmes noted in his journal: 'the Royall Company's flagg was upp at Anta Castle'. He went ashore and arranged for the defence of the place, dismissing all the prisoners except Captain Froome who was brought aboard the *Jersey*. Amongst the many scores to be settled between him and the Royal Company were his activities as commander of the vessel *Christiana*.[12]

It is clear from Holmes's account of the operation and from the sharp note he sent to Brathwait that he was by no means satisfied with the discipline and efficiency of his officers. The fact that he left them in no doubt of his opinion, and indeed turned up in person in the middle of an action to communicate it, speaks for the authority of his command. Anta was the smallest and easiest of the sea-borne assaults that he was to carry out on the Gold Coast. Sending the *Expedition* on ahead to report what Dutch ships were in the anchorage at Chama Bay, he set sail with the fleet for that stretch of coast—Kommenda, El Mina, Cape Coast Castle—where the richest and strongest European forts and factories were clustered.

X

The Capture of Cape Coast

IN THE TWO MONTHS that followed Holmes very nearly succeeded in reversing the positions of the powerful Dutch West India Company and its peaky English rival. A modern historian has justly pointed out that the fruit of successes such as his lasted only so long as local naval supremacy was maintained:[1] a few months after the *Jersey* and her consorts had sailed for England De Ruyter with a much more formidable fleet caused Pepys to bewail the fact that we had been 'beaten to dirt at Guinny'.[2] Yet, without disputing the sense of this observation, it may be argued that Holmes left the basis of the struggle between the two companies that of competitors who grudgingly accept each other and who regretfully abandon the idea of eliminating a weaker rival. After 1664 the English were in West Africa to stay.

Since the whole purpose of the expedition was to sustain the Royal Company, a brief description of its condition may not be out of place. At the Gambia and Sierra Leone Holmes, as we have seen, found matters more or less as he had left them in 1661. The Gold Coast, however, was new to him. The *Jersey* had already called at the small trading posts of Antho and Takoradi. Besides these the company had factories at Kommenda, Anashan, Ardra and Wiamba [?Winneba] and a fort at Kormantin,[3] which was its administrative headquarters in Africa. In addition it had claims, as had the Swedes and the Danes, on Cape Coast Castle, after El Mina the strongest and most important of European bases. Known also as Cabo Corso or Cape Corse, the castle had changed hands even more often than it had changed names. For the past year it had been in the possession of the Dutch, whose governor Valckenburg had threatened the Royal Company in the bluntest of terms.[4] The Company's ability to withstand these and other shocks was reduced by the fierce dissensions between its officers. On December 18th Thomas Holder, the secretary of the Company in London, had written to Holmes:

> . . . you have a Busyness of great concerne to the R^ll Comp.^a on your hands: I meane the discoverie of the truth of those complaints which have been made against Mr. Selwyn. 5 [the chief factor]

A month later Selwyn wrote a long—indeed a very long—and injured letter to the Company from Kormantin Castle.6 His exertions in their service seem to have reminded him of St. Paul:

> I can boldly say it, and can Justifie it, I have laboured more in your service & . . . don more than all you have sent out . . . night and day employing my head and hands and shoulders to all even the heaviest offices, which some unable or unwilling leave to me . . . By sea and land have I in all weathers and seasons ventured when the least appearance of your occasions have seemed to invite me, through hazards none but I would adventure—I speak without offence—to the wonder of many who have beheld it etc etc.

The resources of his eloquence are concentrated on clearing himself of two charges: first, that of collusion with Sir Martin Noell, one of the directors of the Company, in private trading; second, that of threatening the natives of Kormantin with slavery. The second charge touched off an explosion against his accuser; Selwyn's whole policy was based on cultivating the friendship of the Kormantin tribe under their remarkable leader John Cabissa as a counter-weight against the Dutch.

> That . . . is soe far from my thoughts as the words were ever from my uttering, that I am almost distracted with astonishment what divell invented it. I have heard Mr. Davies* declare that before his time for the E.I. Comp.^a should expire he would lay John Cabissa his house levell with the Ground and ship him for Barbadoes, who is the most considerable Black for your service Guinea ever bred . . .

This judgment at least was true: when De Ruyter appeared off Kormantin in February 1665, it was Cabissa and his men who put up the stoutest resistance and in spite of inferior numbers succeeded on the first day's

* His accuser: it appears from this letter that he was employed by the East India Company.

attack in driving the Dutch back to their boats. When in the end superior force decided the issue Cabissa, unlike the European servants of the Company, chose death rather than surrender. Had he lived he intended paying Charles II a visit.[7]

It was not to be expected that the conditions and nature of the service would attract men of much quality. 'To be in Guinea is itself unpleasant enough', wrote Selwyn: and on this subject at least few of his colleagues would have disagreed with him. Their letters, fawning, whining, boasting, do nothing to encourage a favourable impression. 'I find but few of those you employ fitt for anything unless it be Mr. Selwyn', Holmes wrote to Coventry on May 9th.[8] Captain Valentine Pyne of the *Expedition* writing his dispatch at the same time put it even stronger: 'But the Truth is, were it not for an honest Blacke at Cormentine all the Company's servants ashore were little enough these distracted times, if the shippes were gone.'[9] These two, Selwyn and Cabissa, Holmes was shortly to meet.

In the early afternoon of April 12th the *Jersey* anchored off Kommenda within sight of El Mina and Cape Coast Castle. Next morning a letter was sent off by canoe to the Dutch governor at El Mina complaining of the injuries suffered by the Royal Company. Although his boats were not allowed close in Holmes noted four ships at anchor there, including a well-manned warship, and sighed for a fireship to send in among them. To protect his own fleet he kept the *Galliot* and four or five of his boats out all night between the English ships and the shore. On receiving a non-committal answer from the Dutch he left the *Welcome, Dover Merchant* and *Katherin* to watch El Mina and sailed with the rest of the fleet for Cape Coast. Next day, the 15th, the tempo increased. The *Sophia* and the *Reliefe* were sent to Kormantin to fetch Selwyn and John Cabissa: the Dutch prisoners aboard the *Jersey* and the *Expedition* were sent ashore in '2 great Canoas from Castle de Mina with their chests and cloathes along with them': lastly an officer from the Danish fort at Cape Coast came on board to offer 'friendship' in any attempt against the Dutch-held castle. On the 17th 'some Blacks from the Dye of Foutou' offered to surprise the castle if given suitable support. On the two following days the Dutch obligingly opened fire unprovoked on the *Galliot* and on a canoe which contained the precious person of Mr. Beavis, the East India Company's Agent at Kormantin. No further pretext was needed. On the afternoon of the 19th it was resolved at a council of officers and factors to take Cape Coast Castle with the assistance of the Africans and the connivance of the Danes.

At two o'clock the next morning the *Jersey* and the *Expedition* weighed anchor and cleared for action. They stood off a little to the westward so as to join forces with the *Welcome, Dover Merchant* and *Katherin* which had been hastily summoned from El Mina. This concentration was the more necessary because some natives from Anta had just reported a fleet of seven sail to windward. Furthermore Captain Brathwait of the *Dover Merchant* had apparently been refusing to obey the orders of Captain Cubitt of the *Welcome*, the Senior Naval Officer before El Mina who was to succeed to the command of the ships left behind on the coast when Holmes sailed for England. 'It is strange to me that you would suffer such impertinency to the great prejudice of the R^{ll} C.', wrote Holmes sharply. 'Had I not thought your orders sufficient to him I would have sent mine.' The *Dover Merchant* was, admittedly, not a King's ship; but it is doubtful if the distinction would have meant much to contemporaries. Certainly indiscipline of every kind was to be common in the Navy for many years yet.[10]

The ships rendezvoused at half-past ten, formed themselves into a line and stood in to the shore till they were abreast of the castle in four and a half fathoms:

> The *Welcom* being the headmost fired the first broadside at the Castle, wee next, then the *Dover Merch^t*, the *Katherin* and lastly the *Expedition*. Then wee tackt and made 3 or 4 boards plying our Guns at the Castle till 4 in the afternoone.[11]

The only effect of this prolonged cannonading, as Holmes afterwards admitted in the letter to Coventry already quoted, was on the morale of the Africans, who were much impressed. But the ships were too far away from any source of replenishment to use up munitions on a firework display. A council was called on board the *Jersey* to arrange for the landing

of men and guns 'to Batter the Castle'. In the end four twelve-pounders
and two six-pounders were got ashore over several days and at the cost of
several boats. On the first day a canoe carrying one sank close by the shore.
Even in calm weather it would have been quite a feat of seamanship. As it
was, hardly a day went by without a tornado or gales of wind and rain.

At this council of war it was reported by the 'Cabisheers', as Holmes
called Cabissa's tribesmen, that the Dutch were sending out a squadron of
three ships from El Mina to recapture Anta. The *Expedition* was ordered to
intercept them. Just short of Anta she came up with them and captured the
Black Eagle of Groningen,[12] rejoining the fleet with her prize two days
later. This vessel, a merchantman of nearly four hundred tons, had left
Holland bound for the Gambia. Calling at Goree shortly after Holmes had
left and suspecting nothing she had sent her boat ashore. Its failure to
return woke her Captain to the truth. He sailed at once for El Mina to
give the alarm. The Dutch governor took out all her cargo, put forty men
aboard and sent her for Holland with intelligence. Her capture thus had a
value beyond her six-pounder guns which were at once landed to play
against the castle.

Not that even ashore these pieces seem to have made much impression
on the castle. Increasingly Holmes's mind turned to direct assault. Very
likely there was nothing in the report of those seven ships sighted off Cape
Three Points, but if a Dutch fleet were to steal up behind him when
perhaps a fifth of his men and a considerable part of his ordnance were
stuck ashore there would be grave risk of a devastating defeat. Every day
he sent a few more men, even stripping the prizes of a handful here and a
handful there, until by the 24th Captain Muschamp had nearly a hundred
men under his command. The Company's officers who might have been
expected to give a lead seemed noticeably hesitant to expose themselves.
And the Africans of whom such great things were expected turned out to
be virtually useless except for hauling ordnance about.[13] As for the Danes,
their Governor 'was somewhat dissatisfied with some of our people' and
had to be pacified.

As day succeeded day two problems gave cause for alarm: water and ammunition. The *Brill* was sent along the coast to Anashan 'to keep your Boat constantly bringing of Water on board you . . . and to take care that it be not embezzled by the Blacks'. Ammunition was a much more serious difficulty. Partly the batteries were at too safe a distance; partly the shooting was so abysmal. 'I have observed', wrote Holmes to Selwyn on the 28th, 'some shotts made out of the last gun planted, and where one is plai'd I see six goe over. Unless care be taken to make better shotts wee shall want both Powder and shott to supply you.' On the 29th he peremptorily ordered the Royal Company's officers to raise a battery nearer the castle and sent the *Sophia* close in shore in support. On the 30th he could stand no further delay. The *Jersey* weighed anchor and stood in for the shore at which 'all the Officers and Factors came on board and dissuaded me from it until the Busyness on shore should be in better condition'. Reluctantly he agreed to wait but kept his ship cleared for action and ordered the *Expedition* to be ready to follow him in.

On Sunday morning May 1st John Cabissa came on board to tell Holmes that the Dye of Foutou 'being the Chief man in those parts amongst the Blacks was very earnest to storm the Castle'; whereupon Captain Bowen of the *Sophia* was sent ashore with a present to sustain his enthusiasm. This had, it seems, communicated itself to the officers of the Royal Company who now moved their guns very close to the castle. Holmes was determined to wait no longer. The *Jersey* and the *Expedition* hauled in their anchors and made sail. As they did so a white flag appeared on the castle and another one was to be seen being waved down by the shore. By midnight the terms of surrender had been agreed.

The hundred Dutchmen and thirty Africans who constituted the garrison were allowed to keep their arms and personal possessions. They marched out on the morning of May 3rd and embarked on the *Welcome, Sophia* and *Galliot* for El Mina. Proper courtesies were observed; the Dutch Governor and factors came aboard the *Jersey* to pay their respects before sailing to rejoin their compatriots that evening. When they arrived at El Mina, however, they encountered a reception much rougher than anything they had experienced during the siege of Cape Coast Castle. The

H

wrath of the Governor at hearing that Dutchmen had been 'abused and plundered by the Blacks soe terrified the rest that they refused to goe ashore but came back again soe farr as the shipps could come'. On the following day the ex-Governor of Cape Coast and one of his officers made the voyage from El Mina in a canoe to persuade them that they could now return in safety. This disposed of the problem for the moment, but it was to recur when other ships and forts were captured.

Why should surrender, so long an established convention of European warfare, bring down the anathemas of the Dutch West India Company on the heads of its servants? The imperialist struggles of the mid-seventeenth century were conducted at a distance from European bases and at a proximity to strange, fierce and unsubjugated peoples that made any sort of *guerre à outrance* more than usually unattractive. In any case fighting to the last man and the last round requires some kind of deep personal commitment of principle, of honour or belief. It cannot simply be ordered by credit account customers, which is precisely what the Royal Company and the West India Company were. Their officers had not come to Africa to proclaim the merits of Parliamentary government or to convert the heathen. They were not citizens defending their own homes. They had in fact no very strong inducement to risk getting hurt. In such a situation the moral element, tenacity, willpower, thrust, always important becomes overwhelming. Holmes has recorded his astonishment at the surrender of Goree when he had had, though he does not say so, rather the worst of the engagement. Again at Cape Coast it was the attackers not the defenders who had the best reason to give up. In the crucial action at Luanda in August 1648 when Portugal, at her last gasp, had broken the Dutch stranglehold on Angola and the all-important slave trade, it had been exactly the same story. The Dutch in an impregnable defensive position had astonished, almost embarrassed, their attackers by capitulating just after the disastrous failure of the main Portuguese assault.[14] If the West India Company could not instil into its servants the will to fight, it hoped to make them a little less ready to surrender. In the battles of the Second and Third Dutch Wars, perhaps the hardest-fought naval actions of the days of sail, Holmes was to learn as well as any man how formidable an enemy he had stirred up.

For Holmes the surrender had indeed been timely. Besides the shortage of powder which had already become serious, discipline amongst the men on shore had deteriorated 'to that disorder and insolency that they will not obey the officers appointed to command them'. Holmes's immediate threat of death without mercy seems to have been effective. And the plunder of the castle which was split between the Africans and the men landed from the ships no doubt made tempers easier. At a council of officers and factors held on board the *Jersey* on May 7th it was resolved to leave Captain Muschamp and fifty soldiers to garrison the castle

and that Mr. Gilbert Beavis at present Agent for the hon^ble East India Company be desired to be Chief Factor there for the management of the R^ll Comp.'s Affayres, the which if he undertake, that he promise to write to his friend in England to give the R.C. security for his performance according to the custom of their other Factors and that he either condition with us for the same salary he formerly had of the E.I. Comp^a or referr it to his friends in England to agree with the R.C. and that two Factors shall be placed with him for his Assistants.

These secondments from the East India Company do not seem to have had happy results. Davies, as we have seen, was still agitating the Royal Company by his accusations against Selwyn. And Beavis, on being relieved of his appointment at Cape Coast in 1667, was to lead a party of Africans in an assault on the place and carry off both his successor and a large part of the Company's goods.[15]

Besides this inauspicious settlement of civil affairs it was agreed to reduce the Dutch forts of Anamabo and Aga* that lay between Anashan and Kormantin. Holmes, we know, would have liked to have attacked El Mina but recognised, regretfully, the limitations imposed by lack of manpower.† The *Sophia, Katherin, Dover Merchant* and *Welcome* were ordered to Aga, the *Brill* was again sent to Anashan for supplies of water and two

* The orthography of this place name defeats me: Adia, Egya and other variations are common.

† See his letter to Coventry quoted above p. 104.

frigates belonging to the Royal Company, the *Reliefe* and the *Brittain*, were sent off with reports and letters for the Company in Sierra Leone and England respectively. On May 13th the *Jersey*, in company with the *Goulden Lyon*, *Expedition* and her prize the *Black Eagle* sailed from Cape Coast at eleven in the morning and dropped anchor off Aga at four in the afternoon.

Holmes was still determined to find a technique of naval bombardment that would be effective against coastal fortifications. At Aga he hit on the idea of turning the prize the *Black Eagle* into a floating battery. He put some guns on board her, unrigged her, lowered her topmasts on to the deck and had her anchored in three fathoms within musket shot of the castle. Unfortunately the weather upset his plans. A steep sea got up and ran so high that the *Black Eagle* had to cut her cable and make what sail she could on her lower masts to escape being pounded to bits on the shore. The experiment was not repeated.

The resources of local diplomacy were also exploited. The King of Fantine, reputed to be in league with the Dutch, was asked to remain neutral in the event of an English attack on Aga. He declined on the grounds that he preferred to 'have two sorts of white men to trade in his Countrey'. Holmes swiftly countered this balance-of-power argument by promising to hand over either Aga or Anamabo to the Danes and offering him two pounds of gold to clinch the deal. The monarch remained firm: not until his deposition had been engineered ten days later was it thought prudent to land men for the assault on Aga which capitulated instantly.

Meanwhile Holmes had been occupied with a variety of administrative and social duties. On the 18th Selwyn and his accuser Davies were ordered aboard the *Jersey* 'bringing with you your Journall, Ledger and Cash booke' to be strictly examined before Holmes, Pyne and other officers. The accusations were pronounced totally false and maliciously grounded. For the rest he was constantly to and fro between Kormantin and Cape Coast: watering at Anashan, celebrating the King's birthday and Restoration (May 29th), giving a dinner party on board the *Jersey* for the Danish Commanding Officer and the Dye of Foutou 'with diverse others whom I caressed and very well presented to secure their friendshipp to the English', and last, but not least, reconciling the factors.

And then there was the problem of the prisoners—more than a hundred in all—taken aboard the *Black Eagle*. The Governor of El Mina was even more savage than last time 'allowing the Blacks to riffle, plunder and abuse all the whites that should be landed, whereupon towards night they returned to us to Cape Coast'. This was a serious nuisance. Holmes wrote to the Governor a civil letter pointing out that in the *Black Eagle* he had captured all the provisions and liquor consigned him out of Holland to last him a whole year. Holmes himself was more than adequately victualled and would be pleased to supply him if he cared to send three or four boats or canoes. When they arrived the opportunity of filling them with the prisoners was too good to miss,

> which the Generall of De Mina perceiving drew his men out of the Castle to oppose their landing, fireing at them with great and small shott. Whereupon they returneing back I ordered some Boats to be mann'd and arm'd to keep them from coming near us. Upon their fireing at them with their small shott and Guns that some Boats carried in their heads they forced their way ashore, where being landed the Generall fell cutting and slashing of them and ordered diverse of them into the dungeon.

An unpleasant scene; but it ended the matter.

It was followed a couple of days later (June 2nd) by a much uglier one. After the taking of Aga:

> . . . the Dutchmen, being taken into mercy, inviteing our people into their warehouse with assurance of great quantitie of treasure and riches they most treacherously with trains of powder (lay'd to that end) blow up above fourscore whites and Blacks, which soe exasperated the Blacks that notwithstanding all our endeavours to protect them (as our people did 7 or 8 with apparent danger of their own lives) the Blacks in just revenge of the Dutchmen's treachery fell upon them and cutt off the heads of soe many of them as they could arrest out of the hands of the English. One of our men haveing a Dutch habitt contending earnestly for the rest of the Dutch was mistaken for a Dutchman and soe suffered the same disaster.

Dutch accounts of this horrid incident, predictably, charged Holmes with employing methods of barbarism. Such accusations, as we all too tediously know, are the small shot of propaganda in the wars of nations. Holmes himself habitually practised the same technique. The very next day, he claims in his journal, he sent a drummer—the conventional equivalent of a messenger under flag of truce—to the fort at Anamabo to warn the Dutch that the Africans were in a dangerous mood 'and desireing to prevent any further Effusion of Christian blood I offered (if they thought fitt) to receive them into my protection, but they instead of a right sense of this my charitable humanitie . . . [fell] upon the poore drummer under their walls, and having most barbarously cutt and mangled him, they stript him and left him for dead upon the place . . .'

The pious horror conveyed by this self-conscious borrowing from the Authorised Version induces a certain scepticism. Nothing that we know of Holmes or of his adversaries, the officers of the West India Company, suggests that either were too tender-hearted for the rough world in which they met. But this does not compel us to accept every charge of frightfulness that each brought against the other. Holmes, it may be, was a tough, but he was not a bully; he was hard, but not cruel; he was avaricious and unscrupulous, but he was not a beast. In the moist haze of a permissive age such distinctions are easily lost sight of.

True or false, the pretext of uncivilised conduct was eagerly seized on at a council of factors and officers which resolved on an immediate attack on Anamabo. The *Jersey* and the *Expedition* sailed there next day, Saturday, June 4th. At half-past four on Sunday morning the Blacks opened up with small shot and 'our people plyed a great Gun'. Men were landed from both ships but before the morning was out the Royal Company's officers and factors came on board to ask for the honour of taking the place without naval assistance. Holmes, who was anxious to get ready for the voyage homeward, consented, recalled the men, and sent the *Expedition* off to Cape Coast. He himself stood off a mile or two to the westward so that, without spoiling the Royal Company's fun, he would be at hand if they made a hash of things. Sure enough on Wednesday Selwyn came aboard with his tail between his legs. Wearily Holmes altered his plans and dispositions, recalling the *Expedition* from Cape Coast, the *Brill* from Anashan, the *Goulden Lyon* from Winneba, a trading post thirty miles to the east of Kormantin. Next morning the Dutch defenders 'understanding that I was resolved not to depart the Coast till that the place were taken, and fresh supplies going ashore, capitulated and surrendered the place'.

Holmes did not even bother to go ashore. He had a great deal to do. The next two days were spent taking in wood and water. Then he sailed to Kormantin to settle all outstanding civil and military matters with the Royal Company and to take on board the gold and ivory that was so eagerly awaited in London. On June 13th he sailed in company with the *Brill* and the *Galliot* for Winneba where he found the *Expedition* and the *Goulden Lyon* expecting him. He left the *Galliot* there as a parting present to the Company and put to sea with the others at seven o'clock in the morning of June 16th taking with him a packet of letters and dispatches from the Company's servants. From among these a letter from Dr. Lister, a doctor, it appears, of civil law, to Thomas Holder, the Secretary of the Company may be quoted:

> Those great services wch he [Major Holmes] hath don upon the Coast for the Royall Comp^a will merit greater acknowledgement then is fitt for me to prescribe to my masters . . . Upon my creditt his bountie and courage have both been soe eminent that it would puzzle a wiseman to say which exceeded and by them he hath made soe perfect a conquest of this whole coast that nothing but want of men hinders our intire possession.

Holmes would have qualified this by insisting on raising the standard as well as the numbers '. . . and those you do send not worth the bread they eat' he had written to Coventry. He gave his own summary in the Tower when he was being examined several months later:

> And thus I left the Coast of Africa haveinge served our Nacions interest soe well as the small force I had admitted of. I endeavoured by all wayes and meanes an adjustment of damages and regulation of trade as farr as in me lay. I avoided all Acts of hostilitye but in order to the aforesaid ends.[16]

XI

Return via São Tomé

RUMOURS OF HOLMES'S ACTIVITIES on the coast of Africa had reached Europe by the end of March. Early in May the taking of Goree and the capture of Dutch vessels on the coast was common knowledge in London and Amsterdam.[1] By the end of the month, on the very day that Holmes was arranging the *placement* of his farewell dinner party for the Dye of Foutou and the Danish General, Pepys and Coventry were shaking their heads over the outrageousness of his conduct and looking forward, the one with appetite, the other with apprehension, to the war that he seemed likely to precipitate.[2] Coventry stressed that Holmes had acted 'without any commission', a view consistent with his retrospective survey of events already quoted* but not, it may be thought, with the instructions which he himself had drafted or with the findings of the Examination which he and Arlington were to conduct in the following spring. The instinct of a politician to disavow the actions of a Commander-in-Chief has not diminished with the improvement of communications available in our own day. And when we hear Coventry go on to explain to Pepys that the country's economic troubles are caused by defects of national character and by the slackness of our business men† we recognise that history is indeed a seamless garment. Holmes as we know from his letters to Coventry was perfectly alive to his danger and habitually asks indulgence if he has exceeded his instructions. It was, no doubt, a formality. He was too much of a realist to expect mercy if the whole military and diplomatic gamble did not come off.

According to the letter of his instructions he was, after loading the

---

* See above, pp. 85–6.

† 'Our pride, and the laziness of the merchant', as Pepys has recorded him.

The Royalist and Parliamentary Fleets at Helvoetsluys. This contemporary Dutch print shows Rupert's ships to the right, Warwick's blockading squadron in the foreground and the Dutch force commanded by the elder Tromp in the left background ready to interpose.

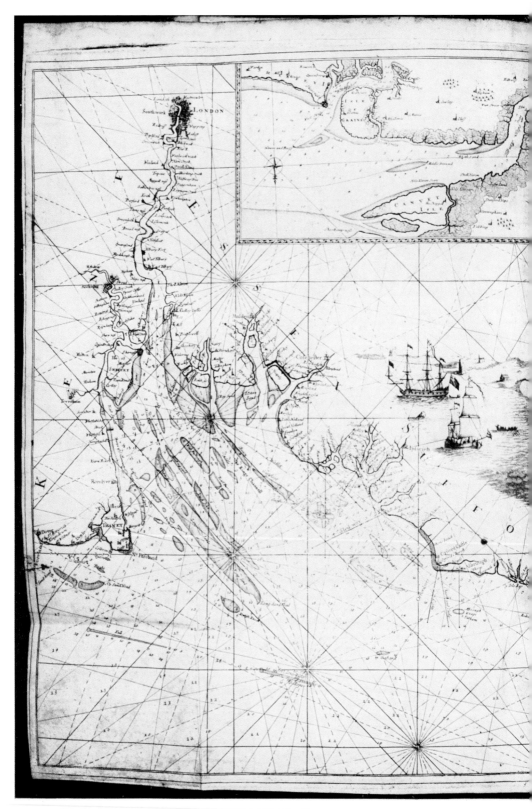

Map of the Thames Estuary from Grenville Collins's *Coasting Pilot*.

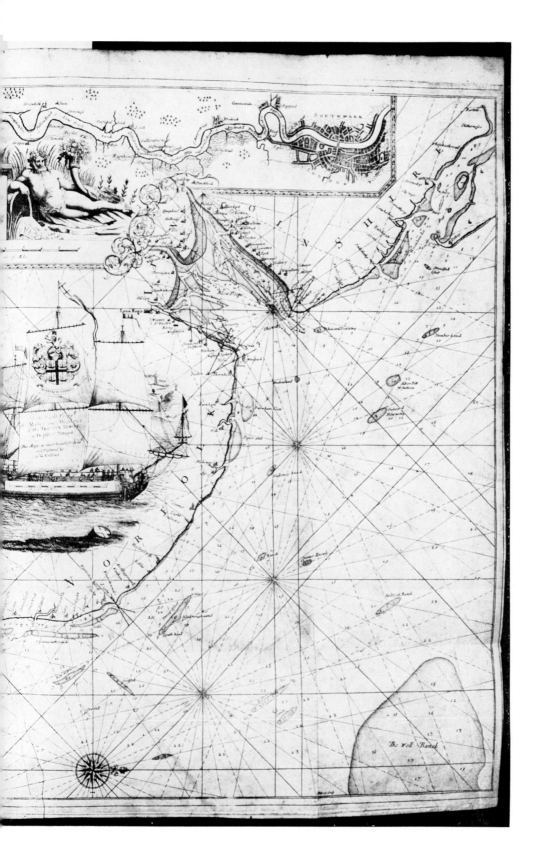

El Mina. From an enlargement of the border decoration to Blaeu's Atlas of 1638–40.

Third Rates in a squall. Among Holmes's commands the *Henrietta*, the *Reserve*, the *Revenge* and the *Defiance* were vessels of this type. From the studio of Van de Velde.

Map of West Africa. From Blaeu's Atlas of 1638–40.

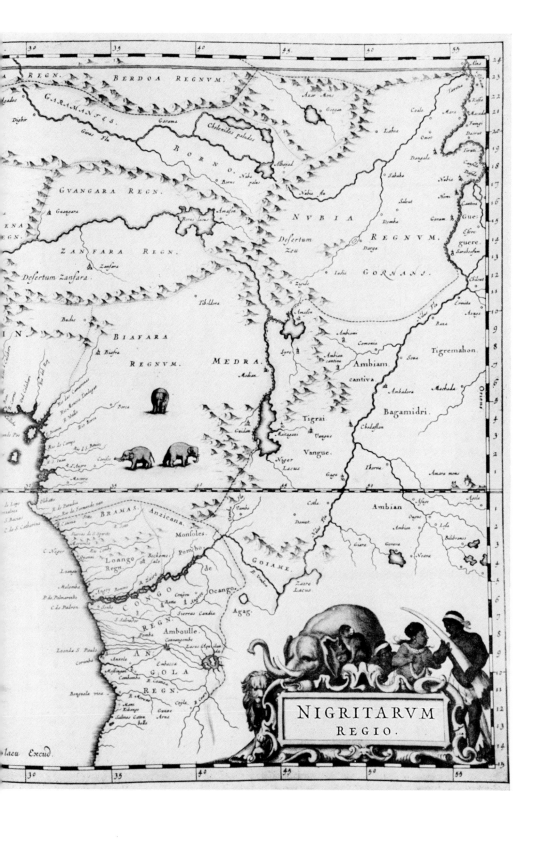

Prince Rupert by Lely. One of the famous series of portraits known as the Flag Men of Lowestoft.

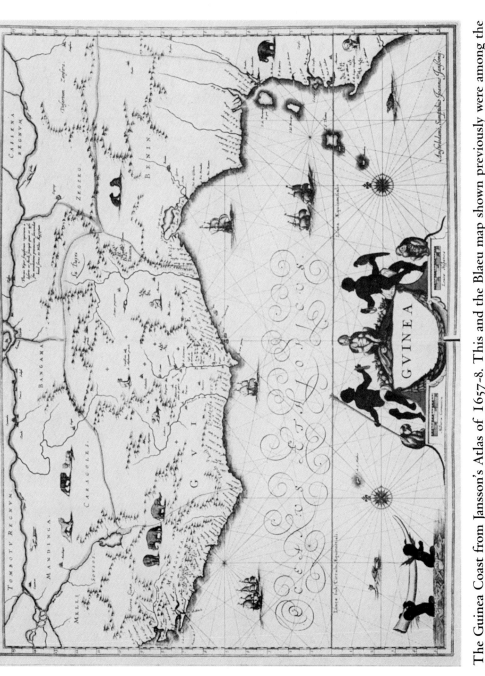

The Guinea Coast from Jansson's Atlas of 1657-8. This and the Blaeu map shown previously were among the best available to mariners of Holme's time.

Sir Frescheville Holles (left) and Sir Robert Holmes by Lely.

James, Duke of York, by Lely.

Sir Jeremy Smith by Lely. Smith, Monck's protégé, quarrelled bitterly with Holmes over the conduct of the St. James's Day Fight.

Van de Velde was present at the Four Days Battle as official war artist. The carefully annotated series of pen-and-ink wash drawings from which this illustration is taken is thus an authentic eye-witness record by the greatest of marine artists. Two points

The St. James's Day Fight from the print by Hollar. No Dutch artist has depicted this English victory. The fleet flagship, the Royal Charles, appears at the nearest point of the bulge in the line. Holmes as Rear-Admiral of the Red in the *Henry* must have been some way astern. Even this highly schematic

are particularly noticeable: first the overwhelming Dutch preponderance that characterised the first three days of the battle;
and second the difficulty of maintaining any tactical formation
once an engagement had begun.

representation, with every ship tidily keeping station as they never did in real
life, shows how impossible it was to co-ordinate and control a line of battle
that stretched over so huge a distance. It should be compared with the contemporary diagrams reproduced on pp. 144–5.

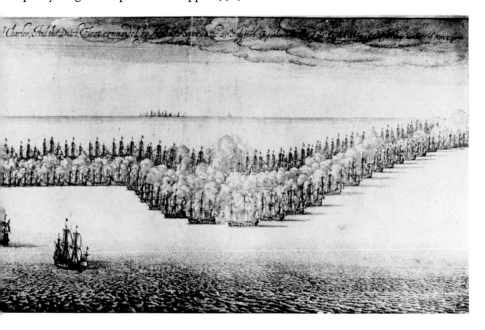

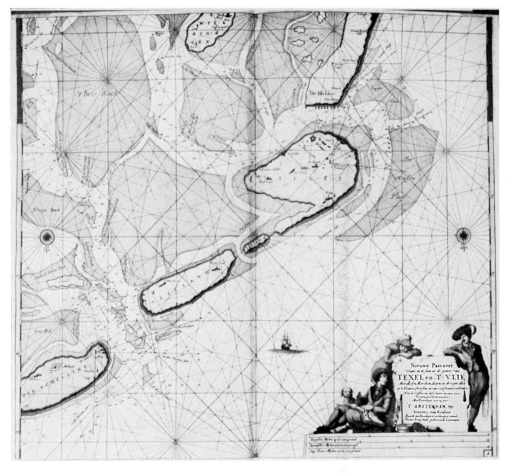

This contemporary chart of the Vlie makes vivid the dangers and difficulties of these narrow, shoaling waters in which Holmes achieved so signal a success. He entered by the easterly of the two channels and anchored in Schelling Road. The Dutch merchantmen were riding in Vlie Road a few miles to the south-west. The beacon (*Brandaris*) at the western end of the island of Schelling where the landings took place on the following day is clearly shown.

A detail of J. Kip's *Prospect of Whitehall* (1724) showing Sir Robert Holmes's house on the extreme right.

Van de Velde's drawing of the Bonfire. Note the beacon in the right foreground where the landing-parties are coming ashore to burn the town of Wester-schelling. Most English contemporary accounts call the place Brandaris, the

Dutch word for beacon, and the mistake is perpetuated on Holmes's monument (see Appendix II).

This model of the *St. Michael*, Holmes's last ship, is not one of those built for the Navy Board and may well have been made for him. See page 190.

An engraving of Yarmouth dated 1801, showing (right) the house Sir Robert built for himself (now the George Hotel) and (left) the castle which he restored to military effectiveness.

Solebay: the tapestries now in the Royal Collection executed from drawings by Van de Velde. The first shows the position just before the engagement with the Dutch coming on in line abreast and the English hurriedly trying to form a line ahead but with many of their ships masking each other. The second shows the action in the afternoon. The blazing wreck to the left is that of Sandwich's flagship the *Royal James*.

Sir Robert Holmes's monument in Yarmouth church.

Company's gold and ivory at Kormantin, to make the best of his way home. To do so at that season a ship would steer well to the southward of the Gold Coast so as to pick up the South West Trades. In fact Holmes sailed south-eastward for ten days, eventually making his landfall at Cape St. John in Spanish Guinea. He continued southward along the coast for several days, keeping a careful record of pilotage. On June 30th they sighted a sail off the mouth of the Gabon, the only ship they were to meet along that empty coast of red and white cliffs and sandy bays. She proved to be a pinnace of the Royal Company's, bound for her base at Kormantin.

Still sailing south Holmes reached Cape Lopez Gonsalves on July 5th. He spent the next four days refitting; tallowing, scraping, tarring and taking in wood and water. A few days later they at last turned on to a westerly course and early in the morning of the 14th sighted the Portuguese island of São Tomé. São Tomé was not only well-sited to control the coast of Angola and the Bight of Benin but of direct economic importance both as an entrepot for slaves and as a principal producer of sugar. Its capture by the Dutch had been a heavy blow to the Portuguese empire and its return in 1648 only less valuable than that of Angola itself.[3] If, by an unlucky turn of the wheel, the Royal Company's ships and servants were to find themselves driven from their bases on the Guinea coast, São Tomé offered a useful rallying-point. Holmes had therefore decided to land a considerable quantity of stores there in case disaster should overtake the Company once he had gone.[4] His account of the colony is not without interest:

The Governor of the Castle sent me a present of 7 cowes, some sheep, Goates, Hoggs, henns and fruit. The next day I sent him double or treble the value of his present, these sort of Governors expecting alwaies to be soe dealt withall, which caused great kindness and good understanding between us all the time I stayd there; and nothing he could get in the Island but he sent me.

This Island has great plentie of provision, as Cowes, sheep, goates, hogges and poultrie in abundance; good fish. All the fields full of black Quailes and other birds. I had a mind to see the shore by the watering place and the King of Portugall's house and the Castle. The Governor did not seem to deny it but, as I understood, he had no mind that I should see his poore and weak condition.

However I was resolved to goe in my well day (for I had got an Ague at Cape
Lopez Gonsalves). The next well day in the morneing I sent him word that I
intended to come ashore, but desired him to take no notice of me. But he did,
and put himself in the best posture he could, and received me with the best
countenance he could shew. But before I came away he begg'd a Barrell or two
of powder of me, supposing that I had a good quantity on boord. I sent him 2
Barrells of Powder, and at my going away he sent to me to let me know that he
was in some apprehension that the Dutch had a designe to take the Island from
the Portuguese and desired me to let him have 3 or 4 Barrells more. Otherwise
he would not be in a condition to keep the Castle or secure the Royall Com-
panie's shipps when they should come there. I sent him 4 Barrells more and
when he found me soe free he was every day begging something or other.

That which I took most notice of on this unfortunate shore was that all the
women were in armes formed into Companies with Captains, lieutenants and
Ensignes in good order and 7 or 8 Companies of them. The reason is that the
males do not live long upon this island, but the females doe, and they have 10
Females for one male.

Altogether Holmes spent four weeks in this curious outpost of Empire.
Most of the time he was either landing stores or superintending the
cooperage of additional water casks against the long voyage ahead. He also
found an opportunity of sending his master to survey the approaches of
the harbour. He saw a slave ship leave for Brazil and saw her limp back
again four days later 'being very leakie'.

Was it perhaps the slave trade that led him to take so detailed an
interest in the coast of the Congo and Angola? When, on August 11th, he
at last left São Tomé (to the relief, no doubt, of the Governor and his
regiment of women) it was not for England but for Cape Lopez that he
directed the course of his ships. Sighting the Cape on the 13th they
cruised down the coast for a fortnight till they were two hundred miles
south of the Equator. Most of the time, however, they seem to have been
too far out to sea to obtain any nautical or commercial intelligence. On the
28th Holmes called the commanders on board him and ordered them to
keep station abeam of each other six miles apart so as to minimise the risk
of collision at night. The fleet turned on to a course that should bring it
home by way of the Cape Verde and Canary Islands. With every imagin-
able advantage of wind and weather it would be many days before they

sighted land. Next to Holmes's navigation the safety of the fleet would thus depend largely on vigilance in station-keeping.

In fact this turned out to be the least of their problems. For the first fortnight fresh gales carried them prosperously onward. But on September 12th the wind fell light. For ten days they made little way. 'Very little wind'. 'Calm all night'. The laconic entries leave much to the imagination. A day without wind is a long day in a sailing ship. On the 23rd the storm broke—but it was not the weather. The commanders of the *Goulden Lyon*, *Brill* and *Expedition* came on board the *Jersey* to complain that they were short of water and to propose an immediate alteration of course for the Barbadoes which they believed to be near at hand.

Holmes was furious, both at their incompetence in running short of water and at their slovenly navigation:

> I chidd them very severely . . . I called for their Journalls, as alsoe all the Journalls of the officers that kept any on board of all the shipps, and finding them all too much to the westward I told them I thought they were all mistaken. For that observing my pendulas I had on board, which I constantly attended, either they could not be true or . . . we must be much more to the Eastward . . . for that by my reckoning Fogo one of [the] Cape de Verd Islands bore of me N.E. by N. 36 leagues and since they dealt no better by me nor the King's Service in not getting water enough as I directed them, I was resolved (presuming upon my pendula's) to try 48 houres in steering for Fogo as it bore by my own Reckoning . . . and if in that time I found my pendula's in an error it was but bearing up at last for Barbadoes.

The combination of personal and professional authority sweetened by a diplomatic appeal to reason carried the day. A fortunate easing of the wind enabled the fleet to make good the course Holmes desired. Two days later,

> . . . in the afternoone wee had a great shower of Rain. At 3 of ye clock wee saw land which were the Islands of Fogo and Brava being 2 of the Cape de Verde Islands. Fogo bore N.E. by N. and Brava N.N.E. ½ E. distant by estimation 11 leagues.

They had been out of sight of land for between five and six weeks. By any standards this was good navigation.

It was also a triumph for Huygens who was awaiting Holmes's return with impatience. '*Vostre Capitaine Holmes demeure fort long temps a revenir,*' he wrote to Moray on November 11th after the *Jersey* had been sighted in European waters. His anxiety may have been sharpened by the French *savant* Chapelain who suggested to him that it would in any case be naïve to expect the English to give a truthful account of the performance of the watches. In fact, within a month of Holmes's return to London, Huygens was professing himself delighted with his reports and was asking Moray to question him further about the behaviour of the watches in rough weather. The master of the *Jersey* confirmed Holmes's report that they behaved perfectly '*non pas lors que le vaisseau estoit a l'Ancre en temps d'orage . . . que les vaisseaux roulent et dansent de tous costez*'. And Holmes at dinner with Moray added that it was only the watches that enabled him to perceive that he had been carried eighty leagues to the eastward during the time that the ships were becalmed. [5]

To return from this navigational digression to the vessels themselves, which we left approaching the Cape Verdes. As they came up to the islands the wind fell away to a whisper. Holmes had decided to wood and water at the uninhabited island of St. Vincent but it took him four days—and some towing by his boats—to get into the anchorage. He found a French ship of about one hundred and fifty tons that had been there for nearly two months turning and salting turtles for sale in the West Indies. During the three days he spent there watering the ships 'our men turned diverse turtles on shore and brought them off, which was a great refreshment to them'.

Sailing early on October 5th they soon found too much wind rather than too little. At dawn on the 11th sighting two sail to the north on a north-westerly course they gave chase. After a few hours the *Brill* and the *Goulden Lyon* had dropped so far astern that Holmes ordered the *Expedition* to pursue the chase while he waited for them. By late afternoon they were close enough for Holmes to make sail after the strangers who were exchanging shots with the *Expedition* as darkness fell. The wind dropped during the night and by midnight they were close enough to see the light of one of them. At daybreak the *Expedition*'s boat came alongside to report that the two ships were Spaniards bound for the West Indies; the smaller had escaped but the larger was hove to under the *Expedition*'s guns. Holmes's account of this incident is printed here partly for the light it throws on the Law of the sea as it was then understood and practised and partly because of its unexpected disposal of the uncertainty surrounding the loss of Prince Maurice, Holmes's old Commanding Officer, in the Sombrero hurricane of September 1652:*

She was a Dutch built shipp of 25 Guns bound for Porto Rico with a new Governour, Don Francisco Velasco who with the Captain of the Shipp and others came on board me and dined with me. And complaineing much for want of water I spared them two hogsheads. All this forenoone it was calm.

This Gentlman was very much afraid that I would make a Prize of him. I might very well answer to doe it being on the other side of the Tropicke† & fireing at the King's shipp, and his Matie since his happie restoration haveing made no peace with ye Spaniards.

Amongst some others that came along with this Gentlman there was a Dominican Friar who spoke good English and lived many years upon the Island of St. John Porto Rico. I asked him whether he was in that Island about that time that prince Rupert was in the West Indies. He told me he was. I asked him whether he did not heare of any prisoners, Englishmen, that were brought thither about that time. He told me that he heard of none, but withall that there were severall of the best officers of that Island and other Gentlmen that lived upon the same 30 or 40 yeares on board their shipp, which were able to give me the best account of anything I had a mind to know. I desired him to write their names which he did of 8 of them. I desired him to speak to Don Francisco De Velasco to send for them, which he did grant and they accordingly came like a Bear to the stake, not knowing but that they were all to be prisoners. When they came aboard (and) found it otherwise, then they began to recover themselves of their Fright. Then I got this Father to tell them the storie how wee lost prince Maurice in a Hurricane about that Island and some people did say that the prince did save his life But was kept prisoner in a Dungeon at St. John Porto Rico. They assured me there was no such thing as any prisoner there; nor any men saved; but [that] about that very time I spoke of, upon the Southward side of the Island they found a shipp cast away and several pieces of the wreck came ashore; and amongst the rest a Goulden Lyon wᶜʰ some of them saw and a great quantitie of pipestaves markt MP as all prince Maurice his cask[s] were. This confirmed me that he was lost thereabouts.

* See above, p. 49.
† Holmes refers to the traditional doctrine of 'No Peace Beyond the Line'.

Holmes asked Don Francisco to let him know if he was able to find out anything more which was gladly promised and they parted the best of friends:

> I made much of ye Dons and supplied them with water and what other things they wanted and let them goe freely away to their great satisfaction and content. They gave me all the Guns they could fire, which I answer'd. They stood their course and I stood mine. [6]

The gunfire of the salutes, an appropriate funeral volley for Prince Maurice, sounded over the ocean that had earlier claimed the *Constant Reformation*, a last echo of the Royalist fleet.

On November 5th after two or three weeks of very stormy weather in which it proved impossible to keep his ships together Holmes sighted the Rock of Lisbon. Entering Cascais Roads he met a merchantman outward bound for Dartmouth and stopped her while he dashed off a letter to Coventry, 'to let you know of my arrivall here after a long and tedious passage occasioned by contrary winds, calms and foule weather'. His last letter had been written from Cape Coast on May 9th. Six months was a long interval to leave in the communications of a Commander-in-Chief to his political superiors even by the slow irregular standards of the seventeenth century. Clearly reports of his activities must have reached Europe. What might not be made of that unfortunate affair after the surrender of Aga when the blacks went on the rampage?

> I know not how my Actions upon the Coast of Guyny are resented at Court, nor how my Condition stands: I shall desire you to doe me the favour to write a letter for me to Capt Gallois to the Isle of Wight where I intend to stopp at my coming into the Channel and give me account of my affayres and how my behaviour on the Coast is resented.

Anxious as he was to get back to England as quickly as possible he was too experienced a seaman to take undermanned and defective ships across the Bay and up the Channel at so dangerous a season and at a time when, as the Captain of another English frigate in the port informed him, war with Holland might break out at any moment. Both the *Jersey* and the *Brill* had suffered severely from their recent buffeting and all the ships were short of their proper complement. Holmes was determined to press every English seaman he could find under any foreign flag, including that of our Portuguese ally:

> . . . and seeing one of the King of Portugall's Frigatts coming in, commanded as I understood by a Knight of Malta, on board of wch I was informed were great many English seamen, I sent my Lieutenant before in my Pinace to demand them, which he refuseing to deliver just under Bellile castle I closed my wind with intention to be aboard him . . . etc., etc.

Hostilities were narrowly avoided, but to Holmes's annoyance the Knight got all his Englishmen ashore and gave them enough money to make themselves scarce. Next day, November 22nd, the refit completed, they sailed on a fine fresh south-westerly gale. It was the last time Holmes was to call at the great port that had given him and his friends protection in adversity.

Two days out they met two English ketches homeward bound from Oporto out of which Holmes pressed a couple of seamen. On the morning of December 6th they sighted the Dodman and steered in for Plymouth as the *Jersey* was leaking badly. Hardly had she dropped anchor in the Hamoaze before John Holmes was away to London with another letter from his brother to William Coventry. In addition to the other matters already raised Holmes meant to lose no time in obtaining official clearance for the supernumerary seamen he had collected in Lisbon.[7] He might be in trouble for over-zealous interpretation of his instructions but he was not going to be caught in the same trap he had fallen into on his return from his previous expedition to the Gambia.*

Whatever private misgivings Holmes might feel about his reception, others considered him a very fortunate man. 'Major Holmes is come from Guinny, and is now at Plymouth with great wealth, they say,'[8] noted Pepys. And Colonel Norwood whom Holmes had taken out to Lisbon in the *Reserve* sent to their old host, the ambassador Sir Richard Fanshaw, 'happy tidings (of) . . . the return of poor—nay rich—Robin Holmes from his conquest of the river Gambo with Dutch prizes.'[9] None the less, in

* See above, p. 72.

spite of the wealth and the prizes, in spite of the political tide that was running for a war with the Dutch, Holmes had good reason for anxiety. In August the great Dutch minister De Witt had sent secret orders to Admiral De Ruyter in the Mediterranean to sail at once for the Guinea Coast to redress the situation. By October 11th De Ruyter appeared off Goree and retook it, capturing a number of English ships. Within a few weeks he had made a clean sweep of the Guinea Coast, with the single exception of Cape Coast Castle. The first news of this reversal had reached England a few weeks before Holmes's return. Full confirmation of its extent arrived while he was bringing his ships round from Plymouth to the Thames.[10] Although a fleet was being fitted out to be sent against De Ruyter under Holmes's old chief Prince Rupert, although the unheard of sum of £2,500,000 had been proposed and was shortly to be voted by the Commons to prosecute such a war, the swiftness and completeness of the Dutch success might strengthen the peace party. And if there were to be no war Holmes would be in a most unenviable position. Had not the King himself in the very speech in which he had called for supply against the Dutch specifically repudiated Holmes action in taking Goree* and promised a strict examination and exemplary justice? News of this would have come to his ears at once which perhaps explains his dawdling over the last and easiest passages of his long voyage. He spent twelve days in Plymouth, sailing at last on December 18th. On the 19th he anchored off Portsmouth and spent another six days there. It was convenient, no doubt, to settle his affairs in the Isle of Wight before becoming involved in whatever was awaiting him in London. And every day brought encouraging signs. Coventry had written in reply to his letter from Plymouth:

> I suppose haveing begun so severely already you need no incouragement to seize and bring with you what Dutch you can. It is now the generall order and therefore if you doe it you shall not want paper for it when you come, if I cannot have it sent now wch I shall endeavour.[11]

* 'The King assured the Ambassador upon his Princely word "That he had given no Commission or Order to Captain Holmes for that purpose, nor did know upon what Grounds he had proceeded to that Act of Hostility".' *Lords Journals*, XI, 625. 24 Nov. 64.

The Channel was alive with English warships. Off Portland the *Jersey* came up with the *Colchester* frigate. Off the Isle of Wight Sir William Berkeley, Rear Admiral of the Red, came on board. Further up the Solent they found Sandwich and the main part of the fleet riding at anchor. The supernumerary men whom Holmes had pressed at Lisbon were discharged to swell their complements. Sailing from Spithead on Christmas Day they anchored in the Downs on the 27th. Shortly after they came in they saw the *Mary* and five sail more weigh and go out by the Longsand to cruise to the north-westward. Delayed by contrary winds they were kept yet longer in this anchorage by the accident of the *Forrester* frigate running aground on the Woolpack sand. They lent her their boats and their pilot. It took two or three days, and the further assistance of a Margate hoy, to get her off. That done, they made sail and ran over the flats to Sheerness, letting go the anchor for the last time at three in the afternoon of January 3rd, 1665.

The Royal Company who had instigated the whole enterprise were feeling somewhat cooler towards Holmes as the news of their losses arrived with every ship from Guinea. On the day before he entered the Thames they petitioned the King that Major Holmes's Dutch prizes might be made over to them as compensation and on January 7th a warrant was issued to that effect.[12] The petition glitters, even in that dark hour, with the radiant expectations that illuminate its arguments and gild its statistics. £100,000 p.a. in elephants' teeth, wax, hides, dyeing wood and Guinea grain was expected from Gambia, Sierra Leone and Cestos: £200,000 in gold and about £100,000 in 'servants for the Plantations' from the Gold Coast; and, to round things off, £86,000 a year in Spanish silver for a contract they had made to supply the Spaniards with 3,500 negroes from Old and New Calabar.[13] Set against such huge sums Holmes' loot was small beer; but it had the advantage of verifiable existence and they meant to have it. On January 9th Holmes was committed to the Tower. 'I perceive', Pepys observed in his *Diary*, 'it is made matter of jest only; but if the Dutch should be our masters, it may come to be of earnest to him, to be given over to them for a sacrifice, as Sir W. Rairly [Raleigh] was.'

I

His examination by the two Secretaries of State Sir William Morrice and Sir Henry Bennet took place on January 14th. Bennet, later Lord Arlington, was a politician of the same generation and background as Holmes who was assiduous in courting his favour. On this his most recent voyage he had brought back some horses for him, presumably from Lisbon.[14] Full transcripts of this and of his subsequent examination on March 3rd, together with two rough drafts of each in the handwriting of William Coventry, are in the Public Record Office.[15] Together with Holmes's own full narrative delivered to his examiners on March 6th[16] they tell, somewhat more glibly, the story already unfolded. Questioned about the treasure he had brought home he replied that he had brought between two and three thousand pounds in gold together with hides, wax and teeth to a value he was not sure of and he confirmed that he had not as yet disposed of any of this. On January 23rd a warrant was issued to the Lieutenant-Governor of the Tower to hand him over to a messenger who would keep him under surveillance.[17] This partial liberty was probably connected with the Royal Company's anxiety to get what it could while it could. On the 25th Sir Martin Noell and two other of its representatives signed a receipt for 799 ounces 2 pennyweight of gold from Major Robert Holmes[18] and on the following day ordered him to deliver 'all such wax, teeth, iron and other goods as you have aboard the *Jersey*'. It is an index of the ambivalence of his status that the Duke of York's warrant ordering him to hand over the gold was directed to 'Captain Robert Holmes, Captain of his Majestie's shipp *Jersey*' though dated January 13th when Holmes was certainly in the Tower.[19] On January 29th and again on February 10th the Dutch ambassador reported him still at liberty though under guard.[20] On February 14th he was recommitted to the Tower and, as we have seen, underwent a second and final examination on March 3rd. The Dutch declaration of war on February 22nd doubtless helped his judges to put a favourable construction on his actions. On March 6th[21] a warrant was passed for his release, on the 10th the Dutch ambassador reported that he was already at liberty[22] and on the 14th Pepys was among those who attended a lavish banquet given by the

Lieutenant-Governor in the Tower to celebrate Holmes's enlargement.[23]
If Pepys was correctly informed, Holmes had the day before given the
Lieutenant-Governor a douceur of fifty gold pieces, which suggests that
the Royal Company had not had things all their own way. On March
23rd he was granted a full pardon and release of all debts and demands
concerning shipping and ammunition as well as of all felonies and offences
committed in England or elsewhere up to that day.[24] Four days later the
Dutch ambassador reported to the States General that the King had given
command of his ship the *Revenge* 'to Major Holmes who declared he would
maintain the name of his ship against the enemy'.[25] His previous record
no less than his subsequent achievements show this no empty boast.

XII

The Second Dutch War

THE SECOND DUTCH WAR of 1665–7 is chequered by victory and defeat, by professionalism and amateurishness, by courage and incompetence, so that even at the distance of three centuries it seems to retain the disorder and unpredictability of immediate experience. A supremely well-informed contemporary such as Pepys was perpetually in the dark as to what was going to happen next. Generally fearing the worst he appears to have been incredulously delighted by the successes which brilliantly and bewilderingly diversified the heroic failure of the Four Days' Battle and the ultimate humiliation of the Dutch attack on the Medway. And all these vicissitudes, like the origin and conduct of the war, were naval. Diplomacy had little to contribute. Soldiers were employed either to make good the deficiencies in naval manpower or, on occasion, to beat the woods and copses near the ports for runaway seamen.[1] The two most formidable maritime powers of Europe, a remarkably even match for each other as to ships and sailors, were in the ring for the trade of the world.

This, as we have seen, is what Holmes had been gambling on. It now remained for him to bring off a double by seizing the opportunities of a war that he had been active in provoking to make a name and perhaps a fortune as a commander. The words with which the late Lord Birkenhead fluttered the dovecotes of Glasgow University: 'The world continues to offer glittering prizes to those who have stout hearts and sharp swords'. would no doubt have struck Holmes as an apt summary of his situation and prospects. The fleet in which he was now serving was a very different force from any in his previous experience. In size and firepower it was much superior to the ship-money fleets of Charles I or even to the

Commonwealth Navy in which so many of its officers and men had learned
their trade. Ninety-eight men-of-war were ready to meet the Dutch in the
spring of 1665 and, in the event, to give an excellent account of themselves. What is more this vast force was articulated into squadrons and
divisions, each controlled by a code of fighting instructions and signals, so
that the fleet would fight as a fleet, not as a seaborne horde.[2] It is not easy
to realise how ambitious and how novel a departure this was. A fleet of
this size sailing in line ahead—and line ahead was the formation dictated
by the broadside until the rotating gun-turret revolutionised naval tactics
—would stretch over several miles of sea. Its mobility was limited by the
wind, its ability to maintain formation by the sailing qualities of the
individual ships. In action the smoke from the guns would not only make
signalling all but impossible but might easily blanket a ship from her next
astern and ahead in the line. The admirals of the Restoration Navy were
trying their hand at a job so daunting in its technical difficulties that one
can only wonder at their undertaking it, as if a prima ballerina were to
dance in gumboots.

Some among them seem indeed to have felt that once battle had actually
been joined it would be better to leave each individual Captain to join
uninhibitedly in a general free-for-all. Monck and Prince Rupert were
regarded as the protagonists of this school, while James, Duke of York,
supported by Sandwich and Sir William Penn, was the champion of
formal tactics. When Holmes received his commission as Captain of the
Revenge, the Duke of York was in personal command of the fleet as Lord
High Admiral. As such he commanded the Red or centre squadron;
Prince Rupert the White or van; and Sandwich the Blue or rear. This
pattern of command was reflected in each of the three squadrons, a Vice-
Admiral commanding the van division and a Rear-Admiral the rear so that
there were nine flag-officers in all. Holmes in the Revenge was assigned to
the Admiral's division of the White so that his first fleet action, like his
first experience of life at sea, was to take place under the direct command
of Prince Rupert. Indeed in the Order of Battle drawn up on April 7th,
1665, the Revenge is stationed next astern of Rupert's flagship with only a

sixth-rate, the *Merlin*, in between.³ When the fleets came to close action
the *Merlin* would not be expected to keep her place in the line but to deal
with fireships. After the flag-men, Sir Christopher Myngs commanding
the van and Robert Sansum commanding the rear, Holmes was thus in the
most senior position within the squadron. Yet the whole notion of
seniority, though within a few years of crystallising, was still fluid. It
could be argued, for instance, that Valentine Pyne who had been junior to
Holmes as Captain of the *Expedition* on the Guinea coast was now senior to
him because he was commanding the *St. Andrew,* a second-rate of 60 guns,
as opposed to the *Revenge,* a third-rate of 58.⁴ The chances are that he did
so regard himself: and the chances are that Holmes would indignantly
have pressed his own claims. The quarrelsome assertiveness of the
Restoration officers has already been remarked. It was not, it was emphati-
cally not, the Navy of Nelson's band of brothers.

The *Revenge* was in fact much the better ship of the two. Built under the
Commonwealth at Limehouse in 1654 she had a good deal of life left in
her while the *St. Andrew,* a survivor from James I's time, was tottering to
the end of forty-odd years of service. Even in the matter of armament,
facts do not always correspond with figures. For instance in the spring of
the next year when Holmes was commanding a brand-new third-rate of
64 guns, the *Defiance,* the Commanders-in-Chief supported his complaint
'that the men appointed for the *Defiance* are too few, being it carryes, as
many and heavier Gunns as the *Swiftsure*' (shewn in contemporary lists as a
second-rate of 66).⁵ As with the fiscal rating valuations of our own day,
administrative convenience must have tended to conserve the rating of a
warship even when it no longer corresponded exactly with the realities it
was supposed to represent. Indeed a powerful third-rate seems to have been
the most desirable command for a private Captain. Thomas Allin, Jeremy
Smith, Edward Spragge, were among those, soon to be Holmes's seniors or
his rivals as flag-officers, who in the spring of 1665 sailed to fight the
Dutch in ships of this description.

As the fleet prepared for its first encounter a number of courtiers
hurried aboard to give the crude, unpolished seamen the inspiration of

their presence and the benefit of their advice. On April 10th the Duke of Buckingham arrived. On the 12th he stormed off back to London because the Duke of York refused to admit him to a council of war on board the *Royal Charles* in spite of 'being a Privy Councillor, and also for his Quality sake'.[6] On the 17th another clutch of noblemen appeared, among them Lord Castlemaine who was assigned a berth in the *Revenge*. Four days later the fleet weighed anchor and stood over for the Dutch coast.[7]

To follow in detail the campaigns and battles of the Second Dutch War is not the purpose of this book. It would in any case be superfluous as there are already admirable accounts available.[8] Briefly the aim of the English fleet was twofold: to intercept the great convoys of Dutch merchantmen that were believed to be homeward bound by the northern route round Scotland and to force the Dutch fleet out of harbour in defence of them. This initiative failed and the English returned to their anchorage in the Gunfleet (in the mouth of the Thames) about the middle of May. While they were riding at anchor there Coventry who was serving afloat as Secretary to the Duke of York reported to Arlington that his master kept on board the flagship a libellous picture about Holmes in Guinea.[9] In view of what was to follow, this piece of tittle-tattle is perhaps worth remembering. But a few days later there was far more important intelligence: the entire Dutch fleet was at sea and had captured an English convoy homeward bound from Hamburg. On May 30th the English fleet sailed for Southwold Bay—Solebay as our ancestors called it. Two days later the Dutch fleet of about a hundred sail were sighted to the east-south-east and the English altered course towards them.

The Dutch who had the advantage of the wind made, inexplicably, no use of it, so that two days were spent in manœuvring until a change of the wind in the small hours of June 3rd transferred the initiative to the English. They at once bore down on the enemy, supposedly in the new rule-book pattern of action in which the two fleets filed past each other on opposite tacks, giving and receiving broadsides as they went, the van of each fleet going about as soon as the enemy's rear had left nothing but open sea to fire at. Naturally it didn't work out quite like this. The Dutch came into action 'pell-mell' and the English, in many cases, 'in ranks 3, 4 or 5 broad'.[10] It was thus from the start a hot and confused battle. The hottest part, to begin with, was experienced by Rupert's squadron which, having passed down the enemy line, tacked and stood back towards them. The subsequent course of events kept them heavily engaged till late in the afternoon—the action had begun at three in the morning—when the Dutch line was broken and their flagship blew up. A complete rout ensued and the Dutch were only saved from annihilation by the frivolous futility of a courtier aboard the English flagship who pretended to have the Duke of York's authority in ordering the pursuit to be called off.

The battle of Lowestoft, though hard-fought, had not cost the English so many casualties as most battles with the Dutch were to do. It had however, claimed the lives of two flag-officers one of whom, Robert Sansum, was the Rear-Admiral of Rupert's squadron. Rupert himself recommended Holmes, whose valour was particularly mentioned in several reports of the battle,[11] for the vacant flag. The Duke of York, however, decided to give it to his own flag-captain, Harman. The upshot is recorded by Sandwich in his journal entry for June 13th:

> This day, after Council [i.e. of war], the Duke went aboard the *Royal James*, to see Prince Rupert, who had kept his chamber of a sore leg. Whilst he was in that ship, Major Robert Holmes (for whom the Prince had moved to be Rear-Admiral in the room of Sansum), but his Royal Highness thought more fit to give that flag to Capt. Harman . . . The Major, as before said, being hereat discontented, came to the Duke and told him he saw that he had enemies about him that would do him prejudice and never suffer him to rise, and expressed his unwillingness to continue in the service. The Duke most graciously endeavoured to content him and advised him to consider before he absolutely resolved on that course, but in the close Major Holmes presented him his commission and the Duke took it, and when he came on board the *Charles* cancelled it and gave his ship to Capt. Langhorne of the *Bonaventure*.

Next day Coventry (Holmes was surely hinting at him in the interview recorded by Sandwich) reported the news to Arlington. A few days later he gave an even fuller account to Pepys who had come to court to see 'the Duke and his courtiers returned from sea. All fat, and lusty, and ruddy by being in the sun'.[12] Pepys's conclusion was: 'Yet Holmes would do it, like a rash, proud coxcombe. But he is rich, and hath, it seems, sought an occasion of leaving the service.' Both explanations, though mutually contradictory, are unflattering. Of the two the first seems more probable.

On one point, at least, there can be no dispute; it was a colossal gamble. Several times in his career Holmes had shewn himself ready to put his all to the touch. But what makes his resignation at this point so astonishing is that he had, against formidable odds, gone far towards winning the game. There were few officers of the Restoration Navy who combined such experience of independent command with such a reputation as a fighter. And of that few, all but two or three had Parliamentary rather than Royalist antecedents. As Sir William Coventry noted against his proposals for maintaining the Navy on an annual charge of £200,000:

> There are in his Majestie's service at sea more than twenty Cap^s whoe have served the K^g soe that his Ma: will have Commanders enough of his owne party to command the Fleets herein proposed, whereby the Fleet will be made safe for his Ma: service against domesticke dangers though against forraigne it must be confessed the former [i.e. Cromwellian] Commanders are more capable.[13]

This advantage was, however, diminishing with every year that passed and with every battle that was fought. At Lowestoft the ex-Cromwellian Jeremy Smith was singled out by the Duke of York for honours and promotion. Before long the two streams of the Civil War would have merged into the river of national loyalty.

Holmes retired to his civil and military appointments in the Isle of Wight, Deputy Governor of the island, Governor of Sandown Fort and Captain of his Independent Company of Foot. Later in the summer the King visited the island in his pleasure boat but refused to see Holmes because he had not made his peace with the Duke of York.[14] How and when the reconciliation was effected we do not know. It cannot have been very long delayed, for early in the following year Holmes was appointed to command a powerful new third-rate, the *Defiance*, while she was still on the stocks at Deptford. The *London Gazette* reports her launching on

March 27th, 'a very stout and promising Fregat of 64 guns'. The King, the Duke of York and Prince Rupert graced the occasion, 'His Majesty having been pleased at the same time to Confer the honor of Knighthood upon Captain Robert Holmes who is designed to have the command of this ship.'[15] Here was a fatted calf indeed.

The presence of Prince Rupert was especially appropriate both because of his lifelong connexion with Holmes and because he and Albemarle had been appointed joint Commanders-in-Chief for that year. On April 10th the *Defiance* was assigned to the Admiral's division of the Red squadron. On the 28th she was reported to be ready to sail in four days' time. In mid-May orders were given to victual her for three hundred and thirty-two men. On the 20th her commander was ordered to Sheerness 'to take a view of H.M. ships now there and to see what forwardness they are in, to learn the cause of their so long delay and to hasten their dispatch to the Fleet'.[16] The Commanders-in-Chief had every reason to hustle. The Dutch fleet might come out at any moment and the French, who had now allied themselves against England, were known to have sent their fleet out of the Mediterranean and were presumed to be attempting a junction of forces. At the end of May alarming (and, as it later turned out, false) reports reached London that the French fleet was off the western approaches of the Channel. The fateful decision to divide the English fleet was taken by the Government. On May 29th Prince Rupert, in command of some twenty ships, was detached to intercept the French.

Rupert's command was formed by withdrawing ships from each of the three squadrons to compose what was in effect, if only temporarily, a fourth squadron. Among the vessels so detached was the *Victory* in which Sir Christopher Myngs had been flying his flag as Vice-Admiral of the Red. Sir Joseph Jordan, who had been serving as Rear-Admiral, thereupon took his place and Holmes in the *Defiance* was made acting Rear-Admiral of the Red. Within a few hours of hoisting his flag he was to play a notable part in the hardest-fought action of the war.

Earlier in the year Pepys had heard the Duchess of Albemarle express the wish that 'the King would send her husband to sea with the old plain sea Captains, that he served with formerly, that would make their ships swim with blood, though they could not make legs as Captains now-a-days can.'[17] Holmes, we know, was courtier enough to make a leg, but even so coarse and horrible a woman as Monck's Duchess could hardly have found the 'tweendecks of the *Defiance* in the Four Days' Battle too insipid for her rank tastes. Whether her husband ought to have accepted battle on such unequal terms is a much more open question. Without Rupert's squadron he only had about sixty ships against a Dutch strength of well over eighty. James, Duke of York had, while leaving him entire discretion, suggested that a defensive position within the Gunfleet shoal was the best place for his weakened fleet.[18] None the less when the Dutch fleet was sighted early on June 1st Albemarle, with ample time to have escaped to safety, called a Council of the flag-officers at which it was resolved, though not unanimously, to seek out the enemy and attack him.[19] The action began about twenty miles off Ostend, the strong south-westerly gale that carried the English ships up to their opponents heeling them over so that the lowest and heaviest gun tier was so close to the waterline as to be unusable throughout the engagement. When both fleets had to go about to avoid running ashore the English were caught between the ships they had already been fighting and the as yet unengaged Dutch van and centre under the greatest of all Dutch admirals, Michael de Ruyter. In the murderous action that followed one English and one Dutch admiral were killed, several ships were boarded and taken by hand-to-hand fighting and those that escaped were badly mauled.

During the night the worst damaged ships limped into harbour but the body of the fleet remained together, mending rigging and carrying out temporary repairs to masts and yards. An urgent message had already been sent to recall Rupert from his fool's errand down Channel but this had through the inexcusable irresponsibility of Coventry and Arlington been delayed for several hours. In spite of the fact that the dawn brought no sign of the longed-for relieving squadron Albemarle led his depleted forces once again to the attack. It was a triumph of discipline and of fighting spirit. The fleets opened fire on each other about ten o'clock and kept up a fierce action till late in the afternoon. Pepys, walking, in Greenwich Park shortly before four o'clock . . . 'could hear the guns from the fleete most plainly'.[20] Later the King and the Duke of York who had come down the river by barge climbed Observatory Hill to hear the cannonade. Like Pepys they were on tenterhooks to hear that Rupert had rejoined the main body of the fleet. But there was still no sign of a sail coming up on the south-westerly breeze. Even then it was only the sight of disabled ships standing off for England that induced Albemarle to break off the action and protect their retreat. Once again the English had taken a terrible battering. Pepys heard next day that both Albemarle and Holmes had had their flags shot down and their sails and rigging so damaged as to force them to anchor for a time. Among the ships too crippled to make harbour was the *St. Paul*, a fifth-rate commanded by John Holmes. Albemarle took the men out of her and set her on fire. Although the Dutch pressed the pursuit the wind fell calm just as they came up with their quarry about nine that night.

Early on the Sunday morning a light breeze sprang up from the northeast which would carry the fleet towards the protection afforded by the shoals and sandbanks of the mouth of the Thames. At a Council of flag-officers Albemarle resolved on a fighting retreat 'placing his weak and disabled Ships before in a Line, and 16 of his greatest and best in a Rank in the Reer, as a Bulwark for them, keeping his own Ship nearest the Enemy'.[21] This much-admired manœuvre was successful. But early in the afternoon Monck's look-outs sighted Rupert's squadron away to the south-west. In altering course away from the safety of the Thames to join the Prince, Monck's ships ran foul of the Galloper Sand and the flagship of the White squadron grounded and was surrendered to save a pointless loss of life. The Dutch, unable to get her off, took the Admiral, Sir George Ayscue, and his company prisoner and set her on fire.

Neither Rupert nor Monck was the man to let a battle end on so humiliating a note. It was agreed that evening that the following morning Rupert's squadron with Sir Christopher Myngs in the van should lead the fleet in line ahead to a battle that, if still unequal, was not impossibly so.

It raged from about eight in the morning till seven at night with a fury that left both combatants exhausted. From the start Holmes was in the thick of the fighting. 'Sir Christopher Myngs and Sir Robert Holmes led the van', an eyewitness reported.[22] Although the Dutch were the un-doubted victors of the four days' fighting, losing four ships as against ten English, their casualties may be judged from the fact that no less than three out of their sixteen flag-officers were killed in action. On the English side the greatest loss was Sir Christopher Myngs, Vice-Admiral of the Red, a fine seaman, a brave officer and a commander of rare humanity. Sir George Ayscue, Admiral of the White, had had, as we have seen, the misfortune to be captured. Sir William Berkeley, his Vice-Admiral, had been killed on the first day of the battle and Sir John Harman, his Rear-Admiral had had a leg broken by a yard crashing on to the deck when, sails and rigging ablaze, his ship the *Henry* was summoned by the Dutch to surrender. His answer was a broadside that killed one of the Dutch Admirals. Harman, it will be recalled, had received his flag in preference to Holmes the previous summer. Yet when on the eve of the battle the creation of Rupert's detached squadron had necessitated the rearrange-ment of the flags in the main fleet Holmes had been made Rear-Admiral of the Red—one step higher than Rear-Admiral of the White. By the end of the century this sort of cutting in—indeed overtaking of any kind—would be strictly forbidden in the single lane traffic of the sea-officer's lists.

The traditional toast of promotion-hungry naval officers 'A bloody war and a sickly season' might have seemed supererogatory in the year 1666 when the plague was raging in London and the slaughter at sea must have satisfied even the exacting standards of the Duchess of Albemarle. With so many casualties among the flag-officers it was not surprising that Holmes was confirmed as Rear-Admiral of the Red. He had served, like Monck, his Commander-in-Chief, right through the four days and had, in the words of one report, 'done wonders'.[23] The *Defiance* had been so badly mauled that she was sent to Yarmouth to refit.[24] Holmes transferred his flag to the *Henry*, Harman's old ship, a second-rate of 72 guns, which was refitting at Sheerness.[25] Flag-rank and the command of one of the most powerful units of the fleet marked substantial advancement. But few professional successes are wholly satisfying to the ambitious and the competitive. In the same list of flag appointments Sir Jeremy Smith, the tarpaulin who had won the Duke of York's especial commendation at the battle of Lowestoft, was made Admiral of the Blue and Sir Edward Spragge was promoted to be his Vice-Admiral. That Holmes bitterly resented both these appointments is clear from his subsequent relations with the officers concerned. Smith, of course, belonged to that body of veteran Commonwealth officers whom Pepys and Coventry regarded as the backbone of the fleet. But Spragge was a more particular and thus a more dangerous rival. Like Holmes he was a Royalist who had shared the exile of the Court and had returned to England only at the Restoration. Both had immediately been given commands of small ships: both, as we have seen, had been promoted to third-rates by the time of the battle of Lowestoft. How Spragge had got thus far, except by the friendship of the Duke of York, is by no means clear. But from then on there was no holding him. Knighted in June 1665, made Rear-Admiral of the Blue the following spring, and now Vice-Admiral. No wonder if Holmes felt that he had been slighted in his profession.

Activity left for the moment little time for such reflexions. The joint Commanders-in-Chief wrote to Sir William Coventry on June 10th, less than a week after the battle:

> You know what advantage it would be to His Majesty's service to have out the Fleet again suddenly. There shall be nothing wanting here in (as much as) we give none of our Captains leave to go on shoar . . . and we hope they will be Emulous, who shall set out his ship first, if they may be supplyed with necessaryes for that purpose.[26]

The 'necessaryes' they had particularly in mind were ammunition, beer and seamen. On the 27th they wrote a stirring appeal to the Brethren of Trinity House:

> . . . We hope now the Dutch are coming out there is no seaman will have so little Honour or Courage to keep ashore when wee are going to fight for our King, our Countrey and Trade.[27]

Somehow the men were found. Holmes's squadron which was as short-handed as any received several reinforcements—consisting largely of soldiers—during the last week of June and the first week of July.[28] On the 7th the *Henry* was flying Holmes's flag at the buoy of the Nore having completed her refit at Sheerness.[29] On the 9th Holmes was ordered to go up the river to hasten the ships that were still refitting down to the buoy of the Nore.[30] He seems to have discharged this duty effectively as a few days later the Commanders-in-Chief informed the King of their intention to take the fleet out immediately and to seek an encounter with the Dutch fleet then lying off the mouth of the Thames. Contrary winds kept them from taking the fleet through the narrows till the 22nd.* On the 23rd the Commanders-in-Chief reported the enemy fleet in sight, standing away to the north-east.[31] On the afternoon of the 24th the two fleets converged some thirty-odd miles south-east of Orfordness and on the next day, St. James's Day, they fought the third and last of the fleet actions of the war.

Of all the three it came nearest to the copybook pattern except that the fleets were converging on each other on parallel courses instead of passing each other on reciprocal ones. But though each fleet had formed itself into a line—no mean feat when they consisted of eighty-nine (English) and eighty-eight (Dutch) respectively—the lines sagged and wriggled as the contemporary sketch plan (fig. 1) shows. Holmes in the *Henry* had at ten o'clock a good hour to watch the Dutch line drawing closer before the range would permit him to open fire. By eleven (fig. 2) action is imminent at the centre: in the van the two sides, already heavily engaged, are struggling to weather each other and thus catch the enemy between two fires, while in the rear the two fleets are still nothing like close enough to get to grips. In the closing stages of the battle some six hours later (fig. 3) its fissiparous nature has become clear: the van and the centre though in formal touch are fighting separate actions, while the rear or Blue squadron is on its own in what looks like a very tight corner with the Dutch rear having just

* The fleet consisted of eighty-nine ships and it was essential to bring them all through together on one tide. See the Commanders-in-Chief to the King, NMM DAR/3 f. 63.

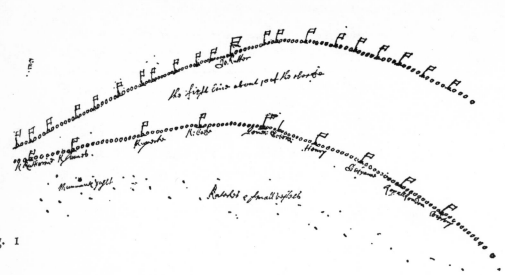

Fig. 1

Fig. 2

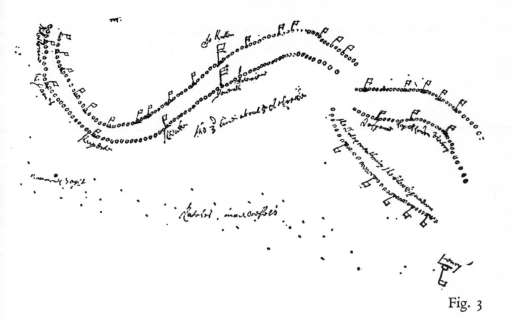

Fig. 3

These diagrams, evidently drawn shortly after the battle when the relative position of every ship was fresh in the draughtsman's mind, give a uniquely authentic impression of how a formal fleet action developed. The English, if in nothing else, had the advantage of a single Admiralty. Compare their nine flag-officers with the twenty-one of the United Provinces as the fleets converge in fig. 1. In the bottom right-hand corner of fig. 3 the *Henry* is clearly shown standing away from the battle to repair the severe damage she had sustained to her masts and rigging. The legend immediately above and to the left of her reads: 'the Dutch weathring the blewe squadron'. The significance of this situation is discussed on the next page.

Reproduced by courtesy of the Trustees of the British Museum

K

succeeded in weathering it. Holmes in the *Henry*, disabled and left behind, looks a sitting duck for the Dutch when they have dealt with the Blue squadron under Sir Jeremy Smith in the *Loyall London*.*

Things did not work out quite like this although the Blue squadron was in fact very savagely handled by the Dutch. But the English van and centre drove off their opponents in complete confusion so that the younger Tromp in command of the Dutch rear, though in a winning position, had to think about making good his retreat to base rather than about pressing on a retreating enemy. Owing to a change of wind during the night the two defeated squadrons got safely into harbour without exchanging more than a few shots with the pursuing English. But this left Tromp in a most unenviable position, with his own particular adversary tailing him and two powerful squadrons ready to intercept him off the Dutch coast.

Holmes had been forced out of his station in the line by the early afternoon.[32] To quote an eyewitness from the Red Squadron:

> . . . when the height and extremity of firing was over with us . . . we kept on our course sailing after the two Dutch squadrons which fled before us. We missed our Rear-Admiral Sir Robert Holmes whom we discerned far to the leeward of the Blue with his foretopmast down and as we might imagine very much disabled in his rigging; his own fireship only was with him. In the night he repaired and joined himself with the Blue Squadron on board the Admiral of the Blue to learn in what condition they were . . .[33]

So far, so good. By late afternoon on the 26th the English van and centre squadrons returning from their pursuit sighted Tromp's squadron with the Blue to windward of them in pursuit. Tromp was trapped. Luckily for him the White and Red squadrons did not anchor early enough in the night, while Smith, apprehensive of grounding on that treacherous coast, stood too far off. At daybreak Tromp, finding no English ships between him and home, quickly slipped into port.

The escape of Tromp's squadron robbed the English of the fruits of a victory that in spite of its decisive character had not much to show in terms

* These plans are taken from BM Add. MS. 32094, ff. 139–140, which was drawn to my attention by the kindness of the Rev. J. R. Powell.

of ships sunk or captured. Holmes made no secret of his opinion that the blame lay with Sir Jeremy Smith. Accusations of cowardice and charges of failure to press the pursuit of Tromp for fear of running aground led in the autumn to an official hearing before the King in Council and, even, it was reported, to a duel. But the quarrel between them appears to have originated over the conduct of the battle proper[34] rather than of the pursuit though no doubt the second issue inflamed the first and, as it was so much more plausible, ultimately supplanted it. Fierce professional jealousy was intensified by party loyalty. Smith was the particular protégé of Albemarle[35] as Holmes was of Prince Rupert. While the two shared the Command-in-Chief the issue was left in abeyance but as soon as the campaigning season came to an end, the flags were hauled down and the ships laid up, it was revived with the utmost vigour. And by then Holmes's greatest exploit had done more damage to the Dutch than the St. James's Day Fight and had made him the man of the hour.

XIII

The Bonfire

CONSCIOUS PERHAPS THAT there was very little to show for what had been a complete victory the English commanders decided to press their advantage up to the very harbours of the United Provinces. At a Council of flag-officers held on July 28th it was resolved that only the badly damaged ships should be sent home, and that the rest of the fleet should sail for the Texel as soon as possible.[1] On the same day the *Little Mary*, a sixth-rate of 12 guns, together with the *Fanfan*, Prince Rupert's pleasure boat, was ordered

> to goe to the Holland coast and to take with her Lauris van Hamskirck and follow such directions as he shall receive from the said Lauris and to return the next day at night to the Fleet.[2]

Lauris Heemskerk, subsequently knighted and given a command in the Navy, was a Dutch traitor whose presumed knowledge both of pilotage waters and of the nodal points of trade was highly valued. His reconnaissance in the *Fanfan* was followed by orders to a squadron of frigates to carry out a northward sweep along the coast taking or destroying any Dutch, French or Danish vessels they should meet before rejoining the fleet between the Vlie and the Texel not later than August 4th.[3] These operations yielded a few prizes but, with the season drawing on, it became clear that dramatic results were hardly to be expected from them.

Accordingly on August 7th a more daring plan was unfolded to the assembled flag-officers. Heemskerk had volunteered the information 'that the islands of Vlie and Schelling were very ill guarded, notwithstanding there were Store-houses both for the States, and the East-India Fleet, and Riches to a good value'.[4] The official account from which these words are taken goes on to add: 'and what did weigh most, a considerable number of good Merchants Ships usually riding there'. But that is official hindsight. The instructions which Monck and Prince Rupert drew up for Sir Robert Holmes, Rear-Admiral of the Red, who was chosen to command the expedition are admirably clear and explicit. The one sentence that deals with shipping: 'You are to seize what vessels you finde in ye Harbour, which you are to make use of in bringing away ye Booty: what are not serviceable you are to sink or Burn', bears out what is plain from this consistent and unambiguous document: that the expedition was conceived simply as a seaborne raid. Holmes's job was to land a force of some five hundred men on the Vlie, burn, loot and destroy as much as possible in a short time, prevent the sailors getting drunk in the exhilaration of the moment and finally to re-embark them. An additional force of four hundred men commanded by Sir William Jennings would meanwhile be making a similar attempt on the neighbouring island of Schelling but it was open to Holmes as Commander-in-Chief to combine and concentrate the two parties as he saw fit. Lastly he was enjoined to give orders 'that no violence be done to women or children, nor the inferior sort of people, unless in case of resistance . . . and you are to take care there be some men allotted to the Dutch Captain (Hemskircke) to preserve him from violence.'[5]

To provide the nine hundred men required each division of the fleet was to send one hundred, two-thirds soldiers, one-third seamen. Again, of each hundred, seventy were to be musketeers and thirty pikemen—each musketeer was to come equipped with twenty-four bullets and two bandoliers full of powder. Three days' rations of bread, beer and cheese were to accompany each man.[6] In fact the total force seems to have been nearer twelve hundred than nine hundred men as, according to the official account in the Gazette, Holmes commanded an additional company of his own; and a larger company of volunteers drawn from the whole fleet was commanded by Sir Philip Howard, a hard-swearing, high-living exquisite. Among the ordinary company commanders was Holmes's brother John.[7] The ships allocated to the expedition consisted of five fourth-rates, three fifth-rates, five fireships and seven ketches together with about fifty boats for landing and embarking the assault force.[8] On Wednesday, August 8th Holmes flying his flag in the *Tiger*, commanded by Captain Wetwang, a Cromwellian officer with a fine record, led his force away from the fleet about eight in the morning and anchored about three miles from the buoys that marked the entrance to the channel between Vlie and Schelling. There he was met by that intrepid pleasure-boat the *Fanfan* which reported a concentration of large merchantmen, estimated at about fifty sail, inside the anchorage.[9] A contrary wind kept Holmes from the Vlie–Schelling channel all that day[10] but by early on Thursday morning it had eased. He entered the channel while the weather was still thick and dark. About eleven the sky suddenly cleared 'so that they could now clearly discern every particular ship in the harbour, and counting them some reckoned 150, others 160, some more and some less'.[11] Holmes himself in a letter to Arlington written three days later put the figure at 'about 170 sayle, small and great at Anchor in Vly road'.[12] The English squadron was at that moment in Schelling road, preparing to land the assault force.

For once in that war so erratically compounded of brilliance and blunders, of efficiency and mismanagement the man and the opportunity were a perfect fit. Even the intelligence provided by the *Fanfan* the day before had not prepared Holmes for this forest of masts that lay across a few miles of shallow and difficult water. But with his strategic flair he saw at once that this was a chance of damaging the Dutch economy so severely as to weaken, perhaps to destroy, their power and will to carry on the war. As a tactician he saw exactly how to do it. And as an officer with long experience of independent command he had no difficulty in making up his mind as to the priorities and methods required by an unforeseen development. It is this readiness, instant and absolute, to read a situation first and instructions second that distinguishes a great from a merely competent commander. The key to everything lay in the fact that 'there were not many men of warr amongst them and . . . that they ridd very thick'.[13] It was the ideal, the classic, occasion for the use of fireships.

This seems so obvious that the daring, originality and brilliance of a raid comparable only with the exploits of Drake, Hawkins and Blake has been largely overlooked. Holmes had been given orders and provided with forces to carry out what we should now call a commando raid: he in fact carried out, with next to no casualties and with devastating success, an operation of an entirely different type. It was a military masterpiece in which the virtues of surprise, improvisation and dash were controlled by a thorough and exact professionalism.

The first instance of this is Holmes's rejection of the services, so much puffed and so amply rewarded, of Lauris Heemskerk. A Danish vessel inward bound to the Vlie had been captured by one of the frigates on the previous day. Holmes reported in his letter to Arlington:

> . . . by much persuasions I got him to Pilot me in, finding the Dutch Capt. that undertooke it before not altogether capable. I did ingage to the Master and Steerman of this Dane in case they should bring me in safe to the place where the Dutch fleet lay, I would give them their shipp and Goods again. It made me the bolder to promise, shee haveing nothing in her but some Deale boards and firewood; I am confident that the shipp and her ladeing at the best Market cannot be worth above six hundred pounds sterl. Since my comeing into the Fleet I find that the Deale boards are disposed of, and that what I have promised will not be made good here. I shall desire that your Lordship may take care that my promise may be performed, else [lightly crossed out but still easily legible] I shall humbly desire to be excused from going to sea any more.[14]

The promise was made good immediately.[15] In spite of Holmes's clear statement Heemskerk was still highly regarded by his superiors and warmly recommended by them to the favour of the King. It is difficult to prefer their second-hand opinion to the evidence of Holmes whose whole career shows him to have been a good seaman and a first-class navigator. It is impossible to believe that he would have risked the safety of his squadron on the pilotage of an unknown Danish prisoner-of-war unless he had good reason. Suppose the Dane had put them aground in an enemy harbour, what would Holmes have had to say for himself at the court martial which would certainly await him if he escaped alive? One can imagine easily enough what Pepys and Coventry would have said about his intolerable pride in choosing to dispense with the services of an expert wisely provided by his superior officers. This was the kind of risk that would only be taken by a man who knew exactly what he was doing.

The same holds true of his instantaneous decision to remodel the whole operation so as to take the fullest advantage of an opportunity unknown and unsuspected by the men who had drafted his instructions.

> I went in with five fire-ships, some ketches and one fifth-rate frigate (leaving some other frigates in Schelling roade). I sent the fire-shipps ahead who soone burned two men-of-warr and other shipps that stood defending the whole Fleet.
>   I immediately sent all my Boats to burn the rest of the shipps wh. had so good success that in a short tyme the most of that great fleet was in a flame, except a Guyny man of 24 guns, and three small Privateers that got together in the narrow of the Channell and protected five saile more that were got ahead of them, that our Boats could not possibly come at them, and the most of our Ketches being on ground.[16]

An ampler and more graphic account is given by the unknown eyewitness already cited:

> All the longboats were presently manned with seamen and soldiers. The volunteers were appointed aboard the galliot-hoy taken but that morning upon that coast by one of the ketches. Sir Robert Holmes went aboard the *Fanfan* with some other officers and she bore his flag, the *Tiger* staying behind near the Schelling shore, the *Hampshire* and *Sweepstakes* riding further off at sea. When the men were thus disposed of, then without further delay they made into the port; the fireships going before, the *Pembroke* frigate to the leeward of them, and the *Dragon* frigate by keeping too far to the windward ran aground. The *Fanfan* went before the longboats, the ketches sailed in some to windward, some to leeward and some before the Flag, sailing in thus and coming in within half a league of the shipping. There bore towards us two sail, one with a pendant on the maintop, the other with a flag there, firing at the fireships, which now were got within a pretty distance of them. They thus firing, a fireship commanded by Captain Browne, being headmost, had got near the chiefest of them and with the advantage of the wind laid him aboard and so fired him; soon after one other of the fireships had come very close to the other man of war and thinking to have grappled him set fire, but ere he had closed with the man of war the fireship was aground and so the flames reached him not. However the terror of the approach of the flame and the smoke of the other ship and fireship caused the men to quit the ship and betake themselves to their boat, and being gone out not far perceiving their ship free from the flame and thinking to recover her

again made towards it with all the speed they could, but our fireship's men perceiving their boat and men were off, they also hasten to board her and now both boats strive to out-row the other for a man of war, but our boat being swiftest first made the ship and entering her got presently to the stern chase guns which they fired upon the Dutch boat and so kept it off with powder and a bullet into the bargain, and within a while after she was fired in good earnest. When the fleet riding there perceived that those men of war were taken and destroyed wherein consisted their safety, the men forsook their vessels and got away in their boats down the water towards Amsterdam followed by an infinite number of boats from the Vlie; the people running away thence as fast as they could. The longboats were now commanded to bear up to the shipping and so fire as many as they could master without further delay, the which they did without any further direction, so that of a goodly number of shipping which were there proudly riding about one of the clock in the afternoon there remained nothing but so many consuming keels at 8 in the evening; save only one Guinea-man (some say a privateer) who continued firing at our boats and by that means kept them off and sheltered 1 sail* more than himself from the general destruction. The game of burning being ended here about 8 of the clock, care was taken to bring ourselves away thence, it being a very nice place to sail through and we having but one man of war in the place, the *Pembroke* by name, and she within a foot water of ground and the weather beginning to be unkind, a violent rain following attended with thunder and lightning. Order was given as soon as the flood tide came to sail thence with ketches, boats, vessels and hoyes to the rest of the men of war which were riding at Schelling, and those that were not on float to set on fire, Sir Robert Holmes sailing away before and all the rest following his light. We set on fire of our own a hoy taken from the Dutch and a fireship, and the wind serving we were up with the *Tiger* at Schelling by 12 of the clock that night, where we anchored, resting ourselves as well as we might and not without thoughts of the next day's business. Many of the ships that were consumed at the Vlie were richly laden, some homeward some outward bound, some from Guinea, some from the Straits, some for Russia, some for Danzig and some from West India and other places.[17]

The flames and smoke were visible far out to sea. 'We saw divers smokes arise upon the land,' Sir Thomas Allin noted in his journal, 'which made us judge that Sir Robt Holmes was prosperous, and they continued burning within the night'. Like Allin, the Commanders-in-Chief naturally assumed that the columns of smoke on the horizon came from burning warehouses. On this premise there could not be much left in the

* The figure is uncertain.

island worth setting a match to. They therefore issued this anxious and peremptory recall:

To Sir Robt. Holmes.   [9 August]
    Sir
        Wee hope you have proceeded with success in ye Expedition, wherein you have been now engag'd. In confidence whereof we have thought fitt to send you our further directions, that you doe forthwith ship such things, as are to be shipped of your spoyle, whereof you are possessed, and make all hast as soon as weather & wind will permitt to return back to ye Fleet again; For we presume by ye Smoak which we ourselves have seen, that ye Countrey by this time may be alarmed to such a degree, that they may possibly pour over some sudden forces upon you, which may be too powerfull, and bring some danger upon you, which therefore we take this care to prevent. Wee desire you to give ye like directions to S^r Wm Jennings.
                            Wee remain
                          Your assured Friends
                          R[upert]: A[lbemarle][18]

Holmes does not mention this letter in his report to Arlington.* Certainly he paid no attention to it. It is of course possible that it never reached him though it is difficult to see why. The obvious explanation is that he regarded it as an irrelevance, based on inadequate intelligence. He had just destroyed a sizable proportion of the Dutch merchant marine in an afternoon, while his superior officers were still thinking in terms of a coastal raid. Holmes had no blind eye to put his telescope to; perhaps he had neither the theatrical instinct nor the whimsicality to do so; but the principle was the same. As his letter makes clear his original intention was to land his men on the Vlie as soon as he had destroyed the merchant fleet. But, as he had explained in his brief account of that action printed on p. 152, most of his ketches had run aground.

This hindered the landing of our men upon the Fly but wee resolved to doe it the next morning, & had accordingly proceeded, had not in the night a Gust hap'ned, & so much Rain faln that spoyled great many of our Men's Arms &

* In the official *True and Perfect Narrative* a letter requiring immediate return to the fleet is handed to Holmes just as he was evacuating his expedition twenty-four hours later. No doubt this version of events satisfied everybody.

Amunition on board the Hoyes, Ketches & Boats. However I went with eleaven companyes on shore upon the Schelling. Wee saw some scattering fellowes but no great opposition. I burned the Chief towne upon that Island, which (by all relation I could get) was very rich. I had burn't all the villadges there, but that it was almost high water, & could not lose that opportunity of getting out again to sea, which I thought to be more considerable than to stay 24 houres (at least) to demollish one or two small villadges, and the Channel betweene the Buoyes very narrow & not bold without a franck Wind.

. . . Upon the Schelling I kept out with five Companyes upon the skirts of the Towne, lest any Enemy should surprize us, whilst I sent five companyes more to burne it (leaveing one Company to secure our Boats) whom finding so slow in executeing that office that I was forced to set fire in some to the houses to windward of the towne to occasion the hastening of our men away, which tooke so good effect that in half an houres tyme the most part of the towne was in a flame. Otherwise it would have been a hard task to get our men away so suddenly.[19]

The evidence of the unknown eyewitness who served in Sir Philip Howard's company of volunteers suggests that Holmes had to use even more drastic methods. Discipline comes naturally to Englishmen if they are properly paid and looked after. But to the comon soldiers and seamen of the Restoration, cheated and bilked by officialdom, plunder was much the most promising means of remuneration. Small wonder if they did not instantly obey a recall from golden opportunity to a leaden present. They were not going to be showered with sinecures and grants of fee-farm rents in recognition of their gallant services when they got back to England. Half an hour's looting was likely to be more profitable than two years' good conduct.

The witness whose account follows shows himself an excellent war reporter:

. . . About 5 in the morning order was given to the ketches and hoys to weigh and to stand nearer the shore with directions for the men to be in readiness and the longboats to be fitted to receive them. And at 7 of the clock the several ketches and hoys were under sail with the longboats manned, ready to receive command for landing. About 8 directions were given to the several captains and officers to take care to land their men. Sir Robert Holmes approaching the shore in the *Fanfan* and Sir William Jennings being commanded with a shallop to go before to observe the fittest place to secure landing and to discover whether there were any enemy in ambush, as we were thus making close to the land one horse-man appeared on shore, at whom the *Fanfan* fired one of her guns, the which so startled the horse that down came the rider (this the strict observer affirms he did see), but as we were within a stone's cast of the shore there was a shot made at us by a person that lay under the bank, at which we gave a great shout and the man in a great fear ran away, whereupon each boat strove to get the soonest ashore and within less than half an hour all the men were landed and drawn up ready to march. Thus safely landing in a fair sandy creek we marched towards the town in very good order, expecting every instant some kind of resistance, the place through which we marched being a sandy place full of banks and hillocks beside which men might have been securely placed and done us no little hurt, to prevent which as near as could be several persons were ordered to march a good distance from the body to discover anything of lying in wait. As we marched towards the town the persons that were appointed as scouts found a Dutch flag set on a kind of sheep-fold which stood on the north side of the place where we marched and from thence the word was given to be used in fight if any happened. The seamen had taken the Dutch colours. When we came within sight of the town the body was divided in order to the secure entering that place, Sir Robert Holmes drawing on the south part of the town with 3 or 4 com-panies, Sir Philip Howard with the persons under his command, marching directly to the east part of the town, having received commands to fire it. When we were entering the town there came out an old man about 80 years of age who craved for mercy, but being asked where the people of the town were, he answered they were dead of the sickness and run away. We marched through the town, the houses being all shut and the windows closed up, no inhabitants appearing, having the day before and that morning got thence. When the town was entered and no appearance of any resistance, the soldiers fell to plunder; but the town being fired to the windward they had not above an hour's space for it; the wind being pretty high increased the flames exceedingly. This town is situated in a very sandy place where nothing grows naturally but rushes, yet they had gardens where by their art and industry they made vines to bear; there were also some apple trees. The houses generally but of one story high but well contrived and very clean and sweetly kept and boarded before the doors. It had a new and pretty fair Town House and as nearly as I can imagine it consisted of about 800 or 1000 houses and one church. Springs they had not any as I could see; so that what water they have is from above, which when it falls they receive in vessels and preserve it in leaden cisterns placed in vaults under ground, which I tasted of and found sweet, though not altogether so fresh and good as the spring water. Sir Robert Holmes all this while had not himself been in the town, but with 200 men or thereabouts kept his guard less than half a quarter of a mile southward of it. And when he perceived that the fire had mastered the town, gave orders for the drums to beat up to call away the men; the which they were very loath to do, so that he was forced to fire into the town to compel the men to return. We marched back to the water side as well as we could, missing many of our number, who were gone before to the sea side with burthens and were ready to go back again for more; but were disappointed of their purpose, the fire having left little or nothing behind. When we came to the water side the long-boats were there ready to receive us and in less than an hour's time were all aboard and under sail bearing for the fleet which was about 8 leagues to the westward of us. Only a ketch was left behind with directions to take care to get aboard any stragglers of ours which peradventure by debauchery and carelessness might stay behind. The ketch remaining there till the latter end of flood tide and then weighing discovered 2 persons with burthens making towards the water side, to meet whom the boat was sent ashore; but ere they could get ashore these 2 were pursued by 6 others, who falling upon them killed the one of them and carried the other with them miserably wounded; but when these 6 saw the boat so near they fled away. The boat's crew not daring to adventure out of sight of their boat for fear of a surprise came back again to the ketch and made sail away for the fleet.[20]

Although two of the frigates, the *Dragon* and the *Garland,* had run aground during Thursday afternoon both had been successfully refloated that night, after the *Dragon* had been lightened by heaving eight guns and twelve tons of beer overboard.[21] The whole force was thus extricated without the loss of a single vessel and at a total cost of a dozen casualties. Holmes's own summary is worth quoting:

> I cannot give an exact accompt of what dammage the Dutch might sustaine by us, but certainly it must be great. I suppose your honour may have a most full accompt of it from Amsterdam. Our own loss was not very considerable, haveing not above twelve men kill'd & wounded. The number of the ships burn't I suppose to be betweene 150 & 160 sayle.[22]

These figures accepted in the English official account have been disputed by some Dutch authorities, one of whom puts the total at a hundred and fourteen.[23] What the value of the cargo destroyed amounted to is even less easily determined. A million pounds was the estimate generally accepted at the time. But of the central, crucial fact that, in Allin's words, 'So great a loss the Dutch never had', there can be no doubt. Beside it the burning of the town of Westerschelling was, as a contemporary remarked 'as bonfires for his good success at sea'.[24] The phrase caught on: and the action has ever since been known as Holmes's Bonfire.

News of it was received with immense enthusiasm. The carpenters in Harwich dockyard shouted and rang the church bells. The douce citizens of Edinburgh went further and let off guns in a *feu de joie*.[25] Pepys, who had been out on the tiles till three or four in the morning, was roused from a profound slumber by a letter from Sir William Coventry giving him the news. Later in the day,

> . . . the Duke of Yorke with his books showed us the very place and manner, and that it was not our design or expectation to have done this but only to have landed in the Fly and burned some of their store . . . We were led to this by, it seems, a renegado captain of the Hollanders, who found himself ill used by De Ruyter for his good service, and so come over to us, and hath done us good service; so that now we trust him, and he himself did go on this expedition. The service is very great, and our joys as great for it. All this will make the Duke of Albemarle in repute again, I doubt, though there is nothing of his in this.[26]

The Lord High Admiral had grasped the fact, skilfully disguised in the Commander-in-Chief's report, that what had been achieved was far beyond and utterly different from what had been intended. But once again Heemskerk is represented as the central figure. That both Holmes and De Ruyter did not think him as indispensable as he thought himself is not without interest. De Ruyter's judgment was surely justified by Heemskerk's treachery. Holmes thought too little of his professional competence to trust him, preferring his own sources and observations. His own master's mate, Anthony Cockarell, whom he had taken with him from the *Defiance* to the *Henry* after the Four Days' Battle, had served for seven years as upper steersman in Dutch ships of 50 and 60 guns.[27] By the hand of Sir Philip Howard, who carried the dispatch announcing the victory, he sent his own draught of the channel and the harbour he had just left together with 'exact draughts of five or six more of their principle Harbours in Holland, which will be a great Light to us hereafter, in case the Dutch should have a fleet in any of those Ports'.[28] It was a character-

istically professional touch. And throughout the operation, in which his
conduct and courage were praised without reserve, he had been, the same
letter tells us, in poor health.

Speculation as to the nature of a seventeenth-century ailment is un-
profitable. Medicine was barbarous and the terms in which patients
described their symptoms generally obscure. Holmes, unlike Pepys,
eschews elaboration; 'not well', 'in some indisposition of body', is the
usual extent of his clinical vocabulary. Very likely he had picked up some
form of malaria in his long periods of service in the tropics; the ague to
which he referred on his visit to São Tomé might be considered as evidence
supporting such a conjecture; but conjecture it remains.

What is clear is that Holmes never, until the very end of his life,
allowed his illness to interfere with an active and energetic prosecution of
business. Two days after he had written his account of the Bonfire to
Arlington, 'aboard H.M. ship the *Henry* 17 leagues from the Vlie', the
whole fleet had returned to Solebay 'being necessitated thereunto by the
great want of beer, water and ammunition'.[29] Nothing would have been
easier than to ask for a spell ashore and to take the opportunity of appearing at Court in the sunshine of victory. But there was still a good chance
that the Dutch might come out again: and there was much for everyone
to do if the fleet were to be in a fit state to receive them. The letter
book of Rupert and Monck bristles with demands for powder, provisions, the fitting of new masts and the transfer of men and equipment from damaged or defective ships to those that are fitting for sea.
Next to the shortage of men and the delay in providing fireships by far
the most acute problem was drink. Nettled by Pepys's allegations that
they had too easily accepted the bare affirmations of the Pursers about
stinking beer supplied in woodbound casks, the Commanders-in-Chief left
both him and the Lord High Admiral in no doubt of the urgency of this
matter:

> . . . But wee humbly desire your Highness if it be possible, that wee may be
> supplied with beer, and that those supplies be immediately dispatched unto us,
> and if that cannot be, Lett us but have plenty of water, and if wee take a

prize of Wine and Brandy wee shall be able to make a wholesome beverage thereof.*

A recent wine-prize with which they had intended to relieve the necessities of the fleet had been taken into the Thames, which not only meant that her cargo would be sold off by the Prize Commissioners but would give the prize crew an easy opportunity of deserting:

> If this vessell could be suddenly sent us back again, or some other effectuall course taken that wee may have drink for ye seamen, we may be able to doe some further service for his M^ty's and your satisfaction; But if this bee not done, and that very suddenly we shall not be in a condition to visitt ye Dutch coast again at this season though we much desire it.[30]

A week later they heard that De Ruyter was at sea with a fleet of eighty sail 'designed for as speedy a Conjunction as they can with ye French Fleet'. Even at that grave moment their first thought was to present the King with an official complaint in measured but forceful terms.

> ... when wee send up our demands, instead of having them answered, wee have accounts sent us, which are prepared by Mr Pepys, of what hath been supplyed for ye fleet, whereas that will not satisfye ye need of the shipps.[31]

The Admirals were particularly incensed by Sir William Coventry's assertion that the whole fleet was supplied sufficiently to last up to October 6th. They had, in fact, less than a month's provision of most essentials including beer. They might well be forced to return to port prematurely. Having established the responsibility for this contingency they then put to sea.

Holmes had by this time recovered his strength. In a letter to Arlington written from Southwold on August 22nd he thanked him for a letter which had evidently contained wise counsel

> which I shall be very careful to observe. What hath hitherto faln from me in my heat, I thought was not unseasonable at that tyme because I would make my usage knowne. But hereafter I shall take care to give no advantage to my enemyes in that kind.

Finding himself better he was returning on board that evening.[32]

---

* A generous ration was envisaged. By an order of September 6th the allowance was set at two gallons of French wine for six men *per diem*.

Contact was established off the North Foreland on the afternoon of August 31st. Violent weather made it difficult to maintain formation and the English who were to windward had to check their attack because several of their ships ran aground on the Gabbard. Next morning the wind was so strong that it was impossible to carry topsails. About two in the afternoon the Dutch were sighted off Calais, making for Cape Gris Nez. 'The weather was so tempestuous that it was impossible to fight them orderly. We designed to get between them and the French shore and so to drive them to seaward.'[33] In spite of head seas and a wind that made the larger ships practically unmanageable Holmes 'with much ado' brought off this manœuvre. But by then, 'the night drawing on, the shore so near, the weather so violent', the action was broken off, 'it being impossible for us to do the enemy any damage, having work enough to keep our sails to the yards and our masts standing'.[34] Although the two fleets were to be in sight of each other again some three weeks later, this was in fact the last action of the year.

Hardly had the storm-beaten ships found the shelter of St. Helens before news reached them of the Fire of London. On the 5th Monck was recalled by the King to assist the Government in this emergency so that Rupert was left in sole command of the fleet. On the 6th Monck was given a farewell dinner by the Governor of Portsmouth and on the 7th Rupert on the first day of his command paid Holmes the distinguishing compliment of dining as his guest.[35]

A week later the fleet put to sea in the hopes of intercepting the French fleet which had now arrived at Dieppe. Holmes took no part in any of the minor actions which ensued but when on October 2nd the fleet was brought into the river for the winter he was given the honour of carrying the Commander-in-Chief's final dispatch to the King.[36] It had been well earned.

L

XIV

Scandals and Rewards

WHEN HOLMES APPEARED at Court early in October personally charged to represent the deplorable conditions over which the Navy had triumphed in that eventful summer his own standing was high. His lapse of temper the year before was blotted out by his eminent services in a year of hard-fought battles. Of his closest rivals Harman was still unfit for sea service, Spragge had no outstanding exploit to his credit, while Sir Jeremy Smith, his senior officer as Admiral of the Blue, had still to face the charges that Holmes himself had brought against him of cowardice and misconduct during and after the St. James's Day Fight. In the cold war between the sea-officers and the Navy Board things were going Holmes's way. On the same day that he left the fleet at the Nore, Pepys woke up 'mightily troubled in mind, and in the most true trouble that I ever was in my life, saving in the business last year of the East India prizes.' The first rumblings of the Parliamentary storm that was to break over the peculation and inefficiency of naval administration and supply had been clearly audible at a Committee before which Pepys had been summoned the day before. That he and his colleagues had a good deal to hide is obvious from his state of mind when he mislaid, for a few hours, the file of documents which he had prepared for the meeting: 'This, added to my former disquiet, made me stark mad, considering all the nakedness of the office lay open in papers within those covers.'[1] Behind the menacing and uncomfortably well-informed questions of the Committee might lurk sea-officers like Holmes and his crony Sir Frescheville Holles; and always ready to make trouble was Prince Rupert himself. He had returned from sea with his grievances against the administration intensified by the tepidity of his reception: 'it pleases me to hear that he did expect great thanks and lays the want of it upon the fire, which deaded everything, and the glory of his services.'² Pepys had been unwise enough to imply in an off-the-cuff defence of his office before the King in Cabinet that Rupert had brought the fleet home in a condition that suggested negligence or poor seamanship. 'I had no sooner done, but Prince Rupert rose up and told the King in a heat, that whatever the gentleman had said, he had brought home his fleete in as good a condition as ever any fleet was brought home . . . I was not a little troubled at this passage, and the more when speaking with Jacke Fenn about it, he told me that the Prince will be asking now who this Pepys is, and find him to be a creature of my Lord Sandwich's, and therefore this was done only to disparage him.'³

In this dangerous position Pepys found some consolation in the divisions of his potential adversaries. '. . . the Duke of York and Duke of Albemarle do not agree. The Duke of York is wholly given up to this bitch of Denham.* The Duke of Albemarle and Prince Rupert do less agree.'⁴ The quarrel between Holmes and Smith was widely regarded as a public expression of this antagonism. Gauden, the Victualler of the Navy, told Pepys:

> He observed while he was on board the Admirall, when the fleete was at Portsmouth, that there was a faction there. Holmes commanded all on the Prince's side, and Sir Jeremy Smith on the Duke's, and every body that come did apply themselves to one side or the other; and when the Duke of Albemarle was gone away to come hither [i.e. when he was recalled to help restore order in London at the time of the fire], then Sir Jeremy Smith did hang his head, and walked in the Generall's ship but like a private Commander.⁵

Pepys ran into Holmes at a Naval party in Sir William Batten's house on October 15th. He was surprised to find him 'exceeding kind to me, more than usual, which makes me afeard of him, though I do much wish his friendship.' Both judgments, given the circumstances, display their maker's usual shrewdness.

At least the scandal of an open row between two flag-officers might

* Lady Denham was the Duke's mistress at this time.

distract attention from the more questionable transactions of the Navy Board. Holmes had originally drawn up his articles against Smith in August.[6] They are perfectly clear and detailed; briefly Smith is accused of over-caution both in the conduct of the battle and subsequently in standing toward the coast of England instead of following Holmes's robust advice to the Admiral's Lieutenant 'that he would do well to gett his flaggs together and fall in upon the Body of the Enemy'. A series of irate but courteous exchanges concluded thus: 'The Rear-Admiral desired the Lieutenant to tell Sir Jeremy Smith that he would be more kind to him than Sir Jeremy Smith was to the said Rear-Admiral, that he would stick by him, whatever he did, whereupon the said Lieutenant departed.' In the event Smith persisted in rejecting Holmes's advice and Tromp's squadron escaped. Smith answered Holmes's recriminations by adducing the sworn evidence of his pilot who declined the responsibility of taking the ship any closer to the Dutch coast.

Both submissions were laid before the King on October 21st.[7] On November 3rd the Royal answer was promulgated in terms distinctly favourable to Holmes:

> ... His Majesty found no cause to suspect that the said Sir Jeremy Smith ... had been wanting either in courage or faithfullness but the said Sir Jeremy Smith on the 26th at night having too easily yielded to the single opinion of his pilote without consulting the Masters or Pilotes of any other ships (w[ch] the weather would have permitted and the consequence of the businesse did require) having muzzled his ship & by it obliged the rest of the Squadron to doe the like gave opportunity to the enemy to escape w[ch] otherwise might have been driven into the body of H.M. fleet ...[8]

Three drafts of this statement are in Sir William Coventry's hand and the phrasing bears the stamp of his sharp and logical mind. Holmes must indeed have had the better of the argument to convince so hostile a judge. Monck and his supporters naturally made the most of the fact that Smith was cleared of a false imputation on his courage. It was not to be expected that any ruling could compose so broad and partisan a quarrel. Even before its publication Pepys was told that 'the whole city rings to-day of Sir Jeremy Smith's killing of Holmes in a duell, at which I was not much displeased, for I fear every day more and more mischief from the man if he lives.'9 According to a newsletter the rumour was only dispelled by their simultaneous appearance in Westminster Hall. The character and situation of both men certainly make it highly probable that a duel did take place. In spite of the good advice given in Arlington's letter, Holmes was showing himself no less combative in the flush of success than in the bitterness of disappointment.

Rewards were now beginning to flow in upon him. In October he was given the *Tulip* of Amsterdam together with twenty tuns of brandy on board her.10 This was a mere apéritif. Early the following year he was appointed Commander-in-Chief of a squadron to operate from Portsmouth and the Isle of Wight. He was at his post by the end of April and his first prize had been brought in by May 7th. 'Nothing', he wrote to Joseph Williamson, Arlington's secretary and editor of the *Gazette*, 'can stir in the channel without notice.' Three days later the *Dragon*, one of his frigates, captured the *St. George* a French privateer of 16 guns in a long engagement off the Isle of Wight. Holmes at once asked for the loan of her so that he could fit her out as a privateer on his own account. Not only was the request immediately granted but five months later the loan was converted into a gift 'as a mark of our Royall favour & bounty to him'.11 The very next day another of his frigates brought in a Danish flyboat of three hundred tons laden with deals, and three days after that a small Frenchman laden with figs and honey, having narrowly missed a convoy of twenty-two French merchantmen, protected only by two small warships.12 Provided that the peace negotiations which had been in progress for some months did not mature too quickly it looked like being a profitable summer.

Early in June the Dutch descent on the Medway, the most brilliant stroke of the whole war, changed all this. Holmes had, not surprisingly, been alive to the danger of an attack of this kind. Pepys had noted on December 16th: '. . . but such is Sir R. Holmes's pride as never to be stopt, he being greatly troubled at my Lord Bruncker's late discharging all his men and officers but the standing officers at Chatham, and so are all other Commanders, and a very great cry hath been to the King from them all in my Lord's absence.'* And it was these same insolent fellows who made desperate attempts to repair the disastrous dereliction of the administration. At the moment of crisis on June 10th when it was known in the Navy Office that the Dutch had come up as high as the Nore and Sir William Coventry had changed his tune and was pressing 'all that is possible for fire-ships' it was Sir Frescheville Holles, Holmes's close friend and companion-in-arms, who came to the office in person to volunteer his services in command of them. But when four days later some of his ship's company came to the office at his direction to demand payment of their wage-tickets Pepys found them 'the most debauched, damning, swearing rogues that ever were in the Navy, just like their prophane commander'.

Even before the Dutch had scored their resounding success, towing away the flagship of the English fleet and burning some of its most powerful units at their moorings, the Government had been toying with a plan to intercept the Dutch East Indies fleet which returned to Europe at this season of the year.[13] Now that public anger at the cost and mismanagement of the war made peace imperative there might yet be time to pull off this *coup*. On June 22nd secret instructions were drafted for Holmes to take his squadron from Portsmouth round the North of Scotland and to cruise off the Western Isles. Prizes were to be sunk if there were any risk of their being recaptured and particular care was to be taken that no French prize passed into the jurisdiction of the Portuguese Government in view of the recent treaty concluded between the two powers.[14] The appearance of two enemy convoys in the channel about this time may have led to the reshaping of the plan. At any rate when Holmes did sail from Portsmouth with seven ships on June 27th he set his course westward. He called at Plymouth and then appears to have received instructions to convoy the merchant fleet, homeward bound from Zante, from the Straits of Gibraltar. He brought them safe into Kinsale by the beginning of September together

---

* Brouncker was a Navy Commissioner. The standing officers, like the standing rigging, were part and parcel of a ship whether she was in commission or not—the boatswain, the gunner and the carpenter. See on this Michael Lewis *England's Sea Officers* (2nd ed., 1948.)

with three ships from the Plantations. None of this had given him much chance of taking prizes. As the peace treaty had been signed at Breda on July 21st a cease-fire was imminent. He set sail therefore to take a broad sweep through the Western Approaches but returned empty-handed to Portsmouth on September 24th. On October 3rd he started to pay off his men and lay up the ships which was completed by the middle of the month.[15]

*　　　　*　　　　*

The ending of the war enabled Holmes to concentrate his energies on what was to prove the most enduring and not the least profitable of his official activities—the civil and military administration of the Isle of Wight. His appointments there consisted of the Governorship of Sandown Castle and the command of an independent company of foot. In order to consolidate his holding he opened negotiations with Lord Colepeper for the purchase of the Governorship* of the island. After hard and prolonged bargaining a sum was at last agreed in September, 1668.[16] Holmes entered on his Governorship on December 28th and the charges then allowed on the castles and forts for which he was responsible amounted to £285 11s. 9d. a year.[17] Holmes, however, saw that these possibilities were not being fully exploited. Even as Governor of Sandown he had spent large sums on rebuilding. Lord Colepeper had not learned to think big. The Isle of Wight was a frontier that required four thousand foot and three hundred horse to defend it. Its Governor ought to have a double sloop to permit him to discharge his duties in a fitting manner. As for the castles at Carisbrooke, Cowes and Yarmouth, they were totally out of repair. 'Carisbrooke has no officer there but myself, and only seven men, five of whom are sixpenny pays, and two eightpenny.' This was laughably inadequate. Four Lieutenants and four gunners at a daily charge of twenty shillings was the very least that would be needed. And an immediate advance of £1,000 for repairs would do to be going on with.[18]

---

* Lord Colepeper, like all his predecessors, had been styled in his patent simply Captain of the Isle of Wight. Holmes was the first to be styled Captain and Governor. I owe this point to Mr. J. D. Jones.

The military potentialities only represented a part of the money to be made. As Governor there would be the usual profits of justice, forfeited estates of suicides and felons and so on. And besides all that there were limitless prospects from rights of Admiralty, wreckage, salvage, prizes and whatnot. Combined with a local command in the Navy the thing could be a 'mountain of purer Gould' than anything to be found in West Africa. But before entering on this smiling prospect Holmes went through some of the most contentious passages of his career.

In January 1668, Whitehall rang with one of the great scandals of the reign—the duel between the Duke of Buckingham and the Earl of Shrewsbury: 'and all', as Pepys succinctly records, 'about my Lady Shrewsbury, who is a whore, and is at this time, and hath for a great while been, a whore to the Duke of Buckingham'. In the duels of that day the seconds took part. Buckingham's seconds were Sir Robert Holmes and a fencing-master called Jenkins, Shrewsbury's Sir John Talbot and Bernard Howard. The unfortunate Jenkins was killed instantaneously and the Earl of Shrewsbury mortally wounded. All the others got off more or less lightly. Shrewsbury's death, which was two months in coming, would leave his opponents liable to be prosecuted for murder. A warrant for Holmes's pardon was issued on January 27th. None the less the death of Jenkins seems to have led to his conviction for murder at the Surrey assizes, as on February 25th a warrant was issued reprieving him and suspending all proceedings against him in the event of a conviction for manslaughter at the next assizes.[19] Buckingham and the others were similarly protected. It is difficult to believe that Holmes did himself any good by his participation in this deeply repulsive affair.

Hardly was he clear of it before the quarrel with Smith over the conduct of the St. James's Day Fight was revived yet again. The humiliations and miscarriages of the war had goaded the House of Commons into an implacable investigation of every dark corner of naval administration and command. Everything came out: the disgraceful story of corruption and inefficiency that had made it possible for the Dutch to sail into our principal naval base without so much as a scratch on their paintwork; the well-concealed secret, that had led to so many quarrels and accusations, of the order to shorten sail when the Dutch were in headlong retreat after the battle off Lowestoft in 1665; and, of course, the charges and counter-charges brought against each other by Holmes and Smith. No wonder Pepys and Coventry paled under their habitual urbanity as they thought of the gunners, pursers and masters queuing up to give evidence of the money they had paid for their places or of the questions that might be asked about arrangements with the various contractors whose supplies, it seemed, were neither cheap nor reliable. Sir Frescheville Holles, in particular, earned their severe displeasure for his inquisitiveness in such matters.[20] When Sir Jeremy Smith told them that he hoped to be able to get Holles into trouble with the House of Commons for his blasphemies Pepys forgot his old antipathy in welcoming so determined an opponent of the Rupert-Holmes faction. Pepys was not alone in feeling that, on this re-examination of the matter, Smith got the best of it and that in any case it was 'a most shameful scandalous thing for Flag Officers to accuse one another of'.[21] The vindication of Smith was emphasised by his appointment a few days later to be Vice-Admiral of the fleet in the Channel under Sir Thomas Allin.

If Holmes's standing had suffered by the events of the spring he was still a figure of importance in his own right and he still had powerful friends. His younger brother John was continuously employed in the much reduced peacetime Navy, serving in the Mediterranean under Allin and Spragge, Sir Robert's great rival. While still ashore John had sur-prised and annoyed a wide circle by a clandestine marriage to Margaret Lowther—

> which I was sorry for, he being an idle rascal, and proud, and with little, I doubt; and she a mighty pretty, well-disposed lady and a good fortune. Her mother and friends take on mightily; but the sport is, Sir Robert Holmes do seem to be mad too with his brother, and will disinherit him, saying that he hath ruined himself, marrying below himself, and to his disadvantage.[22]

Pepys went on to express the opinion, with more reason than delicacy, that Sir Robert's social pretensions were exaggerated. As will later appear the marriage was not in all respects successful though it was blessed with several children.

After this succession of public scandals and family squabbles Holmes retired to Bath to take the waters with his friend Sir Frescheville Holles. Towards the end of July they attended the launching of the *Edgar*, a 72-gun ship, at Bristol in the presence of a crowd of three thousand people.[23] It seems to have been the only naval occasion in which Holmes took part during the year, though when Pepys ran into him in Whitehall in November and told him of Sir William Penn's resignation from the Navy Board his sudden interest frightened his informant into thinking that he might be saddled with him as a colleague. In fact the vacant place was taken by Sir Jeremy Smith, who had now reverted in Pepys's estimation to 'a silly, talking, prating man'. It was from him that Pepys heard that 'Holmes and Spragg now rule all with the Duke of Buckingham, as to sea-business, and will be great men.'[24] No doubt Holmes's mind was turning more and more to the Isle of Wight. Early in the New Year he was firmly established down there, arranging Admiralty courts, rapping Arlington's secretary over the knuckles for not sending him regular news bulletins, projecting, petitioning, ordering. The peace treaty had led to a temporary reversal of alliances so that England might find herself at war with France, in which event the defence of the Isle of Wight would have to be taken seriously. Meanwhile the energetic Governor still had time to engage in trade on his own account. We know about this because of a ludicrous technical error. Holmes, in conjunction with others, had freighted a French prize for a voyage to Leghorn and Smyrna. Just as she was due in the Channel it was realised that as she was not English-built both she and her cargo would be forfeit under the Navigation Act if she were to bring Ottoman goods into an English port. Arrangements were hurriedly made to stop her in the Downs until the necessary licence had been obtained.[25]

In October 1669 Holmes was elected M.P. for Winchester. Although he sat in every succeeding Parliament (except the short-lived Exclusion Parliaments of 1680 and 1681) he left no mark as a House of Commons man. But for the impeachment of Danby in 1678 and the offer of the Crown to William and Mary in 1689 he was a faithful member of the Court party and supported the Government of the day. One of the very few occasions on which he contributed to the counsels of the House was in a debate on whether or not Andrew Marvell had given Sir Philip Harcourt a box on the ear.[26] It appears that he regarded his membership as an adjunct to and latterly as a function of his Governorship. It simplified and accelerated transactions with the Government in London. That he was regarded as a political personage of some importance is suggested by his being chosen to convey Louis XIV's personal envoy back to France in 1670[27] and therefore to accompany the Duke of Buckingham on the second leg of the Secret Treaty negotiations. In the summer of 1671[28] he had the honour of entertaining the King at his new house in the Isle of Wight. By that time the Government had concerted its plans for a second reversal of alliances and a third war with the Dutch.

XV

The Third Dutch War

T O THOSE WHO CONCEIVE of foreign policy in the pure simplicity of conflicting appetites unclouded by such abstractions as honour or morality, the Third Dutch War must shine as a clear deed in a muddled world. Others, such as the contemporary John Evelyn, have deplored it as the diplomacy of smash-and-grab. Cynical, the adjective so often applied to Charles II, seems a just description of his policy and of the pretexts on which war was declared. A yacht bringing the English Ambassador's wife home altered course so as to pass through the Dutch fleet. Because, as Evelyn put it, 'the Dutch Admiral did not strike to that trifling vessel', Charles II professed himself mortally offended and sent Sir George Downing over to The Hague to stir up as much trouble as he could. Even then the Dutch proved exasperatingly good-tempered: but they were too clear-sighted not to notice the flurry of warlike preparation in the French and English Naval bases.

Portsmouth had at least a dozen men-of-war fitting for sea in January 1672. Sir Robert Holmes had been appointed Senior Officer there and given command of the *St. Michael*, a newly-built first-rate of 90 guns. Amongst the Captains in the powerful squadron assigned to him were his brother John in the *Gloucester* and Sir Frescheville Holles in the *Cambridge*. 'The fitting of our ships goes on at a great pace and the sailors come freely', he wrote at the end of the month (having a week earlier intimated to the Navy Commissioners his desire that Lieutenant Edwards of the *Blessing* might press seamen for him). 'If there should be occasion I could set out a good squadron in a very short time.' In the same letter he reproves his correspondent, Joseph Williamson, recently knighted, for not keeping him properly informed:

When Joseph Williamson Esq was in being Sir Robert Holmes had sometimes a letter of intelligence, but since Sir Joseph succeeded I have not had a word of news stirring. Three or four posts have I been heare Commander-in-Chief of His Majesty's Fleet and not as much as a newes book.[1]

It was not in Holmes's character to wait on events or to leave his political masters unaware of the views formed by the commander on the spot. His grasp of strategy and what would now be called logistics is nowhere better shown than in his letter to Arlington, written on January 26th soon after he had arrived at his post.

A Wednesday morning I arrived here and after I had seene the condition of the shipps and speake with what Captains are here & the officers of the Dock I went over for the Isle of Wight to see what condition that was in and to inquire of the number of Dutch shipps that are now in Cowes Roade.

The economy, clarity and speed of a professional makes everything look easy and obvious: but the priorities observed are perhaps worth noting. Certainly the inquiry was well directed: there were no less than twenty-two merchantmen laden with wine and salt sheltering in Cowes Road under the guns of four Dutch men-of-war. Holmes at once saw the chance offered by this cargo.

If my intelligence be true they have hardly salt enough in Holland at this time to salt the meat they must use for their fleet this summer, and without meat they cannot come to sea; and if the salt be stopped you may be confident that they will be in great want.

They will not be able to fish nor provide for their Garrisons or scarce doe anything without it.

Besides the Dutchmen already mentioned there were twelve or thirteen Hamburgers 'as they pretend: I beleeve they are upon the Accompt of the Dutch' similarly laden at anchor in Cowes Roads:

There have not been three Hamburgers at Cowes since I had the government till now, and if the King will permit them to trade, all the ships in Holland will quickly turn Hamburgers.

One of the Dutch saltships that reached Cowes the night before reported twenty more sail off the island trying to make Cowes Roads, but the head-wind was probably driving them into a westerly port such as Plymouth or Falmouth. Yet further to the westward, not yet in the Channel, was another Holland-bound salt convoy protected by two warships.

> My lord, I write you my mind as you are my friend & I hope you will putt it to the best use for H.M. service & I may not be thought too Busy for endeavouring to use my weak endeavours to serve my master . . .
>
> My opinion clearly is that if these fleets now abroad, bound for Holland with salt, can be luckily seized on, it may bee of greater consequence as in order of the ruining of these people, than if you took their East India Fleet. For without salt, nothing can go forward.
>
> If you will doe anything in this matter you must presently send four companies of foot and five or six hundred watermen which may be had in two or three days.
>
> The inclosed is a list of what Dutch & pretended Hamburgers are at Cowes Roades besides two I see just now coming to Spitthead wch I suppose to be of the twenty ships that were off the Island.

As a postscript Holmes added:

> If his Majestie will have quick despatch heare I must have Authority to Act as a Commissioner of the Navy. Otherwise I must desire to looke only after my owne ship. Before I left London I did desire Monsr Blandfort* to speake to the Duke of York about it but have noe Answer.[2]

This letter has been quoted at some length because it pinpoints the climax of Holmes's naval career. It exemplifies, besides the cardinal military virtues of speed and attack, the reasons for his success—his clear analysis of a strategic situation, his adroit tactical sense, his boldness and his opportunism. Had the Government shewn the same qualities by immediate acceptance of his plan, it can hardly be doubted that he would, as at the Vlie, have inflicted great economic damage at a negligible cost. And had the war begun with so assured and professional a victory, Holmes's claims could hardly have been overlooked when the flags were assigned for the coming summer. But the dice fell the other way. It was six weeks before orders were issued to seize Dutch ships on their peaceful occasions.

* The Marquis de Blanquefort, a naturalised Frenchman who was a great favourite with Charles II and James II.

As Holmes bluntly put it in another letter to Arlington written aboard the *St. Michael* at sea off the Isle of Wight:

> You have let slip the best opportunity that ever people had to destroy those I think you will make your enemies . . . The very day I had his Royal Highness's order a fleet of Merchantmen passed through the Channel which I suppose to be their first fleet from Cadiz, another being still behind. Had your orders come but twenty-four hours sooner we could not miss this last fleet.[3]

This was written on March 12th, a week after Holmes had left Portsmouth to cruise in the Channel with six or seven ships. That same afternoon the Admiralty agent at Weymouth reported the sighting of a large convoy, supposed to be the homeward-bound Dutch Smyrna fleet, ten miles south of Portland.

About noon the next day, Wednesday, March 13th, Holmes in company with four of his squadron sighted them off the Isle of Wight. It was indeed the Dutch Smyrna fleet, with another convoy thrown in for good measure. Altogether there were about seventy ships of which four were totally unarmed. Gun for gun and ship for ship Holmes's force was superior to the men-of-war acting as escort: but Smyrna ships, like their sisters sailing to the East Indies, had to be well-armed. One at least was a 40-gun ship and about twenty of the others carried anything from twenty to thirty. Homeward bound 'richly laden, where the seamen that were on board have every one almost all his fortune in private adventure', they were certain to give a good account of themselves.[4]

The English who had been out in mid-Channel had the advantage of the wind which was south-westerly. Forming themselves into a line with the *Resolution*, a 70-gun ship, in the van, they came up with the Dutch, also in a line to protect their merchantmen, about three in the afternoon. The Earl of Ossory in the *Resolution* 'bore in close up to their Vice-Admiral and gave him a warning gun to stryke'. Three times the Dutch refused so that

> my Lord Ossory setting a broad-syde to beare upon him, they called out 'Hold' and told him their Admirall had gone aboard Sir Robert Holmes the King's Admirall at wch the *Resolution* made a stopp. In the meanetime the Dutch Admiral having sent his Lieutenant aboard Sir Robert Holmes and he it seems

given some saucy language to Sir Robt he was Clapt into the hold and immediately Sir Robert Holmes made up to the Dutch Admiral and having given him
first a warning piece . . . ours immediately fitted their small shott and poured
in a whole broad-syde & soe the fight begun wch continued very hott till six a
clocke . . .

By then it had been dark for nearly an hour. The Dutch in spite of suffering heavy casualties had had much the best of the engagement. The
Resolution was disabled and the *St. Michael* so badly damaged that Holmes
transferred to the *Cambridge* (commanded by Sir Frescheville Holles) during
the night. By the morning the *Resolution*'s rigging had been repaired and
reinforcements had appeared in the shape of the *Gloucester* (62) commanded
by John Holmes and two other ships. It was subsequently reported that
John Holmes 'had a severe rebuke from Sir Robert (for having) his
Tomkins* in his canon the first day of the engagement'.⁵ Perhaps it
provoked him to the action here described.

> . . . the next morning by six a clocke the fight renewed againe & soe continued
> all that day off of Rye very Sharpe. Early in the morning young Holmes bore
> bravely in with the Rear-Admirall of the Dutch and without fyreing one gun,
> came close up to arme & arme with him, & then pouring in a whole broadsyde
> tore him down as broad as the syde of a house, plying him againe & againe till
> at last he made him stryke his ancient. Haveing manned him with English he
> carried him in the fleete severall houres but at last he was seene to make two
> totters from one syde to the other & soe to dropp downe right into the sea. He
> has eighty bales of silk on board besides much plate . . .

This was the *Klein Hollandia* of 44 guns. John Holmes himself was among
the many wounded in the course of the day's fighting. Accounts differ as
to the number of prizes taken but it did not exceed half a dozen and seems
only to have included one of the coveted Smyrna ships, taken by Captain
Legge of the *Fairfax* who found eleven Dutchmen lying dead on her upper
deck. Holmes estimated the value of the prizes at £200,000, but this
seems improbably high. In life and limb it cost the *St. Michael* alone at
least thirty-four killed, including a midshipman and the master's mate,
and another fifty-six wounded. Even by the standards of the Duchess of

* Tompions, fitted to the muzzles of guns to keep the barrel dry when not in use.

Albemarle it was a sufficiently bloody affair. The damage suffered by the English ships was proportionate. The *St. Michael* was reported by the Admiralty agent at Deal as 'much battared and torn'; the *Resolution* so shattered that she had to be ordered out of the fight by Thursday evening when the *Cambridge* and four or five others were still grimly hanging on. When darkness eventually ended the action one of the English ships had lost all her masts and two more had lost one or other. It had proved an expensive foretaste of the war which Charles proceeded to declare a few days later.

And there was no denying the fact of failure. Sir Robert Carr might write jovially to Williamson that ' . . . now that the Dutch find that five of ours can beat forty, brandy will not prevail on the phlegmatic rascals to come out' and ask him to tell Sir Robert Holmes that his health was drunk often in Lincolnshire.[6] Holmes knew better. The phlegmatic rascals had fought their convoy through against his utmost efforts. That those efforts had not been puny, the state of the ships returning to harbour could show. That neither he nor his Captains lacked courage or experience might be an argument that the force employed was insufficient for the purpose. But it was too late now to teach Arlington and the rest the principles of war; and it would certainly be impolitic to repeat what he had written on the day before he sighted the convoy: 'Give me leave to remind you of what I write to your Lordship concerning the stopping of the men-of-war and merchantmen in Cowes Roads which were very considerable.' He was feeling ill and querulous and depressed: and the shock of the hideous experiences of battle was not dulled by the intoxication of victory. On March 18th he wrote again to Arlington. He was back on board his own ship the *St. Michael* in Margate Roads and hoped to sail on the tide for Longsand Head and to anchor next day at the Nore. The illness that had prevented his writing earlier required a spell ashore. Lord Ossory would have given a perfect account of what happened up to the time of his leaving for London. What he has to add tells us more of his own state of mind:

Yesterday morning I sailed out of the Downs in the *Resolution* in search of my own ship, which I have met here in a sad condition, never the like, I beleeve,

M

seene or heard of. The night before I sailed from the Downs I issued orders to the Commanders of the shipps that came with me to follow me . . . but none followed me but the *Gloucester* [his brother's ship], notwithstanding I did send orders in writing to each ship. I also sent orders to the Lieutenants on board the Prizes to weigh & make what saile they could over the flatts to the Buoy of the Nore, but they have not stirred as I can see. You may see how the shipps are officered. I can doe noe more than order them to doe theire duty . . . if His Majesty does not take care to have them punished for this and theire other mis- carriages, he will quickly have noe shipps. I am very apprehensive the Dutch may send a squadron and sweepe the Downs of the shipps there, which is very feasible, considering the baseness of some of the officers that are there . . .[7]

Was Holmes half-heartedly anticipating the search for a scapegoat? A more full-blooded attempt was soon made against his rival, Sir Edward Spragge.

Spragge had only that week returned from the Mediterranean. Coming up Channel on Sunday he had sighted Holmes's squadron over towards the French coast and had made towards him. Holmes, to quote Spragge's account, 'eagerly chased till they made who I was. Immediately he called off his ships by firing a gun or two. T'would be for his advantage to have spoken with me to informe himself of the Enimy. I was not able to come to him being three leagues to windward of mee soe I . . . stood away my course towards the Downes.'[8] He dropped anchor there with half a dozen of his squadron about noon the next day. Holmes's letter to Arlington written on March 12th the day before the attack on the Smyrna fleet confirms this and provides a reason:

> On Sunday afternoon I saw Sir Edward Spragge goe by towards the Downes but did not speake because hee was something neare the shoare and the wind at south.[9]

After the failure of the attack it naturally occurred to people that a very different result might have been obtained if Holmes and Spragge had joined forces. Why had they not done so? The obvious answer that they had not (and should have) been ordered to do so might be embarrassing to the Government or at least to the Lord High Admiral. So an initial attempt was made to put some of the blame on Spragge. A young officer from the *Fairfax* (commanded by the Duke of York's friend Captain Legge) who arrived at Court hotfoot from the battle adverted on how

> unfortunately it fell out that the five shipps of Sir Edward Spragg's squadron being ordered to cross the Dutch merchantmen as they sayled here in the very narrow off of Dover & which in all likelyhood had swept the greatest part of them into our ports . . . it so happened that it was (? far) in the night before they reached up to where this squadron of five shipps lay waiteing, & by the Extreame darkenesse of the night & an over-blowing Gale they soe passed them that not one of them was seene as they passed.[10]

There is no evidence that any such orders were ever given. A rival version of affairs, in which Holmes, from avarice and ambition, had concealed his intentions of attacking the convoy when he met Spragge in the Channel, gained wider and more rapid currency. Two inferences may be drawn from the acceptance of this story; first that Arlington and the Duke of York did nothing to discredit it; and second that it can hardly have conduced to better relations between Holmes and Spragge.

The promulgation of the flag appointments in the the following month must have deepened Holmes's jealousy and resentment. Spragge was Vice-Admiral of the Red; and Harman, his other great rival, was Rear-Admiral. Holmes himself was no more than a private Captain though, since the *St. Michael* was the only first-rate not to wear a flag, clearly the senior captain in the fleet. There were in fact three less flag-officers than usual as the French under D'Estrées were to act as the van or White squadron of the combined fleet.

Neither the *St. Michael* nor her commander were given much time to repair the ravages of battle. On April 25th she sailed from Chatham to rejoin the fleet after less than five weeks in dockyard hands.[11] Just over a month later she was riding at anchor with the rest of the combined fleet in Solebay when the insistent gunfire of a scouting vessel roused the sleeping crews to the imminent approach of the Dutch. By dawn the enemy was in sight, to the north-east, coming on steadily on an easterly breeze; by six o'clock the leading squadrons were heavily engaged.

Solebay, Holmes's last battle, was to be as bloody and as hard-fought as any in his career.[12] In spite of a distinct Allied superiority in number of ships and in weight of broadside the English found themselves fighting with their backs to the wall. Partly this was thanks to the tactical skill of the great De Ruyter, partly to a misunderstanding with the French squadron which in effect fought an entirely separate battle, partly to being caught napping on a lee shore with less than no room to manœuvre. Partly too the fleet may have been confused by fighting in reverse order, as it was the Blue, or Rear, Squadron under Sandwich which happened to be moored at the northern end of the line when the Dutch were reported a few miles away to the north-east. Probably it was this more than anything else that caused the French (who had not been told that they were no longer the van but the rear) to stand away to the southward while the Blue and the Red stood north on the opposite tack. The English went into action in what was meant to be line ahead while the Dutch came down towards them in line abreast. Sandwich with the central division of the Blue squadron had been heavily engaged for an hour or more by the time the Duke of York's flagship the *Prince* found herself facing single-handed the attentions of De Ruyter, his Lieutenant-Admiral, and five other ships. It was the Duke's hour: for all the thunder and storm of the guns it was 'quite calm and the water as smooth as possible—as the saying is as smooth as a milk bowl. We being all alone made it the warmer with us: none of our Squadron could get up with us for their lives, they being so becalmed . . . Between 9 and 10 o'clock Sir John Cox (Flag Captain of the *Prince*) was slain with a great shot, being close by the Duke on the poop. Several gentlemen & others were slain and wounded . . . on both sides of the Duke . . . I do absolutely believe no Prince upon the whole earth can compare with his Royal Highness in gallant resolution in fighting his enemy, and with so great conduct and knowledge in navigation . . . to say all, he is everything that man can be, and most pleasant when the great shot are thundering about his ears.'[13]

The *St. Michael* was to leeward of the flagship when the wind dropped and thus unable to come to her relief. But when, about the middle of the morning, the *Prince* was entirely disabled by the main topmast crashing to the deck and bringing most of the rigging with it, it was to the *St. Michael* that the Duke transferred his flag, accompanied by two of his gentlemen, his chief pilot, his footman and the Marquis de Blanquefort.

> There was then little or no wind, which together with the great smoke, was the cause that neither the Duke's own division nor the enemy perceived for some time, he had changed his ship . . . but these found him out first & then plyed us very hard.[14]

The *St. Michael*, still heading north-east, was in danger of grounding on the sandbanks off Lowestoft so both pilots, the Duke's and Holmes's, insisted on tacking to the southwards. The change of course took them into the thick of the battle, right through the Dutch line, and so close to Sandwich's blazing flagship the *Royal James* that they had to bear off to avoid her. The *St. Michael* was still in reasonably good shape but the hot fighting of the afternoon with three Dutch flagships to windward and two to leeward took its toll. By late afternoon she was almost disabled and sailing very heavily with six feet of water in the hold. The *Resolution* and the *Cambridge* which had supported her stoutly were themselves forced to fall away to leeward, but not before the *Cambridge*'s captain Sir Frescheville Holles had sealed his loyalty to his friend and commander with his life. Their place was taken, with a courage outstanding on a day of brave conduct, by the *Phoenix* which 'had no cartridges left, nor paper to make any', and by the *Victory* commanded by the Earl of Ossory who had shared with Holmes the battering in the Channel two months before. But heroism was no substitute for seaworthiness:

> We were now so much disabled and had so much water in hold, that Sir Edward Spragge with some of his Division, and other of our ships went on ahead of us; which the Duke seeing, and that the *St. Michael* must of necessity bear out of the line to stop her leaks and refit, left her, about five, and went on board the *London* [Spragge's flagship], ordering Sir Robert Holmes not to bear away, nor take down the Standard till he saw it up in the *London*. The Duke was near three quarters of an hour in his boat, before he could get on board Sir Edward Spragge, it blowing then a fine gale, where so soon as he came, he put up his Standard, and then the *St. Michael* took down hers, and bore down out of the line.[15]

It was by then nearly six o'clock and the heat of the action was over. The fresh breeze that had hindered the Duke in getting up to the *London* helped both fleets to steer for the separate battle taking place to the southward between the French and the Zeeland squadron which had originally been detached to deal with them. As the noise and the smoke receded to the southward the *St. Michael* in a sinking condition fitted what sail she could bear to carry her to the safety of the Thames. The day had been of exceptional beauty: 'very hot and fair, sunshine, the fairest day we have seen all this summer before'. Now that the fighting was over there was time to notice the wreckage and the corpses drifting silently and horribly by. To seaward to the south, as night came on, 'a fine air of wind and smooth water', the lights of the Dutch fleet could be seen for several hours.

The casualties of Solebay had been heavy, especially on the English side, totalling about seven hundred and fifty killed and about the same number severely wounded.[16] The number killed aboard the *St. Michael* was thirty-one, three more than the figure for De Ruyter's flagship.[17] And De Ruyter himself considered the battle the stiffest of his experience. Apart from Sir Frescheville Holles Holmes had lost his friend Sandwich whose flagship he had seen burning so fiercely that her crew had had to abandon her. His letters written later in the summer still complain of indisposition arising from his injuries in the attack on the Smyrna convoy, so he had by no means recovered when he was called upon to bear the brunt of Solebay. For the second time in two months he was bringing in a ship that could scarcely swim with a crew who had endured the shock and exhaustion of a battle that had been long and bloody. For the second time there was no victory to reward them for what they had been through. All their courage and skill had been needed to avoid a disastrous defeat.

The death of Sandwich created a vacancy on the flag-list. Spragge took his place as Admiral of the Blue and in the consequent promotions Captain Beach of the *Monmouth*, a vessel that had hardly played so prominent a role as the *St. Michael*, was preferred to Holmes. Did the Duke of York perhaps think it unwise to employ two such violent and extreme rivals as Holmes and Spragge as admirals in the same fleet? Holmes's behaviour to Sir Jeremy Smith, now a Navy Commissioner, was fresh in everyone's minds. And the Duke himself would not have forgotten the scene after the battle off Lowestoft when Holmes had lost his temper and demanded the appointment of Rear-Admiral of the Blue. The inter-twining of their naval careers had begun at Helvoetsluys when James, as a mere boy, had claimed the command of the revolted fleet. It continued when both had won acclaim in the brilliant victory of their first fleet action; it had extended through years of the hardest fighting ever experienced by the Royal Navy. It was to end, abruptly, with the present campaign: at the height of their careers, at the height of a war, their services were no longer required. The resentments and suspicions of the King's policy of alliance with Louis XIV were to produce in the following spring the Test Act of 1673 by which James, Duke of York and his co-religionists were to be debarred from civil or military employment under the Crown. Both men had still the summer and autumn to serve at sea but there were no further actions of any consequence during that period.

In spite of the damage and casualties sustained, the *St. Michael* had rejoined the fleet at the Nore by June 18th.[18] She sailed at the end of the month on the fruitless cruise off the Dutch coast which the Government had ordered in the hopes of intercepting the homeward-bound East India fleet. On August 8th the English fleet after six weeks of bad weather, sickness, shortage of food and a total absence of success was at anchor in Bridlington Bay.[19] Sir Joseph Williamson's correspondent there reported: 'Sir Robert Holmes is come from sea something indisposed but I hope he will be fit to return in a day or two.' Four days later Holmes himself wrote to Williamson:

> I have been this month very ill of the bruises I got in the Smyrna business which brought me so low I was going hence to the Bath, but the consideration of our condition at sea and the fresh air I have had hath altered my design though I am afraid my condition will not be able to go through with my resolution.

Next day, however, he felt well enough to return to his ship and appears to have remained with her until the fleet came in for the winter three or four weeks later.[20]

Of the campaign of the following year Holmes was an impotent spectator. The King had countered the disqualification of his brother for the
office of Lord High Admiral by appointing Rupert to command the fleet,
thus maintaining the military prestige of the House of Stuart. Throughout
the whole period of his command Rupert never ceased to press in season
and out for the employment of an officer whom he evidently regarded as
the most capable of all. On May 10th he wrote to Arlington:

> . . . Our want will be undertaking officers. I could have wished your Lordship
> at the Councell wee had when the Dutch appeared. You would have found then
> the weake harts among us. . . . Sir John Harman is sick, Narbrough not like to
> be here. Judge then in what loss I shall be of commanding officers. I have there-
> fore thought fitt once more to desire your Lordship to try for to gett Sir Robert
> Holmes into play, Mr Barthu telling me he was sure Sir Robert desired to go on
> any honourable conditions. Pray, my Lord, propose this way to his Matie which
> is to make him a Lieutenant-Generall, or send him aboard, and I will give him
> the command, when there's occasion and without any disturbance to the
> officers of the fleet; in the meantime he shall go in my ship . . . pray assure his
> Matie I have no other design in this but his service. [21]

On July 27th he sent to the same correspondent from his flagship off the
Dutch coast a summary of the situation, a choice of objectives and a request
for instructions. He set out three possibilities: to attempt a landing, to lie
in wait for the East India fleet, attacking it either on the high seas or in
harbour, and lastly to attack the enemy battle fleet in the Schooneveld. He
added a postscript in his own hand:

> If his Matie will have either of them well done, he must send me Sir Robert
> Holmes. If there were not a necessity of this I would not, after so many denials,
> press it. I do it only to save the King's honour, which, if we do nothing more
> this year will suffer.

A fortnight later the Dutch obligingly emerged to fight the battle of the
Texel in which Spragge was drowned. Surely this removed the last barrier
to Holmes's re-employment as well as creating a convenient vacancy among
the Flag-men. On August 12th Rupert wrote to the King:

> I most humbly desire your commands concerning Spragg's place. I hope you will
> think of Holmes now the other is gone . . .

As if Charles were deaf or inattentive he repeats in a rather louder tone:

> . . . I hope you will send us your pleasure for our flags. Sir Edward being unfortunately drowned, I hope there will be no dispute to have Sir Robert Holmes in his place.

The Royal veto must have been given in equally bell-like tones, for on August 14th Rupert wrote to Arlington that he had completed the disposal of the flags. 'To Berry I have given the command of a division detasche [detached] as I intended for Sir Robert Holmes.' Holmes's younger brother John, who had been knighted the previous year for his gallantry in the attack on the Smyrna fleet, was advanced to Rear-Admiral of the Blue 'The only man discontented', wrote Rupert, 'is George Legge who pretends to have merited more than Sir John Holmes.'

Even after these rebuffs Rupert did not abandon his efforts to secure recognition and employment for a military talent of which his own opinion —and he was no mean judge—needs no elucidation. Much against his will he had had to bring the fleet into the Thames to victual and refit. In what must have been one of the last letters he wrote as Commander-in-Chief he pressed the King 'to send Sir Robert Holmes with the next squadron that goes out, for Harman and Kempthorne being sickly, none is able to do you that service but himself.'

That letter was written on August 24th when, in spite of talk, naval operations for that year were over. During the winter negotiations put an end to a war that had indeed brought nothing about.

XVI

Bashaw of the Isle of Wight

URING HIS SEA-SERVICE Holmes must often have heard the
sentences, new minted in his day, of the naval prayer. He had
now, in its exquisite phrasing, returned in safety to enjoy the
blessings of the land, with the fruits of his labours. And these fruits were
rich indeed. The proceeds of the two voyages to West Africa must have
been considerable: the prize money from the two Dutch wars would alone
have furnished a respectable fortune; and this had been augmented by the
gift of a French prize which, renamed the *Albemarle,* Holmes had employed
first as a privateer, then as a merchantman before selling her back to the
Government to be fitted out as a fifth-rate, renamed the *Holmes.* Besides
these direct profits of naval service there were his offices under the Crown;
Governor and Vice-Admiral of the Isle of Wight, Governor and Vice-
Admiral of Newport, Vice-Admiral of Hampshire. What the value of such
appointments might be can be surmised from an undated warrant preserved among the State Papers granting him two-thirds of the clear value
of all ships or goods, enemy or pretended neutral, as he should seize on the
high and open seas or in the ports, havens, and creeks of his Vice-Admiralty.
When one remembers that the high and open seas in question were and are
among the greatest trade-routes of the world and that in the days of sailing
ships Spithead and the Solent offered an unrivalled anchorage in every
state of wind and tide, one can recognise that this warrant might be worth
having. The independent company, later increased to a regiment, which
Holmes commanded was another useful source of income. And one must
not forget the gentle rain of perquisites that refreshed the arid soil of
justice and administration.

Last but no means least were the gifts of land, rent or cash by which

Holmes's services were rewarded. In April 1662 he had been granted £800 out of an unaccounted balance of pay from Cromwell's army. In June 1672, perhaps as amends for not getting his flag, he was granted rents in the County of Southampton to the annual value of £387, together with others in the Isle of Wight that brought the total up to £563. On December 14th, 1674 he received another immense grant of fee-farm rents in Wales to the annual value of £609 'as well for and in consideration of severall summes of money expended in our service by our trusty & Wellbeloved Sir Robert Holmes K^t as also for and in consideration of the many good & faithful services performed by him unto us.' In September 1675 he received with another petitioner a grant of forfeited lands in Galway and Mayo amounting to 2,927 acres.[1] This was substantial wealth.

Probably the full extent of this royal bounty is still uncharted. Holmes apparently held the keepership of the North Baylywick Walk in the New Forest together with certain lodges that belonged to it, as he is said to have sold the office and its emoluments to the sergeant of the Buckhounds.[2] Certainly he occasionally softened the asperities of his official correspondence with presents of venison.[3]

Holmes's maritime jurisdiction must have given him valuable connexions and sources of information concerning seaborne trade. He seems to have interested himself particularly in the import of French wines, complaining furiously to the Admiralty against the senior officer of the escort when the St. Peter galliot 'loaden with wines for his Ma^{ty} etc. from Rouen' was captured while sailing in convoy in the closing days of the Third Dutch War. Eighteen months later he requested the loan of 'a dogger for the fetching of some wine from Nantes' in which the King was ready to oblige him until it was found that there was only one such vessel in the Royal Navy and that she had already been lent to the Guinea Company. Holmes's activities as a shipper shaded imperceptibly into his career as Governor and Vice-Admiral. Thus in April 1679 he reported to the Admiralty that four Dutch Bordeaux wine ships had lately been cast away on the Isle of Wight and that a boat's crew from the Royal James (now commanded by his subordinate at the Vlie, Sir William Jennings) had been 'overset and lost in their greedy endeavours after purchase from the said wrecks'.[4] A few years later Holmes himself appears to have been responsible for even more outrageous behaviour. The Dutch Ambassador had complained of the 'barbarous usage of a Holland merchantman laded with High Country wines, distressed but not cast away, on the Isle of Wight'. The whole affair, wrote Sir Leoline Jenkins, the Secretary of State, in a very stiff note, was 'a matter of shame and confusion'. Holmes was to rescue the men, restore their property and send a full account to the King who would then decide what punishment to impose.[5] What with wreckage, prize of war and ordinary legitimate imports Holmes should have been able to offer his customers an interesting list.

If commerce and administration provided a broadening flow of profit, landowning and farming and the purchase of house property offered opportunities of diversifying investment. Often too these activities could serve other purposes as well. As a politician and public man Holmes needed a house in London; as Governor he required a large establishment in the Isle of Wight; as a courtier it might be an advantage to have a place of one's own within easy reach of Windsor; as an old campaigner who was beginning to feel his years and his knocks it would be a solace to have a house in Bath. At the time of his death he had all these, besides a second house in the Isle of Wight in which one of his nephews was living.[6] In 1679 he bought a farm (Thorley) close to his house in Yarmouth and settled it on his illegitimate daughter and heiress, Mary, who had been born the year before. This was not its only use to the family; Sir John Holmes rented it for £400 a year until his death in 1683, after which Sir Robert himself seems to have kept it in hand. It was a mixed farm employing twelve carthorses and carrying, at the time of his death, a stock of twenty-seven cows, ten suckler calves, twenty-seven store cattle and sixty-one sheep.

That Holmes's daughter should enter his biography among an account of his possessions and investments is inartistic but not inappropriate. Who her mother was, what degree of affection and familiarity existed between father and child, whether he played with her or bought her toys, we do not know. No letter of his to her survives: and in the thirty or forty letters of the years 1688–90 in the Isle of Wight County Museum at Carisbrooke Castle there is no mention of her.[7] Not that this means much, one way or the other: but the fact remains that all we know about her is that she had a room of her own 'Madam Homes's Closet' next to her father's in his house at Englefield Green and that his Will is based on an iron determination that she should marry one or other of his nephews, preferably Henry, the son of his elder brother Colonel Thomas Holmes of Kilmallock in Co. Limerick.[8] This she did and bore him several children. Her eldest son was created Lord Holmes of Kilmallock only a few months after her death in 1760, thus fulfilling, if belatedly, what one cannot but believe was Sir Robert's grand design. It was fitting that the Peerage, when it came, should be Irish; the family belonged there and Sir Robert, besides obtaining the grant of forfeited lands already mentioned, had purchased others in Limerick.[9] If Mary Holmes appears not so much a creature of flesh and blood as an instrument for conveying property, this may simply be an illusion arising from the type of evidence that has happened to survive. But it is not inconsistent with aspects of her father's character already observed. The acquisition and preservation of wealth tends to be obsessive, as Holmes's contemporary John Aubrey noted with relief when his own was all gone. And Holmes was a very rich man.

Unlike many rich men he seems always to have been a free spender. Pepys, it will be recalled, had commented on the lavishness of his entertainments and the richness of his dress even before he had become the man of substance who, as Governor of the Isle of Wight, exchanged much official correspondence with the secretary of the Admiralty. It was also among the duties of a Governor to entertain the King on his visits to the island. Charles II honoured Holmes by his visits on three occasions, which were admired for their magnificence by such fastidious judges as Pepys and Henry Savile. Nor was the Isle of Wight the only scene of Holmes's royal banquets. John Evelyn records of a visit to Windsor in July 1674:

. . . next day to a greate entertainement at Sir Robert Holmes's at Cranburne Lodge in the forest: There were his Majestie, Queene, Duke, Dutcheses & all the Court: I returned in the Evening with Sir Jos: Williamson now declared Secretary of State.[10]

Eleven years later, when James II was paying his first State visit to Portsmouth, Evelyn records that he was prevented from attending the official dinner provided by the Lieutenant-Governor because of a previous engagement 'to Sir Robert Holmes to dine with him at a private house, where likewise we had a very sumptuous & plentifull repast of excellent venison, fowle, fish, fruit, & what not.'[11] It was thirty years and further from the days of dried goat in the Cape Verde islands.

Of the houses in which Sir Robert lived in such high style the new house at Yarmouth which he built himself survives as a hotel. He was buying property on its site in 1679 and adding to it in 1680 and 1681[12] so that the date of its building may perhaps be connected with the birth of his daughter and his consequent desire to establish a family seat. Its handsome exterior has altered little since his day except for the introduction of sash windows, which were just coming in.* The furniture was, if not quite so luxurious as that of his London house, elegant and comfortable. In the great dining room a dozen gilt chairs stood round the table on a large carpet. In the drawing room the guests would find cane chairs and couches with cushions. There were pictures on the walls, but not very many; and there were two models of ships, one of them very probably that of the *St. Michael*, Holmes's last and finest command, which is now in the National Maritime Museum.† There was even—a rare luxury for that date—an umbrella.

As he moved closer to London his style of life became more fashionable. The contents of his house at Englefield Green were valued at nearly twice the total for Yarmouth. There was a walnut table in the dining room and a Cyprus chest in the hall. Yellow silk, for which Holmes seems to have had a particular preference, curtained the bed and supplied the counterpane in the Parlour chamber and in another of the guest rooms. His own

---

* In his own room in his house in London the inventory specifically mentions 'two shashes'.

† See illustration facing p. 153.

bedstead, which contained a featherbed, was hung with speckled stuff curtains as was the rest of the room. His daughter's room next door was simply furnished:

> one little bedstead. one Callico Canopy. one counterpane. one chest of drawers. one looking glass. four greene Chaires. one spice box.

Not extravagant for so great an heiress.

But the height of magnificence was reached at his house next the Horse Guards 'over against Whitehall'. It contained a White Room, a Green Room 'hung with Greene Bayes', a Red Room with hangings of painted parragon,* a Damask Room, a Brocade Room and a Tapestry Room. In the Brocade Room which was also the dining room there was a glass table and eight cane chairs; in the Tapestry Room, apparently the drawing room, there was a 'scriptore' (?escritoire) as well as a large glass and eight chairs. In Holmes's own room his lifelong fondness for gold found ample expression: 'one yellow mowhair Bed complete with a case of parragon . . . one screene of gilt leather'. The walls were so richly hung that there was little room for pictures though there was one over the chimney in the Damask Room. In the courtyard of the house was a marble cistern with a fountain. The domestic offices and equipment were proportionate to the splendour of the establishment.[13]

Such were the rewards of his service as a sea-officer. For the rest of his life Holmes was to owe his public importance to his Governorship of the Isle of Wight. That he was exceptionally qualified to discharge the military functions of such a post in an age of European war and domestic revolution is obvious enough. And it was to this side of his duties that he applied himself with notable vigour from the date of his appointment. Sandown, Carisbrooke and Yarmouth castles were extensively repaired and remodelled and their garrisons brought up to strength. Early in 1676 the King instructed Danby to pay Holmes well over £2,000 as reimbursement for the sums he had spent on these works during the preceding six years.[14] Obtaining timber, corresponding with the Ordnance Commissioners, employing labour, recruiting soldiers, all these took time, and the record

* A mixture of silk and camel hair.

of them is scattered at large through the State Papers. But to a man of Holmes's experience and achievements they were small beer.

What of his other activities as Bashaw of the Isle of Wight? We have seen that he provided hospitality worthy of his position. Worsley, the historian of the island, writing at the end of the next century, pronounces: 'He supported the dignity of his office with great propriety, and by constantly residing in the island, acquired great popularity.'[15] It might be thought that the public acknowledgment of a bastard daughter showed no excessive concern for propriety; and 'constant residence' is putting it a little high for a man who seems to have spent a good part of each year in London, at Bath or in Windsor Forest. His own letters written at the time of the Revolution are far from claiming or giving evidence of popularity. Indeed, as the embodiment of a civil power whose relations with its subjects were chiefly repressive or rapacious it is difficult to see how he could have been.

Almost the first instruction he received in his capacity as Governor was to proceed against those who hold 'at severall places within the Isle of Wight numerous & scandalous meetings upon pretence of Religious Worship contrary to the Law & the publicke Peace.'[16] That such persecution of Dissenters was congenial to him is clear:

> ... Disaffected knaves who want noe Art to do all the mischief they can, but I neither value them nor their black Art here ... I had information given me of frequent meetings at the Towne of Newport: some Nonconformist Parsons & others that came from Southampton, Portsmouth & other places ... but their black consciences would not permit them to stay ...[17]

These quarterdeck rumblings were immediately provoked by the successful spiriting away of Lord Grey of Wark and others suspected of complicity in the Rye House Plot:*

> ... Lock, an inhabitant of Yarmouth of this Isle, was master of the vessel that carried off some people that escaped about Chichester ... I have so waylaid him here that he will never come into these parts. He is easily known, being a black tall man with a wooden leg. He lost his leg with myself in his Majesty's service. I had formerly taken care of him and made him a gunner here, till I

* To assassinate Charles II and James Duke of York as they passed through Hoddesdon on their way back from Newmarket.

knew of his qualities and preaching; then I turned him out of the King's service.

In practice as in profession Holmes was an uninhibited full-blooded supporter of authority. At Parliamentary elections he understood that it was his job to secure the return of the Government candidate and went about his task with gusto. Sometimes with too much gusto. In 1677 he appears to have behaved in the most unscrupulous manner to obtain the unopposed return of his brother Sir John Holmes as member for Newtown at a by-election.[18] In the spring of 1685 he clashed with Sunderland, James II's chief minister, over the management of the elections in the island. Sunderland wanted a seat reserving for Heneage Finch, the Solicitor-General. Holmes who had no objection of principle was alarmed that the financial arrangements already made might be upset and that he might be left to foot the bill:

> ... If I do not hear from you I will conclude that Mr Solicitor is provided for & will send another in his room who will give his vote as heartily for the King & his concerns, though it may be his tongue is not so well hung. I will defer choosing members in one of our corporations till I hear from you, that is to say, for ten or twelve days longer.[19]

To question whether a retired naval officer of conservative opinions, sitting for a Hampshire constituency and suffering from the gout, may properly be described as a tory appears perhaps as pedantry run mad; and in the loose and general sense of the term he was a pure pre-phylloxera specimen. But in his day the term was specific, referring to the great controversy over the Exclusion of James, Duke of York from the succession to the throne. The names 'whig' and 'tory' originated in the abuse hurled at each other by the two parties into which Parliament found itself divided by this issue. 'Tory' meant an Irish bandit and this, surely, was an apt, if offensive, label for Holmes. But the inconvenient fact remains that on this grave matter Holmes was unsound. Although he voted on the tory side in the first of the three Exclusion Parliaments he did not stand for those of October 1679 and March 1681. One reason was certainly ill-health;[20] but in 1682 he got into serious trouble with the King for presenting an address from his illegitimate son, the Duke of Monmouth, the Whig

N

candidate for the succession, in which there were some highly offensive references to the Duke of York. These expressions Monmouth subsequently disavowed, saying that they 'could only be Sir Robert Holmes's private sentiments without any commission'.[21] Whether or not anyone believed Monmouth, the fact that Holmes should have so far embroiled himself as to present an address containing such subversive matter earned him the King's severe displeasure. Such grants as were revocable were revoked: and, as most of his offices had been granted for life, a hostile scrutiny of his transactions in them replaced the indulgent winking at the accepted peculations of an old servant. In the spring of 1684 it looked as if he faced dismissal for mismusters (i.e. making fraudulent claims for pay and allowances) as Governor of the Isle of Wight. A warrant was drawn up granting the Governorship to the Duke of Grafton and a court martial was summoned to try the charges. Holmes, who had displayed some tactical skill in putting off his pursuers by enlisting the sympathy of the Secretary at War, now counter-attacked in a letter to the Secretary of State, challenging the competence of the court:

> Having perused an order for a court-martiall of twelve Captains, Colonel Strode president, I doe humbly conceive an officer of my quality ought to be tried by field officers by reason that I ought to be treated as a Generall Officer, considering the station I now act in, so that I desire the Councill of Warr may consist of Field Officers, being I think it my due to have it soe.
>
> I am colonel of a foot regiment in the Isle of Wight and by virtue of my power as Governor thereof I give commissions to colonels, lieutenant-colonels, majors and all other inferior officers as well as to the Lieutenant-Governor.
>
> So that I desire a councill of warr of field officers, believing myself to be in the same rank with them.[22]

Whether the court sat at all we do not know, still less its final composition. But if it did, Holmes must have been acquitted since he remained Governor of the Isle of Wight to his dying day. The King after all had not many servants who had given more eminent proof of their loyalty.

Politics, in short, added nothing to Holmes and gained nothing from him. He became a politician as a man becomes a surtax payer, not from principle or rational choice, but simply as the consequence of other

activities and in the furtherance of other interests. Since his life had been
spent and his fortune had been made in the service of the Crown it was
natural that he should identify himself with the King's government. That
he should have been involved with Monmouth is more puzzling. Holmes
had been, it is true, a friend of Buckingham, who had often spoken and
acted against the Court. But Buckingham, though professing himself the
champion of Protestantism, was notably cool toward Monmouth and
friendly towards the Duke of York. A more probable link is suggested by
Holmes's relations with a somewhat shady financier named Lemuel
Kingdon. Lemuel's father, Richard, had under the Protectorate wormed
his way into the immensely profitable traffic in Irish lands. With com-
mendable agility he had leapt, money-bags in hand, from bandwagon to
bandwagon in the confusing transitions of 1659 and 1660, ending up in
1669 as a Commissioner and Farmer of the Irish Revenue. Lemuel
inherited his father's aptitudes and offices, becoming in 1675, the year in
which he attained his majority, one of the New Farmers of the Revenues
of Ireland. Holmes not only belonged to an Irish family but had himself
been granted lands there and had invested capital in extending his holding.
These activities might have originally occasioned and would certainly have
strengthened his connexion with Lemuel Kingdon. And Lemuel was an
out-and-out Monmouth man, becoming his attorney in 1677 and entering the House of Commons through his interest as Member for Hull in
1679. In the last two Parliaments of the reign, however, he sat, along
with Holmes's brother John, for the Isle of Wight constituencies of
Newtown and Yarmouth respectively. Besides this evidence of their
association a London gossip writer reported in January 1680:

> Lem[uel] is removed out of his house to the great grief of his neighbour Sir
> Robert Holmes, who is fallen into a great intrigue with his wife . . . Lem[uel]
> bears all very contentedly.[23]

The lady in question, Theodosia Kingdon, long survived her husband. In
Queen Anne's time she contested a Chancery action brought by one of
Holmes's nephews concerning a keepership in the New Forest, originally
granted to Sir John Holmes and subsequently voided by him in favour of

Lemuel and Theodosia. In 1680 she was twenty-one. Holmes's illegitimate daughter had been born two years earlier, so that if Theodosia was the mother the child would have been born during the first year of her marriage. Not even Lemuel, it may be surmised, would have stood for that: and Theodosia was in any case occupied in bearing his own children. This piece of scandal throws more light on Holmes's political affiliations than on his daughter's extraction.

For the rest, Holmes's vestigial Parliamentary activity reflects the characteristic preoccupations of a retired officer—though 'retired' is of course an anachronism. In January 1675 he defended his conduct in attacking the Dutch Smyrna fleet, an issue which had been raised in the proceedings against the Duke of Buckingham. Probably it was in the debate on increasing the fleet in the autumn of that year that he irritated Pepys by dogmatising on the size of capital ships:

> I would observe how hard it is for anything to be well understood in the Navy
> . . . And again in the measures of our new ships when Sir Robert Holmes gave
> his ignorant and foolish but popular, faithless and ungrateful opinion in the
> House of Commons that 1,100 tons (which was the measure of the *St. Michael*
> which he had happened to be in) was big enough for the biggest first-rate.[24]

But even Pepys admitted his expertise to the extent of summoning him to a conference on the gun establishment of naval vessels in July 1677 and to recording his statement that he had found a 24-hour glass the truest measure of time at sea.[25]

Not the least of his interests in the service was the promotion of his family and kinsmen. He assisted his brother Sir John by making him a regular allowance of at least £50 a year and generally more from 1672 to his death in 1683.[26] And Sir John's naval career was crowned by the command of the Channel fleet from 1677 to 1679. His elder brother industriously consolidated the family interest by obtaining for him the Governorship of Hurst Castle, thus turning the Solent into a Holmesian lake, and by securing his return for Newtown, Isle of Wight for which constituency in the Parliament of 1679 his fellow-member was John Churchill, the future Duke of Marlborough. The relations between the two colleagues seem to have been both more and less than parliamentary. In June 1679 Churchill somewhat ungallantly knocked an orange-girl about in the Duke's Theatre, as a result of which he was challenged by Otway, the poet. In the duel that followed both men were wounded but Otway got the best of it. Sir John Holmes related these transactions to the King in a manner which Churchill resented. He challenged Holmes who fought him and disarmed him.[27]

In spite of his professional success and of his wife's money Sir John seems to have left little but debts to support his widow and children when he died at his brother's house near the Horse Guard on May 28th, 1683.[28] The vacancy at Hurst Castle was promptly secured for Henry Holmes, Sir Robert's future heir and son-in-law, the son of his eldest brother Thomas.[29] Neither of Sir John's sons were old enough even in those days of nepotism to hold a military appointment of such importance. In fact they were still at school, boarding with the schoolmaster in Newport until the elder, Robert, was sent to Winchester in 1685.[30]

To judge from his school bill Robert's career as a Wykehamist must have been brief. Perhaps he had already shewn signs of that spoilt, ungovernable temper which was to cause his uncle so much trouble. At any rate he was packed off to sea as a volunteer aboard the *Happy Return* bound for a Mediterranean cruise. By January 1687 the ship was back in home waters and Lady Holmes hurried round to ask Pepys to grant her son leave to come to London. Pepys, considering the young gentleman '. . . soe far gone and cherished in liberty as I found him to have been through the goodness of my Lady his poor mother . . .' urged her 'for God's sake that she would lett fall her Request and both incourage and require him to keep on board his shipp; & she seem'd to mee to goe away satisfied'. In fact she sped down to Deal where the *Happy Return* was at anchor and appealed to the Captain in person. Good-naturedly the Captain granted the request for leave, but one of the other volunteers, a Mr. Elloways, was, it seems, unwise enough to venture some sneering remarks, perhaps about favouritism and maternal solicitude. Young Holmes lost his temper, drew a weapon, and blood was spilt. He then apparently left the ship and accompanied his mother to London.

Not many posts later Pepys was writing to the Captain for a full report:

. . . with respect to the Discipline fit to be preserved in the King's Navy to enquire of you the truth of this young Gentleman Mr Holmes's behaviour dureing his voyage with you, both as to his sobriety, obedience to order, & application to, and proficiency in his studdy of navigation as also of ye Ground & Event of this Quarrell & whether he be come up to Towne with your knowledge & leave or not. This I shall desire you to give me for His Majesty's and Sir Robert Holmes's information . . .

The report, recommending immediate discharge from the service, came by return. Pepys and the King accepted it entirely. Forwarding a copy to Sir Robert, Pepys wrote that the King

commanded mee to lett you know that out of particular respect to you he would forbear to proceed with that severity towards him (by calling him to a Court Martiall in order to his being publicly censured for his misbehaviour and disobedience) . . .

and added for his own part

. . . True it is the proof wch he has hereby hapned to give of his manhood carry's something with it that's very laudable, & I doe not wonder that y^r good nature is inclined to interpret to his advantage a Virtue of which you are so great a Master.

The Captain's recommendation, reinforced by both Pepys and the King, of

. . . disposing him in the Merchant service upon some long voyage and with some Master that will keep a strict and hard hand upon him in hope that time and such usage may reforme him,

seems to have been acted on. At any rate when eighteen years later he brought his suit against Theodosia Kingdon he claimed that he had been abroad at sea since the age of fifteen, serving his King and country. No doubt this was an exaggeration, but there was probably some truth in it.[31]

Perhaps the most interesting, certainly the most attractive, feature of this tale is the gentleness and consideration that Pepys shows towards a man against whom he had formerly been so virulent. Familiarity had bred tolerance, perhaps respect. The heat of ambition and of rivalry was cooling with age. Both had little more to hope for and much to fear. Pepys was a mellower figure than the acrid, impatient young bureaucrat of genius who had never a good word for his colleagues. And the gouty, arthritic Governor of the Isle of Wight was past his duelling days. The correspondence of the two men reveals common interests beyond those of administration and failing health. Pepys undertakes to acquaint the King of Holmes's proposal touching red-legged partridges; he encourages him to work on his Guinea papers[32]—doubtless the journal now in his own Library at Cambridge; and when the storm clouds of Revolution darken overhead the two men are united in sympathy and trust.

Was it perhaps Pepys who recommended Holmes for the last independent command of his career, that of a squadron to be sent out to the West Indies to suppress the buccaneers, or was it a tardy act of amends on the part of James II? At any rate his commission, countersigned by Sunderland the principal Secretary of State, was issued at Bath on August 21st, 1687. In November he was granted all such goods as he should take from pirates and in January 1688 all the Governors of the West Indian colonies were ordered to publish a proclamation against the pirates and to afford Holmes every assistance in suppressing them. In August his agent in the West Indies, Mr. Lynch, complained bitterly that, so far from assisting him, the Governor of Jamaica had countenanced the pirates committed to gaol in Port Royal in issuing warrants against him. In spite of all this pother there is no evidence that Holmes ever sailed on what would probably have been an exciting and remunerative expedition: and there is a good deal of evidence that he didn't. The melancholy significance of the place at which the commission was issued—Bath—should not be neglected. A voyage to the West Indies, at his time of life and in his state of health, was beyond him. It was in fact Sir John Narbrough who commanded the expedition that sailed in September 1687 to deal with the buccaneers.[33] Holmes was in England in the summer of 1688: he had spent August and September organising the defences of the Isle of Wight against possible Dutch invasion.[34] At last the equinoctial gales permitted a relaxation of vigilance. Holmes thankfully retired to Bath where on September 27th he received news that sent him hurrying back to his command that very day.[35]

XVII

A Conflict of Loyalties

T HE REVOLUTION OF 1688 presents a striking contrast between its political and its military modes. Politically an observer from the Martian landscape of the twentieth century can only marvel at the maturity, the subtlety, the assurance of the technique displayed. Militarily both sides showed a lack of professionalism astonishing in two nations so versed in the uses of sea-power and ruled by two such experienced commanders as James II and William of Orange. No wonder Holmes could hardly believe his old enemies capable of so amateurish a gamble as an opposed landing on an easily defended coast, with a powerful English fleet still intact, at a time of year when the weather was certain to be rough and might well, if the Dutch task force were caught in an open anchorage, pound it to pieces in a few hours. On the other side the strategy, tactics and dispositions of the English, in particular the decision of the Commander-in-Chief, Lord Dartmouth, to anchor within the Gunfleet, seem equally questionable. It is difficult to imagine Holmes adopting a policy that so denied initiative. And Holmes might very well have commanded the fleet. That he had been offered and actually appointed to the West Indies command in preference to Narbrough a bare twelve months earlier showed that his professional qualifications were not undervalued. As a stout, indeed a ruthless, opponent of religious toleration he could not be tarred with the Papist brush. Had his health served him but a little better he might easily have been preferred to Dartmouth who as Captain of the *Fairfax* had fought under Holmes's command in the attack on the Smyrna convoy sixteen years earlier. But Bath, that long, tolling monosyllable, speaks its own explanation.

Holmes even if old and ill was still a professional. The energy and pertinacity with which he discharged his duties in the Isle of Wight would be impressive in a younger and more active man. The island was considered a likely objective for an invasion and Holmes, though under no illusions as to the sympathy of the inhabitants, had prepared his plans and issued his instructions on this assumption.[1] News of the Dutch putting to sea was received on October 20th. Holmes, sceptical of its truth, passed the report to the central government. It was in fact correct but a change of weather forced the fleet back almost as soon as it had sailed. A few days later the wind changed again. For two days, inexplicably, the Dutch remained at their moorings. At last on the evening tide of November 1st the great expedition sailed on a northerly course. Next day with the strong easterly still keeping the English fleet windbound in the Thames the Dutch changed on to a south-westerly course that would take them down Channel. About midday on Saturday the 3rd they entered the Straits of Dover, altering formation to line abreast so as to impress the onlookers who crowded both the French and the English shore. At daybreak on Sunday Holmes received reports of two hundred sail off the island. Soon he saw them himself standing—no doubt to his relief—to the westward: 'the great ships with their topsails at cap and with their lower sails brailed up, which I suppose was their men-of-war staying for their loaded ships.' That evening three Dutch ships that had become detached from the main body of the fleet anchored in St. Helens Road, sending five sailors, of whom two were English, ashore on the island to buy provisions. The insolent confidence of these proceedings seemed only too well justified. Until the militia arrived to spoil things their reception was obviously friendly. Holmes sent a report of all this to Lord Preston who laid it before the King on November 6th. Even on that dark day he had time to reply:

> We were in great apprehension for you lest they might have made some attempt upon your island, but this afternoon we have had advice that the Dutch fleet did appear yesterday near Torrebay.

On that day Holmes who was passing on sighting reports every few hours recorded that a great fog arose in the afternoon reducing visibility to five or six miles. The mild weather that produced it enabled William to get his army ashore while Dartmouth's fleet, at last clear of the Thames, was becalmed off Beachy Head. It would take a lot to stop the Revolution now. Holmes, ignorant of this disaster, yet reflects the situation in microcosm when he writes again to Preston at one o'clock in the morning on the 6th that he cannot undertake to hold any of the island

> ... except the little forts and castles may hold out for some time ... Part of the militia is grown mutinous already ... for want of one troop of horse to keep this militia in awe the island will be lost without striking one stroke for it; God knows how I shall be dealt with by this militia I have drawn into Yarmouth and Hurst ... [2]

Hopeless, menacing even, as the turn of events might appear, Holmes did not relax his efforts. He had served a long apprenticeship to desperate endeavours and his will-power was not weakened by the wealth and position he had won. On November 12th he made new dispositions of his forces in view of the successful landing at Torbay and included detailed orders for the seizure of any Dutch ships that should come into St. Helens.[3] On the 28th he wrote a long letter to Pepys giving the fullest intelligence he could of the movements and probable intentions of the Dutch fleet. Pepys thought the letter worth forwarding to Dartmouth, to whom Holmes wrote direct on Sunday, December 9th from his forlorn stronghold at Yarmouth. Food, Holmes told him, had been running so short that he had sent his senior lieutenant out to forage. The junior lieutenant took the opportunity of his absence and of the foulness of the night to abscond with the greater part of the garrison with whom he attempted—unsuccessfully—to capture Hurst Castle. Holmes thereby

> is left in this desolate condition having no men to stand by him. The townspeople are ready to declare.

He begs Dartmouth for three or four frigates to ride between Yarmouth and Hurst Castle and particularly requests that if any ships are sent 'let Jack Tirrell's be one'.[4] Holmes was presumably unaware that Tyrrell, then commanding the *Mordaunt*, was an ardent supporter of Revolution principles.[5] Three days later in spite of the knowledge that '500 of the

Princes' Dragoons were advanced as far as Ringwood to countenance this villainous business' Holmes wrote that he hoped by this defection:

> to have a better Companie than I had before for I am rid of villaines & rogues that might perhaps doe me a worse turne hereafter. [6]

His resilience, his stout-heartedness and his personal loyalty shine brightly in what for him must have been days of darkness and disaster. He was old and infirm; the cause of the Stuarts whom he had served without romanticism but with honour and fidelity, never more conspicuous than in extremes of misfortune, was manifestly lost; but until the King admitted defeat Holmes would not desert him. As it happened this event had already taken place twenty-four hours earlier; on December 11th James had fled from his capital, dropping the Great Seal in the river as he left. On December 12th Dartmouth accepted William's appeal to bring the fleet over to his side in a letter[7] which defines with candour, dignity and good sense that acceptance of realities, without cynicism, without sycophancy, without fanaticism, which alone makes civilised life possible. It is a letter that foreshadows the great age of English politics. Where the Commander-in-Chief of the fleet led the Governor of the Isle of Wight was content to follow. On December 17th Holmes drafted terms of surrender and sent them to the Prince. 'The revolution since [my last letter] has been great', he wrote to his friend William Blathwayt, the Secretary at War, 'wee are unanimous for this cause'.[8]

Holmes like Blathwayt and the great majority of office-holders was continued in his employment by the new government. Naturally so staunch a servant of the Stuarts was suspected and secretly accused of Jacobitism but no evidence of treasonable activity or correspondence has survived. It seems unlikely that the new King would have entrusted so crucial a command to a man whose loyalty he had reason to doubt. He knew, of course, of the accusations brought against him. A Jacobite agent convicted of treason and subsequently pardoned for turning informer told the Earl of Nottingham that Holmes had promised to deliver the Isle of Wight;[9] and an anonymous letter 'left by one well-hors'd' at the Earl of

Monmouth's house at Parsons Green outlined a plan to assassinate the King at Hampton Court and to carry the Queen to the Isle of Wight to Cowes Castle 'where they . . . expect French vessels for her transport to France, in the interim to fire the city and suburbs . . . there are divers persons gone to the island, and they say they are sure of Sir Robert Holmes.'[10]

Holmes, especially in his gouty old age, was too explosive to make a good conspirator. He had as a member of the Convention Parliament voted openly against offering the crown jointly to William and Mary, but that was a very different thing from conniving at the violent overthrow of the established order, to say nothing of the murder of the man whose service he had entered and whose pay he had taken. This rather than any heather-scented yearnings for the House of Stuart probably explains his censure of the Revolution—'this villainous business'—in the first place. It was the violation of a professional code about which he felt strongly. A letter to Blathwayt, written on the very day of the plot in which he was alleged to be involved, makes the point with particular emphasis. The people, he says, are 'very tumultuous and readie to goe into mutinie against the Governor as well as against the Government.' He therefore desires the King to let him have:

> . . . a Company of my owne in this Island that I might be sure of soe many men that would stand by me on all occasions.
>
> These men [i.e. the regiments quartered in the Isle of Wight] are so farr from doing anything of that nature that I doe question, if the King did command them anywhere they did not like of, whether they would goe or not. I am sure all their Officers did declare that they would not goe for the West Indies which I look upon to be a very ill thing from People that receives Pay.[11]

The men of Holmes's generation had not altogether forgotten the system of feudal obligation which money had largely replaced. Pay was in a sense the badge of loyalty and troth. Thus the *Gazette* for March 5th–8th, 1666 carried the following story with a Marseilles dateline:

> Monsr de Beaufort* continues his severe usage to the English prisoners, to

* The French Admiral.

force them into their pay: He caused four English Marriners to be hanged, that
had received pay, for leaving him upon the news of a War with France. An
English Pilot that served him in his own vessel, craving leave upon the same
score, to quit his service, was licensed, but with the loss of all his pay . . .

In this, as in much else, professionalism yields on the whole the most
satisfying and consistent explanation of Holmes's character and actions. If
we attempt to derive his moral and political standards from the regiment
or the quarterdeck the results usually make sense. Discipline was the
keystone of his political and social philosophy. Not, to judge from his will,
benevolent from principle he seems to have been punctilious in discharging his obligations to those who had served under him. One thinks at
once of Lock, that wicked radical, who repaid Holmes's good offices by
turning nonconformist and helping the Rye House plotters to escape. But
there were many others. In the summer of 1665, on the eve of the battle off
Lowestoft, Holmes secured a generous pension for the widow of William
Pestle, late master of the *Jersey*, who had been killed at the taking of
Goree fifteen months earlier. In 1668 he recommended the ex-chaplain of
the *Henry* for a living in Essex; after the attack on the Smyrna convoy in
1672 he claims, successfully, for pensions for the widow and children of a
midshipman and a master's mate; at the same time he asks Pepys for
printed passes to exempt his men from the press; a year later he is claiming
a month's pay for his First Lieutenant who had to spend that time in
London getting men.[12] In return his officers and men seem to have chosen
to serve with him more than once. There was his coxswain in the *Henrietta*;
there were the sailors in the *Jersey* who remembered the planting of the
orange trees at Sierra Leone on the earlier expedition; and the First
Lieutenant of Holmes's last ship the *St. Michael* seems to have served with
him in the same capacity in the *Defiance*.[13]

Holmes was both in his qualities and in his limitations a rough-hewn
prototype of the professional officer. Polished by three generations of
eighteenth-century civility he would cut a creditable figure in the novels of
Jane Austen. Such are distinguished from the mercenary commander or
condottiere by the fact that they are animated in the first place by

patriotism and in the second by loyalty to lawfully constituted authority. Secret societies of officers, Generals' *coups*, Colonels' régimes, are corruptions, excrescences, of a conception touched with nobility. In 1689 both patriotism and the duty of giving support to the civil power must have weighed strongly against Jacobitism, for James was now the protégé of Louis XIV who had declared war on England. Could a veteran of the great wars against the Dutch have any doubts when the enemy was France or Spain? National as well as professional pride was touched when in July a merchantman returning from Jamaica was taken and burnt off the Scillies, 'I am sorry to heare', growled the old man 'that the French are so Busy in the chopps of our Channell especially when our Fleet are out.'[14]

So far indeed from retreating into crypto-Jacobitism Holmes seems to have flung himself with all the energy that age and ill-health permitted into the prosecution of the new war. In February and again in April he advised Shrewsbury, then Secretary of State, on the defence of trade and on counter-measures against enemy shipping. In June he came up apparently to have an audience at Windsor on the signing of a commission for his Lieutenant-Governor but wrote from his house at Englefield Green 'I intended to have waited on his Majesty today but have been violently taken with the Gout these three days that I cannot stir out of my bed.'[15] This seems to have been the only occasion on which he left the Isle of Wight during the best part of a year. He had indeed a great deal to do there. First of all there were the elections to be managed. And then there was the infliction of 1,500 Irish dragoons, part of James II's army, who had been hurriedly shipped to the Isle of Wight until arrangements could be made for their disposal oversea. The billeting of troops was, in the seventeenth century, one of the most fiercely resented of all governmental impositions. When at last they did leave in April and May 1689 Holmes wrote to the Secretary at War to have their pay stopped to meet the debts they had left behind them. Quite a number had taken the opportunity to desert: 'These Irish do skulk in the country . . . [I] will hale and hunt them out of all the Bushes and Coppices.'[16] Besides these domestic preoccupations the Governor faced the supreme task of maintaining the island's

defences at instant readiness, and the hardly less onerous duty of watching
all movements of shipping in the busiest sea-lanes of the world. There were
privateers to be reported, prizes to be seized, intelligence of enemy
activity to be obtained. Ten or twelve years earlier Holmes would have
revelled in all these opportunities of action, of bustle and of profit. But
with age and infirmity the grasshopper had become a burden. Each letter
includes an urgent plea to be allowed leave to go to Bath to recruit his
health. At the end of July he was at the end of his tether:

> I am now soe ill of my Limbs that I have not been out of my chamber these
> twelves daies. I want the Bath as an old horse does Grass.[17]

He was allowed to go in August and to stay till the end of September.

But the old horse was to die in harness. In January he was 'in despaire at
the coming of the Queene of Spaine'. The exertions required by a State
visit were beyond him: the King's House at Portsmouth was in every way
more suitable for the reception of visiting Royalty than his own in the
Isle of Wight. His entreaties were disregarded. Four days later he sailed
from Yarmouth to attend Her Majesty at Spithead. Unfortunately during
the short voyage the gout in his feet became so agonising that he could
not climb aboard. He sent his Lieutenant-Governor in his place. In May
his coach overturned as he was coming home 'from the Generall Rendezvous'.

By the end of the month he is recovering but 'the Doctor tells me that I
must hasten to the Bath more particularly for that Bruise as to refresh my
Old Limbs'. His request for six week's leave seems to have been granted
for once fairly easily. On June 24th he had just crossed the Solent and
reached Hurst Castle when he was recalled by the news that the French
fleet were a bare two miles off shore. Invasion seemed a strong probability. He returned at once to the island resolved 'to oppose all I can and
to fall back on Hurst Castle in extremity'.[18]

In a crisis Holmes could still prove alert and active. Making his headquarters at Appuldurcombe where sighting reports from the high ground
could reach him without delay he poured out a steady stream of intelligence

to the Government in London. On at least one occasion he climbed the hills himself as it became plain that a major naval action between the French and the Anglo-Dutch fleets was imminent. But the ships were too far off to make out what was happening.[19] The French victory off Beachy Head on June 30th intensified the danger to the island. In mid-July Danby told the King that Holmes pretended to have certain intelligence of a French attempt on the Isle of Wight but that his own opinion—observing the scene from London—was that they would attack Portsmouth.[20] The French fleet was in sight off the island at the time.

The strain of the summer told upon Holmes's constitution. In February 1691 he was so ill that Godolphin wrote to the King to suggest the appointment of a successor. A few weeks later he had recovered sufficiently to avail himself of the King's permission to go to Bath. In August he was back again at his post of duty when the jackpot of a lifetime came up. A Genoese ship, the *St. Anthony of Padua*, carrying twenty-eight bars of silver valued at 700,000 crowns was cast away upon the Isle of Wight. Exasperatingly the money was consigned for the payment of the Spanish forces in Flanders with whom a breach might at that moment have proved disastrous. Holmes therefore received an immediate command from William's camp in the Low Countries to hand over any of the money that had been recovered and to assist in securing the rest.[21] If Holmes accepted these instructions without complaint or demur it would be surprising.

The spring of 1692 brought another threat of invasion that sent him hurrying down the Portsmouth road to his Governorship.[22] It was in fact the most real of them all. But the battle of La Hogue restored English supremacy in the Channel; and the last months of Holmes's life, unlike so much of the rest of it, were not disturbed by any sudden call to arms. Early in October he was reported to be dying. On the 28th he made his will, 'being in good health perfect sense and memory'. On November 18th he died.[23]

The monument erected to his memory in Yarmouth parish church was, according to a naval chaplain who admired it a few years later, itself a reward of admiralty:

This marble was goeing to France, and the ship being cast away on the back of the isle, was made wrack, and belong'd to this gentleman, who prepar'd all things for his funeral and this monument before his death.[24]

Another version of the story has it that the statue was intended to portray Louis XIV and that Holmes had his own head substituted. If either is true it would be eminently appropriate. The inscription on the plinth rehearses in elegant Latinity Holmes's long career in arms.* It also claims that the monument was erected by his nephew Harry. This seems less than truthful as Holmes left £300 in his will for the express purpose of 'building a compleat and decent vault and monument'. The final complication is that the inscription, carefully noted down by the observer of 1704, bears no relation to the lapidary exuberance for which Harry was responsible. Presumably he felt that his uncle's reputation and his own standing required something more than a few homely hob-nailed hexameters.† Celia Fiennes, that sharp-tongued, sharp-eyed Whig had not been deceived when she visited Yarmouth only three or four years after Sir Robert's death:

> ... Sir Robert Holmes ... was the Governour of the Island and of Yarmouth Castle, and there he is buried where is his statue cutt in length in white marble in the Church and railed in with Iron Grates, he was raised from nothing and an imperious Governor and what he scrap'd together was forced to leave to his Nephew and base Daughter haveing no other, and they have set up this stately Monument which cost a great deal ...[25]

After Harry's effort, which was transcribed in its entirety by his eldest son Thomas in support of his (successful) attempt to obtain a peerage from the Duke of Newcastle in 1760, Holmes has had to wait nearly three hundred years for his biographer. In such brief notices as have appeared in various biographical collections—of which by far the best is Sir John Knox Laughton's article in the *Dictionary of National Biography*—he is invariably credited with the capture of New Amsterdam, an error originated by Colliber in his *Columna Rostrata* (1727) and uncritically repeated by every subsequent writer until two hundred years later the

---

* Inexplicably it omits the two African expeditions that he commanded.
† Both inscriptions are printed in Appendix II.

o

Dutch historian Captain J. C. M. Warnsinck put the matter right once and for all.[26] Was it necessary to trouble his shade with this more extended survey of his life and actions?

An indifferent answer cannot be reasonably expected or truthfully given from its author. And the reader who has endured thus far will have formed his own opinion. It was claimed at the beginning of this book that a study of Holmes's career might yield some insight into the fabric of English history and of Western civilization. The professional military officer who is neither a mercenary nor a feudatory owing, like the medieval knight, service and allegiance to King or Lord is a social phenomenon of the first importance. Society, even the most liberal society, depends upon a known readiness to use force. The more advanced, the more humane it is the more reluctantly it employs its ultimate sanction. The men to whom this duty is committed are generally taken for granted. The decision to employ force and the modes in which it is to be exerted are more often the subject of historical examination or public interest than the lives and ideas of the people immediately, because professionally, concerned. Yet it would be hard to find a nobler statement of general and particular political aspirations than Nelson's prayer before the battle of Trafalgar. Because the navy of Nelson's day, or of Holmes's for that matter, was for the most part a hard and brutal service it has seemed to some to follow that all talk of high or noble conceptions is, in this context, so much cant. And indeed to those who recognise virtue or nobility only in surroundings that have been purified of wickedness and folly, history has little to plead in mitigation of sentence; and the life of Sir Robert Holmes still less. To others it may seem that the idea of the officer, evolved in the era of professional armies and navies, may still have much to offer.

Notes

ABBREVIATIONS

CSP	*Calendar of State Papers*
DNB	*Dictionary of National Biography*
EHR	*English Historical Review*
HMC	Historical Manuscripts Commission
MM	*Mariners Mirror*
NMM	National Maritime Museum
NRS	Navy Record Society
SP	State Papers

CHAPTER I

1 *Diary*, 22 Dec. 1661. All quotations are from H. B. Wheatley's edition.
2 *Diary*, 24 June 1666.
3 Clarendon, *Life*, 883.
4 See below, pp. 184–5.
5 *A Seasonable Argument . . . for a New Parliament.*
6 NMM RUSI Library Naval MSS. 240. The late Elizabethan portrait reproduced in Laird Clowes *History of the Royal Navy*, Vol. ii, p. 282 (London, 1898) as that of Sir Robert may well be that of his grandfather.
7 *CSP* Ireland, 23 Nov. 1612.
8 For what follows see *The Vindication of Richard Atkyns*, ed. Brigadier Peter Young (London, 1967) passim.
9 Rupert's Journal, ed. C. H. Firth, EHR, Vol. XIII, p. 741.
10 For this and most of what follows see Warburton, *Prince Rupert and the Cavaliers*, iii, 236 ff. (3 vols., London, 1849).
11 See, e.g. *CSP* Dom., 18 Mar. 1672, 12 Aug. 1672, 14 July 1681.

CHAPTER II

1 See *passim*, *Documents Relating to the Civil War*, Navy Records Society (ed. J. R. Powell and E. K. Timings), and J. R. Powell *The Navy in the English Civil War* (Hamden, Conn., 1962).

2 *Documents*, 287, 289.

3 Ibid., 291, 294.

4 Ibid., 293, 300, 304, 305.

5 Ibid., 335.

6 Warburton, iii, 249.

7 *Rebellion*, XI, 142.

8 See e.g. *Documents*, 383, 384.

9 Ibid., 384.

10 Ibid., 412.

11 *Rebellion*, XI, 149.

12 For a recent survey of this subject see Christopher Lloyd *The British Seaman* (London, 1968).

13 Warburton, iii, 252 ff.

14 Ibid. A seaman from the *Love*, however, claimed to have cut the hawsers. *Documents*, 402.

15 *Rebellion*, XI, 150.

16 Warburton, iii, 265, 280.

17 Ibid, 281.

CHAPTER III

1 For a comprehensive account of it and for much of what follows see R. C. Anderson, *The Royalists at Sea*, M.M. IX, 34–6, XIV, 320–38, XVII, 135–68, XXI, 61–90.

2 *Documents*, 413.

3 Warburton, iii, 288 ff.

4 R. C. Anderson, op. cit.

5 Ibid.

6 Warburton, iii, 303 ff.

7 R. C. Anderson, op. cit.

8 Warburton, iii, 312.

9 *Adventures by Sea*, ed. E. H. W. Meyerstein (Oxford, 1945).

10 Warburton, iii, 317.

11 *Diary*, 10 Apr. 1667.

12 Warburton, iii, 326.

13 Warburton, iii, 333.

14 Ibid.

15 This is clearly stated in the vivid and dramatic account given by Fearnes, the Captain of the *Constant Reformation* (Bodleian MSS., Firth, c. 8, f. 191) and I have preferred it to the account in Rupert's papers printed in Warburton, iii, 332 ff. which says that the boat was launched from the *Constant Reformation*.

CHAPTER IV

1 For a full exposition of this point see K. G. Davies, *The Royal African Company* (London, 1957), e.g. p. 264; 'To an extent greater than any other extra-European part of the seventeenth-century world, Africa was the resort of ships and traders of many nations.'

2 W. R. Scott, *History of the Joint Stock Companies to 1720*, (Edinburgh, 1910–12) ii, 12–13.

3 Ibid, ii, 15.

4 G. F. Zook, *The Company of Royal Adventurers Trading into Africa* (Lancaster, Pa., 1919), p. 8.

5 Warburton, iii, 351.

6 Warburton, iii, 537. For details and antecedents of these vessels see R. C. Anderson, op. cit.

7 Extracts from journal of the *Swallow* printed in Warburton, iii, 541 ff.

8 Warburton, iii, 359 and 542.

9 *CSP* Colonial, 1574–1660, p. 383 quoted in W. R. Scott, op. cit., p. 15.

10 Warburton, iii, 360 ff.

11 Ibid.

12 Bodleian MSS., Firth c. 8, f. 189–90.

13 Warburton, iii, 363–7 for all the details of this incident.

14 Warburton, iii, 371.

15 This is clear from Warburton, iii, 384.

16 HMC Reports, Heathcote MSS., 134–9.

17 Warburton, iii, 387 and 546.

CHAPTER V

1 Bodleian MSS., Firth, c. 8, f. 203.

2 Ibid., f. 207, 3 May 1653.

3 Ibid., f. 210–11.

4 BM Add. MSS. 18982 f. 202.

5 Ibid.

6 MSS., Firth, c. 8, f, 212.

7 Ibid., f. 215.

8 Ibid., f. 216.

9 *Thurloe State Papers*, VII, 248, 18 July 1658. N.S.

10 MSS., Firth, c. 8, f. 211.

11 Add. MSS 18982, f. 202.

12 *Thurloe S. P.* quot. Warburton, iii, 425–6.

13 For a fuller account and citation of authorities see Eva Scott, *Rupert Prince Palatine* (London, 1899), p. 271 ff.

14 *Thurloe S. P.* quot. Warburton, iii, 427.

15 J. R. Tanner ed. Cat. Pepysian MSS., i, 367.

CHAPTER VI

1 Dalton, *English Army Lists and Commission Registers* (London, 1892), i, 103.

2 Ogg, *England in the Reign of Charles II* (2nd edition), i, 260.

3 Tanner *Pepysian MSS.*, i, 314 and 367.

4 *CSP* Dom, 1660, p. 327.

5 *Diary*, i, 253.

6 G. F. Zook, 8 ff.

7 Ibid. and PL 2698. This MS. in the Pepys Library contains Holmes's journals for both this and his subsequent expedition to West Africa and will be referred to hereafter as 'J'.

8 J., Instructions to Capt. Holmes and in case of his death to the Commander of the *Henrietta*, 1660.

9 See on this K. G. Davies, pp. 103–4.

10 J., 14 Feb. 1661.

11 Dutch sources cited in Zook, p. 30. Holmes does not mention this in his journal but Col. Vermuyden does. Warburton, iii, 539.

12 See K. G. Feiling, *British Foreign Policy 1660–1672* (London, 1930).

13 J., 8 Mar. 1661.

14 J., 18 Mar. 1661.

15 *CSP* Col. America and W. Indies, 24 May 1673.

16 Feiling, op. cit. and Zook, p. 29 ff.

17 J.

18 Printed in Warburton, iii, 538–40.

19 Zook, p. 11.

20 Ibid., p. 33.

21 Pepys *Diary*, 24 Aug. 1661.

22 Ibid., 22 Dec. 1661.

23 For details see Zook, p. 33 ff.

24 Zook, p. 11.

25 *Poems and Letters*, ed. Margoliouth (Oxford, 1927), i, 158.

CHAPTER VII

1 *Diary*, 1 Sept. 1661.

2 *Diary*, 2 April 1663.

3 I owe this point to Dr. R. C. Anderson, M.M. XXXIII, 275.

4 Clarendon S. P. 105 (ii), 122.

5 *CSP* Dom.

6 *Diary*, 29 Nov. 1661.

7 Ibid., 7 Dec. 1661.

8 Lord Braybrooke in his note on Pepys's entry for 12 Nov. 1661 says that Holmes was imprisoned for two months; but the entries in the Diary he is annotating would appear to disprove this.

9 *Diary*, 22 Dec. 1661, 6 Jan. and 3 Feb. 1662.

10 *CSP* Dom., 8 Apr. 1662.

11 Ibid. Presumably after a refit; she had been built in 1650.

12 Ibid., 31 July and 14 Aug. 1662.

13 *CSP* Dom., 25 Aug. 1662.

14 *CSP* Dom. 21 Sept. 1662; Captain of the *Foresight* to the Navy Commissioners.

15 HMC Heathcote MSS. (13 Feb. [N.S.] 1663).

16 *CSP* Dom., Gregory to Navy Commissioners.

17 *CSP* Dom., 16 Mar. 1663.

18 *Diary*, 21 Mar. 1663.

19 Ibid., 22 Mar. 1663.

20 Ibid., 23 Mar. 1663.

21 Ibid., 24 Mar. 1663.

22 E.g. ibid., 2 April 1663 and *passim*.

23 *Profit & Power: A Study of England and the Dutch Wars* (London, 1957), 92–3, 136.

24 This most attractive commander was in fact censured by Coventry for his excessive humanity: '. . . at the beginning of that warre [the Second Dutch War] wee did unfortunately miscarry by the indulgence and popularity of Sr Christopher Mings whoe would not lett the Court Martiall hang a runaway . . . That man escaping which was intended to terrify gave a beliefe to others that running from their ship was not dangerous . . . Next warre some must be hanged at beginning.' Bath MSS., CII, f. 13.

25 HMC Heathcote MSS., 17 and 22 Apr., 17 May and 17 June 1663 (N.S.).

26 See on him Feiling, op. cit.

27 HMC Heathcote MSS., 7 and 9 Aug. 1663 (N.S.).

28 *Diary*, 5 Sept. 1663.

29 *CSP* Dom., Edward Gregory to Navy Commissioners.

30 *Oeuvres Complètes de Christian Huygens* (22 vols., The Hague 1888–1950), iv, 446–51.

31 Ibid, 443. As will be seen, the expedition did not in fact go to Jamaica: nor, as is so often asserted, did Sir Robert Holmes capture New Amsterdam. See above p. 209.

CHAPTER VIII

1 Bath MSS. CII, ff. 3–13.

2 Ibid., f. 5.

3 Ibid., ff. 5 and 5.

4 *Diary*, 2 Feb. 1664.

5 Ogg, op. cit., i, 283.

6 Bath MSS. XCV, ff. 3–5.

7 J. *Note* As this is the main source for what follows in this chapter further references to it will only be cited where there is any possibility of confusion.

8 J., 1–14, Jan. 1664. and in the same MS Deposition of Stephen Usticke, 7 June 1664. See also SP 29/114, ff. 19 and 68 (Holmes's examination in the Tower, 3 March 1665).

9 Bath MSS. XCV, ff. 35–6, 9 May 1664.

10 J.

11 Bath MSS. XCV, f. 7 and ff. 11–14. See also J. and Holmes's examination in the Tower already referred to.

12 Ibid. The chronology, though not the sequence of events, varies slightly in the first two sources.

13 In spite of the fact that John Ladd was one of the eight commanders who attended the conference it is clear both from Holmes's journal and from the order in which the signatures are appended that Robert Fenn was now her commanding officer.

14 Bath MSS. XCV, f. 14.

15 Ibid.

16 Ibid., f. 23.

17 Ibid., ff. 3–5.

CHAPTER IX

1 Bath MSS. XCV, f. 4.

2 J., 12 Feb. 1664. The Admiralty Pilot (Africa, Part I, 8th edition, 1920, p. 322.) notes 'a large red sand dune, quite bare, and visible from a long distance seaward', in the Salum River of the Gambia Estuary.

3 This seems an inescapable inference from J., 8 Mar. 1664.

4 J. 8 Mar. 1664.

5 Details of their size, armament and date of construction may be found in

R. C. Anderson *Lists of Men-of-War 1650–1700* (Cambridge, 1935) in which they are nos. 31, 128 and 137 respectively.

6 See on this K. G. Davies, op. cit. chapter vi.

7 R. C. Anderson *Lists* . . . no 321.

8 Bath MSS. XCVI, ff. 120–2.

9 J., 13 June 1664.

10 See article on Sir John Holmes in *DNB* and authorities there cited. Holmes never in his daily entries in his journal or in his other accounts of the expedition refers to his brother by name or mentions the relationship but there can be no doubt of the fact: and the journal contains his name among the signatories of a council of war held aboard the *Jersey* on 9 April 1664 (also to be found in *CSP* Colonial America and West Indies).

11 Bath MSS. XCV, ff. 35–6. Holmes to Coventry, 9 May 1664.

12 See Holmes's Instructions (in J.) and his examination in the Tower. SP 29/114, f. 19 I.

CHAPTER X

1 K. G. Davies, op. cit. p. 12.

2 *Diary*, 22 Dec. 1664.

3 Zook, op. cit., p. 46.

4 For Cape Coast Castle and its tangled history see Zook, op. cit., 34–6. For Valckenburg see ibid passim. There are abundant references in J., especially in the letters from the Company's servants.

5 J.

6 Ibid.

7 *CSP* Colonial America and West Indies. April 1665, and W. W. Claridge *A History of the Gold Coast & Ashanti* (London, 1915), i, 113–14.

8 Bath MSS. XCV, f. 36.

9 Ibid., f. 31.

10 See on this J. R. Tanner's Introduction to his *Cat. Pepysian MSS.*

11 J., 20 April 1664.

12 Bath MSS. XCV ff. 31 and 35–6. Also J., 21–3 April 64. This vessel is also called the *Black Spread Eagle* and the *Arms of Groningen*. She is evidently no. 323 in R. C. Anderson *Lists* . . ., etc.

13 Bath MSS. XCV ff., 35–6.

14 For a fascinating account of this see C. R. Boxer *Salvador de Sá and the struggle for Brazil and Angola* (London, 1952), pp. 263 ff.

15 Zook, op. cit., p. 68.

16 SP 29/114, f. 19.

CHAPTER XI

1 Zook, op. cit., 51.
2 *Diary*, 29 May 1664.
3 On all this see C. R. Boxer *Salvador de Sá* . . . passim.
4 J., 31 July 1664.
5 Huygens *Oeuvres Complètes* V, 148, 165, 224, 269, 284. The technical problems which occupied Huygens were ultimately resolved by the English watchmaker John Harrison, who produced his first chronometer in 1735. For this and for the subsequent history of Huygens's pendulum watches, see R. T. Gould *The Marine Chronometer* (London, 1923). A summary of Holmes's report is printed in the *Philosophical Transactions of the Royal Society*, Vol. i, p. 13.
6 J., 12 Oct. 1664.
7 J. Coventry to Holmes, 10 Dec. 1664.
8 *Diary*, 10 Dec. 1664.
9 HMC, Heathcote MSS., 15 Dec. 1664.
10 *Diary*, 22 Dec. 1664.
11 J. Coventry to Holmes, 10 Dec. 1664.
12 *CSP* Dom.
13 *CSP* Colonial America and W. Indies, 2 Jan. 1665.
14 J. Coventry to Holmes, 10 Dec. 1664.
15 SP 29/110, f. 87 and 114, f. 19.
16 SP 29/114, f. 68.
17 *CSP* Dom.
18 J.
19 Ibid.
20 Zook, op. cit., p. 64, and *CSP* Dom.
21 Not March 23rd as stated by Zook, loc. cit.
22 *CSP* Dom.
23 *Diary*.
24 *CSP* Dom.
25 Ibid., 27 Mar./6 April 1665.

CHAPTER XII

1 Letterbook of Prince Rupert and the Duke of Albemarle Dartmouth MSS. (NMM DAR/3) passim. I wish to thank the Rev. J. R. Powell and Mr. E. K.

Timings for their kindness in making their photostats of this document available to me in advance of the forthcoming publication of their edition of it for the NRS.

2 See on all this David Ogg, op. cit., Michael Lewis *The Navy of Britain* and, among several NRS volumes, the journals of Sir Thomas Allin and of the Earl of Sandwich, both edited by Dr. R. C. Anderson, and hereafter referred to as *Allin* and *Sandwich*.

3 *Sandwich*, 198.

4 Ibid., 175.

5 NMM DAR/3, f. 13. For a contemporary ordnance List ibid., f. 20.

6 *Sandwich*, 179.

7 Ibid., 180, 198.

8 To the authorities cited in note 2 should be added Mr. A. W. H. Pearsall's illuminating and beautifully illustrated booklet *The Second Dutch War* (London, H.M.S.O., 1967).

9 *CSP* Dom., 23 May 1665.

10 *Sandwich*, lii.

11 *CSP* Dom., 10 June 1665.

12 *Diary*, 16 June 1665.

13 Bath MSS. XCIX, f, 185 n.d.

14 *CSP* Dom., 1 Aug. 1665. Bullen Reymes to Pepys.

15 *Gazette*, no. 39.

16 NMM DAR/3.

17 *Diary*, 10 Jan. 1666.

18 NMM DAR/3, 28 May 1666.

19 For the best account of the campaign and the battle see Dr. R. C. Anderson's introduction to *Allin*, ii, pp. xvi ff.

20 *Diary*, 2 June 1666.

21 *A True Narrative of the Engagement* . . ., quot. Pearsall, op. cit., p. 20.

22 *CSP* Dom., Clifford to Arlington, 6 June.

23 *CSP* Dom., 7 June 1666.

24 NMM DAR/3, f. 37.

25 Ibid., f. 38.

26 Ibid., f. 41.

27 Ibid., f. 51.

28 Ibid., ff. 53, 54, 57.

29 Ibid., f. 57 and *CSP* Dom., Holmes to Batten.

30 NMM DAR/3, f. 58.

31 Ibid., f. 66.

32 'About three Sir Robert Holmes lay by to repair, both his top-masts being disabled.' *Gazette*, no. 75.

33 NRS, *Naval Miscellany iii*, 'Naval Operations in the Latter Part of the Year 1666', ed. R. C. Anderson, p. 12.

34 *Allin*, 25 July 1666. 'A great quarrel arose between Sir Ro Holmes and Sir Jeremy Smith for miscarriages that day.'

35 See, e.g. Pepys *Diary*, 24 Oct. 1666.

CHAPTER XIII

1 *Allin*.

2 NMM DAR/3, f. 67.

3 Ibid., f. 68.

4 *A True and Perfect Narrative of the Great and Signal Success of a Part of His Majesty's Fleet* . . ., published by especial command (London, 1666), cited as *Narrative*.

5 NMM DAR/3, f. 74.

6 Ibid.

7 *Gazette*, no. 79.

8 Ibid., *Narrative: The Daily Motion . . . of H.M. Fleet . . .* July–October 1666 ed. R. C. Anderson in NRS, *Naval Miscellany*, iii. Hereafter cited as *Motion*.

9 NMM DAR/3, f. 76. C.-in-C's report to the King.

10 *Motion: Allin*.

11 *Motion*.

12 SP 29/167, f. 77. This letter written 'aboard H.M. shipp ye *Henry* 17 le[agues] from ye Vly, standing for the Coast of England the 12th of August 1666' is hereafter cited as *Letter*. It is the principal source for the account given in the *Gazette*.

13 Ibid.

14 Ibid.

15 *CSP* Dom., 15 Aug. 1666. Clifford to Arlington.

16 *Letter*.

17 *Motion*.

18 NMM DAR/3, f. 75.

19 *Letter*.

20 *Motion*.

21 *Narrative* and *Allin*, i, 283. Dr. Anderson's doubts as to the presence of the *Garland* (*Allin*, ii, fn. xxxi) surely dissolve in the light of Holmes's letter to Arlington. A collation of this with the relevant passages in *Allin* establishes that she must be the vessel referred to as 'one of the frigg[tts] that went in with me'.

22 *Letter*.

23 J. C. de Jonge cited in Ogg, i, 303.

24 SP 29/167, f. 42. Hayes aboard the *Royal James* to Williamson.
25 *CSP* Dom., 14 Aug., 21 Aug. 1666.
26 *Diary*, 15 Aug. 1666.
27 *CSP* Dom., 10 Dec. 1666.
28 *Letter.*
29 NMM DAR/3, f. 76.
30 Ibid., f. 84, 20 Aug. 1666.
31 Ibid., f. 87.
32 SP 29/168, f. 96.
33 *Motion.*
34 Ibid.
35 *Allin.*
36 *CSP* Dom.

CHAPTER XIV

1 *Diary*, Oct. 2, 3.
2 Ibid., Oct. 24.
3 Ibid., Oct. 7.
4 Ibid., Oct. 8.
5 Ibid., Oct. 20.
6 They are in BM MS. 29597 f.23.
7 *Diary*, Oct. 24.
8 SP 44/23, f. 264: the three drafts in Coventry's hand are in SP 29/177, f. 41. Some confusion has arisen over a nonsensical transcription reversing the names of Holmes and Smith in *CSP* Dom. cited in a footnote to *Diary*, vi, 36–7.
9 *Diary*, Oct. 31.
10 *CSP* Dom., 26 Oct. 1666.
11 SP 44/23, f. 461 & f. 557.
12 *CSP* Dom., 14 May 1667.
13 Bath MSS XCIX, f. 42.
14 Ibid., XCV, ff. 347–8.
15 *CSP* Dom.
16 HMC, Le Fleming MSS.
17 *CSP* Dom.
18 *CSP* Dom., 6 Feb. 1668, 23 Mar. 1669.
19 *CSP* Dom.
20 *Diary*, 26 Feb. 1668.
21 Ibid., 6 and 15 and 18 Mar. 1668.

22 Ibid., 8 Apr. 1668.

23 *CSP* Dom., 29 July 1668.

24 *Diary*, 5 Nov, 4 Dec. 1668.

25 *CSP* Dom., 11 June 1669.

26 *Parl. Hist.*, iv, 858–9. I am obliged to Mr. E. L. C. Mullins of the History of Parliament Trust and to Miss P. Watson for allowing me to see the entry on Holmes which has been prepared for a forthcoming volume.

27 *CSP* Dom., 20, 23 July 1670.

28 Ibid., 16 July 1671.

CHAPTER XV

1 SP 29/302, f. 156.

2 SP 29/177, f. 130.

3 SP 29/303, f. 211.

4 Eyewitness account in SP 29/304, f. 20. I have also used Lediard *Naval History of England* (1735), p. 595, and Dr. R. C. Anderson's invaluable introduction to his *Journals and Narratives of the Third Dutch War* (NRS, 1946) henceforth cited as *J. & N.*

5 SP 29/304, f. 25, I.

6 Ibid., f. 39.

7 Ibid., f. 36.

8 Spragge's journal, NMM DAR/5.

9 SP 29/303, f. 211.

10 SP 29/304, f. 20.

11 Narbrough's journal in *J. & N.*

12 For the fullest account see *J. & N.*, 13 ff.; for an admirably clear short account, Ogg, op. cit., i., 359 ff.

13 Narbrough's journal in *J. & N.*

14 *J. & N.*, 180.

15 Ibid., 183.

16 Ibid., 21.

17 Bath MSS. XCIX, f. 131: *J. & N.*, 405.

18 *CSP* Dom., Holmes to Navy Commrs.

19 The *St. Michael* reported 600 men well and 73 sick. SP 29/328, f. 37.

20 *CSP* Dom., 8, 12, 13 Aug., 1 Sept.

21 *CSP* Dom. and for all subsequent unattributed quotations in this chapter.

CHAPTER XVI

1 *CSP* Dom., and April 1661; 9 Oct. 1667; 4 Jan. 1670; 25 Sept. 1675; SP 29/312, f. 69. BM Harl. MSS. 1220, f. 124.
2 *CSP* Dom. (? 8 Nov.), 1676.
3 E.g. to Williamson, ibid., 20, 23 July 1670.
4 *Cat. Pepys MSS.*, iv, 13, 247, 663.
5 *CSP* Dom., 1 Feb. 1683.
6 The inventory taken at his death is in the Isle of Wight County Record Office HBY/1035 henceforth cited as *Inventory*.
7 Thirty-nine letters and a few fragments henceforward cited as *Letters*. I am indebted to Mr. J. D. Jones for his kindness in making these available to me.
8 Holmes's will dated 28 Oct. 1692 is in Somerset House.
9 To the value of £1,820: Conveyance dated 24 Mar. 1683 in I.o.W. C.R.O. HBY/576.
10 *The Diary of John Evelyn*, ed. E. S. de Beer (Oxford, 1959), p. 600.
11 Ibid., 825.
12 I.o.W. C.R.O. HBY/508, 722, 927, 934.
13 *Inventory*.
14 I.o.W. C.R.O. DOI/11.
15 Richard Worsley, *The History of the Isle of Wight* (London, 1781), p. 140.
16 Arlington to Holmes, 21 June 1669, I.o.W. C.R.O. HBY/183.
17 SP 29/428, f. 146. Holmes to Jenkins, 14 July 1683.
18 *CSP* Dom. Feb. 1677. Petition of Sir William Meux to the King.
19 Ibid., James II, 15 Mar. 1685.
20 *CSP* Dom., 8 Feb. 1681. Jenkins to Holmes.
21 Carte, *Ormond*, iv, 649–50.
22 SP 29/437, f. 80: *CSP* Dom. 3 Mar., 1 April 1684.
23 *CSP* Dom., Gwyn to Earl of Conway, 27 Jan. 1680. For the careers of Richard and Lemuel Kingdon see F. B. Kingdon, *The Kingdon Family* (n.d., privately printed).
24 *Tangier Papers of Samuel Pepys*. ed. Chappell (NRS, 1935), 230.
25 Ibid., 327. *Cat. Pepys MSS.*, iv, 474.
26 *Inventory*.
27 HMC 7th Report. Appendix 473 a. These incidents find no place in Sir Winston Churchill's biography of his ancestor.
28 *CSP* Dom., Gwyn to Conway, 29 May 1683.
29 Ibid., 7 June 1683.
30 *Inventory*, ff. 45–6.
31 Pepysian Library. Admiralty Letters. xii, 434: F. B. Kingdon, op. cit.

32 Ibid., xii, 242, 434. 9 Sept. 1686, 15 Jan. 1687.

33 *CSP* Colonial America and West Indies: *DNB* art. on Narbrough. Quite apart from evidence of Holmes's presence in England during 1688, the silence of his memorial inscription is eloquent. The clinching point seems to be the letter dated 30 Mar. 1688 from Edwyn Stede at Barbadoes to the Duke of Albemarle (HMC, Montagu MSS.) in which he complains that in spite of the King's proclamation he has no news of Sir Robert Holmes and his squadron coming to suppress the pirates.

34 J. D. Jones 'The Isle of Wight and the Revolution of 1688', in *Proceedings of the I.o.W. Natural History and Archaeological Society for 1965*, vol. V, part X.

35 Holmes's Letters 1688–90 in Carisbrooke Castle Museum, calendared by Mr. J. D. Jones, hereafter referred to as *Letters*, 1.

CHAPTER XVII

1 For this and what follows see J. D. Jones, op. cit. passim; HMC 7th Report Graham MSS., 412–14, for Holmes's letters to Lord Preston who succeeded Sunderland as Lord President at the end of October; E. B. Powley, *The English Navy in the Revolution of 1688* (Cambridge, 1928).

2 HMC, loc. cit. The militia in Yarmouth and Hurst had been specially chosen by Holmes as the least disaffected.

3 Printed in J. D. Jones, Appendix C.

4 HMC, Dartmouth MSS. i.

5 For Tyrrell see *Memoirs Relating to the Lord Torrington*, ed. Sir John Laughton (Camden Society, 1889).

6 *Letters*, 2.

7 Printed in Powley, op. cit., 143–5.

8 *Letters*, 17 Dec. 1688.

9 HMC, Finch MSS. III, 372.

10 SP 32/1 f. 110 wrongly calendared as King William's Chest 5, 110.

11 *Letters*, 15, 20 July 1689.

12 *CSP* Dom., 26 May, 21 June 1665, 23 Oct. 1668; 11 April, 6 May 1672; 18 Feb. 1673.

13 John Dawson was certainly Holmes's First Lieutenant in the *St. Michael*. *CSP* Dom., 18 Feb. 1673; and appears as First Lt. of the *Defiance* in an undated list in Bath MSS. XCIX, f. 94.

14 *Letters*, 15, 20 July 1689.

15 *CSP* Dom., 17, 21 Feb., 25 April 1689; SP 32/1 f. 95.

16 *Letters*, 8, 10. Holmes to Blathwayt. 27 April, 1 May 1689. see also J. D. Jones, op. cit.

17 Ibid., 16, 22 July 1689.

18 *Letters*, 24, 26, 28, 30; 23 Jan., 27 Jan., 26 May, 24 June 1690.

19 Ibid., 30–4; HMC, Finch, II, 323, 332.

20 *CSP* Dom., 16 July 1690.

21 *CSP* Dom., 6 Feb., 16 April, 9 Aug. 1691.

22 Luttrell, *Brief Relation*, 16 and 23 April 1692.

23 Ibid. See also his Will for which his nephew Harry obtained probate on November 19th, 1692.

24 Journal of the Rev. Thomas Pocock (25 April, 1704) printed in *Memoirs Relating to the Lord Torrington*.

25 *The Journeys of Celia Fiennes*, ed. Christopher Morris (London, 1949), 52–3.

26 *Mariners Mirror*, XXII, 239. The same point was made at greater length some twenty years later by Professor C. H. Wilson in EHR, lxxii, 469 ff.

P

APPENDIX I

Second Africa Expedition, November 1663—January 1665

List of Ships and Captains that came under Holmes's operational command

Ship	Captain	Source and Remarks
Jersey (RCA 215)	Holmes	State Papers: Bath MSS.: J., passim.
Katherin	Ladd } Fenn }	Instructions in J.
Brill (alias Crown & Brill)	Talbot	J., 27 Dec. 1663. Captured off Cape Verde. On March 30th, 1664 Talbot was appointed Captain of another prize, the Goulden Lyon, and was apparently succeeded by his master, Robert Porteene, as acting Captain. See J., 19 April 1664.
Coaster	Given to Captain Ladd	J., 15 Jan. 1664. A small frigate of the Royal Company.
Neptune	—	J., 20 Jan. 1664. A small Dutch pink captured off Goree roads. Handed over to the Royal Company, she was subsequently sent away with Dutch prisoners. J., 9, 12 Mar. 1664.

Ship	Captain	Notes
Galliot (or the galliot)	—	Holmes to Coventry, 8 Feb. 1664. Bath MSS. XCV, ff. 11–14. Also J., 21 Jan. 1664. When Holmes finally left the coast he presented her to the Royal Company (J., 15 June 1664).
Dover Merchant	Brathwait	
Sophia (RCA 137)	Bowen	J., 25 Feb. 1664, found at Sierra Leone on arrival there.
Expedition (RCA 31)	Pyne	
Welcome (RCA 128)	Cubitt	J., 20 Mar. 1664.
James	Merrett	J., 20 Mar. 1664. In Holmes's letter to Merrett (J., 4 May 1664) she is described as a frigate: and the strict injunction not to sell arms to the natives seems conclusive evidence that she belonged to the Royal Company, not to the Royal Navy.
Goulden Lyon (RCA 321)	Talbot	J., 29 Mar. 1664 for her capture. Talbot's appointment to command her, dated 30 Mar. 1664, is printed in CSP Dom.
Reliefe / Black Eagle alias / Black Spread Eagle alias / Arms of Groningen (RCA 323)	Ewers	J., 6 Apr. 1664. A Royal Company ship.
—	—	J., 21 Apr. 1664. Captured by Pyne of the Expedition off Anta (22 April according to Pyne's own account Bath MSS., XCV, f. 31).
Dorothy	—	J., 25 April 1664. A small Royal Company ship.
Brittain	Cowne	J., 3 May 1664. A Royal Company frigate.

Note: RCA refers to *Lists of Men of War 1650–1700, Part I. English ships 1649–1702* compiled by R. C. Anderson (C.U.P., 1935).

APPENDIX II

(see p. 209)

Inscriptions on Holmes's monument in Yarmouth, I.o.W.

The inscription recorded by the Rev. Thomas Pocock in his journal for 25 April 1704 is as follows:

> Expertus bello sociusque in pace jucundus,
> Et pace et bello bene regno et rege receptus.
> Pregrandi spiritu fecit vir magnus honorem,
> Quem vita longa nunquam nec morte reliquit.

Of which the following is a free translation:

> A professional in war and in peace a convivial companion,
> his worth was recognised by both king
> and kingdom in either circumstance. The honour
> this great man won by his transcendent spirit was
> not tarnished in the course of a long life or in
> the Death that closed it.

The existing inscription, probably carved by a mason who had no Latin, runs as follows:

I.
H. S. I.

Robertus Holmes Miles

Henrici Holmes De Mallow Comitatus Corkensis in Hibernia Armigeri Filius natu Tertius ab ineunte Adolescentia ad acquirendam armis gloriam intentus Militiae nomen dedit et sub serenissimi Regis Caroli vexillis Tyrocinia ponens contra perduelles fortiter feliciterque pugnavit. Pari deinde animo, Pari laude navalibus se immiscuit proeliis et sub Auspiciis Celsissimi principis Ruperti egregie meruit. Cum vero videret Causam Regiam armis ultra defendi non posse, ad exteros sese principes Contulit et in Gallia, Germania, Flandria rebus Belli pulchre gestis inclaruit. Rege Carolo 2ᵈᵒ fauste Tandem prospereque restaurato ab eo Castelli De Sandon in vectis insula praefecturam (tanquam veteris Meriti praemium) accepit et subinde Militis Titulo ornatus est. Anno 1666, Copiarum Navalium quae Rubris vexillis insigniuntur legatus alter Constitutus Portum Batavum De Ulij exigua classe intravit Cumque illic Naves centum et octoginta Concremasset in Scellengam descendit et Branderium istius Insulae primarium oppidum incendio delevit. Ob haec et alia multa praeclare acta eum Serenissimus Rex haud indebitis illius et virtuti, et Fidei praemiis honoravit, Insulaeque vectis ducem et Gubernatorem durante vita naturali praefecit quinetiam Faecialium principi Mandavit ut Ipsius gentilitiis insignibus Leo Anglicus adscriberetur, necnon Crista nempe Brachium Armatum e navali corona porrectum et Tridentem gerens. Hos Honores qua arte acquisivit eadem etiam tuebatur Vir Fortissimus, nimirum bene merendo, fideli semper in Reges et in patriam studio. Obiit An: Dom: 1692 Nov: 18.

Honoratissimo Patruo infra Sepulto hoc Monumentum posuit HENRICUS HOLMES vectis Insulae praefecti authoritate Regia locum tenens.

Which may be rendered:

Here lies buried Sir Robert Holmes, Knight, third son of Henry Holmes esq. of Mallow, Co. Cork, Ireland. From early youth he was bent on winning fame in the profession of arms to which he served his apprenticeship under the banners of His Sacred Majesty King Charles, for whom he fought with courage and success against the rebels. The same qualities distinguished his subsequent incursion into naval warfare under the auspices of His Highness Prince Rupert. But when he saw that the King's Cause could no longer be sustained in arms he betook himself to the service of foreign princes and added fresh laurels to his military reputation on the battlefields of France, Germany and Flanders. On the happy and prosperous, though long delayed, restoration of King Charles II he received from him (as a reward for his past services) the Captaincy of Sandown Castle in the Isle of Wight and was subsequently honoured with a knighthood. In the year 1666 as Rear-Admiral of the Red he entered the Dutch harbour of the Vlie with a small squadron and there, when he had burnt 180 of their ships, he attacked the island of Schelling and burned Brandaris, its principal town, to the ground. For these and many other outstanding achievements His Sacred Majesty, in recognition of his courage and loyalty, honoured and rewarded him, appointing him Captain and Governor of the Isle of Wight for life, and ordering his principal King-at-Arms to augment his bearings with a Lion of England and, for a crest, out of a naval crown an armed arm holding a trident. A man of the highest courage he kept these honours bright in the same way that he had won them, notably by his unswerving loyalty to each succeeding King and by his zeal for his country's service. He died 18 November 1692.

Henry Holmes, by royal authority Lieutenant-Governor of the Isle of Wight, erected this monument to his most honoured uncle buried here.

Genealogical Table

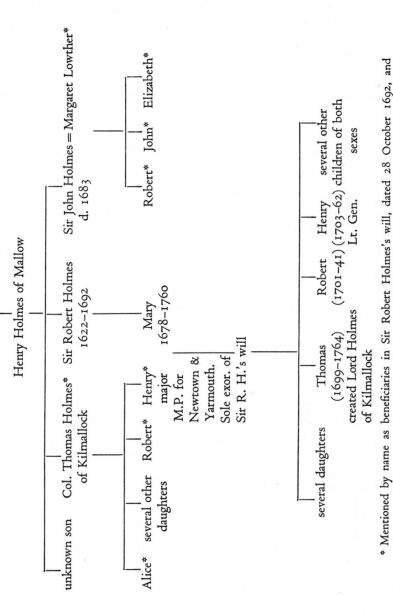

Robert Holmes

an officer in Elizabeth's Irish Wars, Provost of Mallow in 1612

Henry Holmes of Mallow

unknown son   Col. Thomas Holmes*   Sir Robert Holmes   Sir John Holmes = Margaret Lowther*
of Kilmallock   1622–1692   d. 1683

Robert*   John*   Elizabeth*

Alice*   several other   Robert*   Henry*   Mary
daughters   major   1678–1760
M.P. for
Newtown &
Yarmouth.
Sole exor. of
Sir R. H.'s will

several daughters   Thomas   Robert   Henry   several other
(1699–1764)   (1701–41)   (1703–62)   children of both
created Lord Holmes   Lt. Gen.   sexes
of Kilmallock

* Mentioned by name as beneficiaries in Sir Robert Holmes's will, dated 28 October 1692, and
proved 19 November 1692.

Index of Ships

Note: In both Indices the abbreviation H. denotes Sir Robert Holmes

General Index

Note: H. = Sir Robert Holmes

Shrewsbury, Earl and Countess of 168
Sierra Leone 71, 97, 129
Slave Trade 64, 104, 122, 129
Smith, Sir Jeremy 134, 137, 142, 146–7;
the quarrel with H. 162–5, 169; 170,
183
Smyrna convoy, H.'s attack on 175–9,
182
Soldadoes (exotic birds) described by H. 96
Solebay, battle of 135, 179–82
Sombrero 49, 55
Spain, Queen of 207
Spragge, Sir Edward 134, 142, 162,
169–70, 178–9, 181–2, 184
Stokes, Captain 67–8
Sunderland, Robert Spencer, Earl of 193,
199
Surrender, ethics of 114

Tactics: *see* Navy
Takoradi 105, 108
Talbot, Charles 89
Tambo, Duke (in the peerage of Barra) 90
Tangier 78, 83
Teneriffe 66
Test Act 183
Texel, battle of (mentioned) 184
Thorley, I.O.W. 188
Toulon 37
Tromp, Dutch admiral (the elder) 28–9
Tromp, Dutch admiral (the younger)
146–7
Tyrrell, Captain 202

Ustick, Stephen, Governor of James Island
89 f, 216 n. 8

Valckenburg, Dutch Governor of Cape
Coast 108
Vermuyden, John, Prince Rupert's engineer
63, 70
Virgin Is. 48–51

Vlie, The 148–58

Wales, Prince of: *see* Charles II
Waller, Sir William 17, 19
Walmer 25
Warwick, Robert Rich, Earl of, and the
revolted fleet 22–9, 31
Waterford 31
West Africa, trade with 41–2, 129–30;
H.'s first expedition to 62 ff; effects
on health 73; H.'s second expedition
85–130. *See also* Gambia, Guinea, Royal
African Co.
West India Co. (Dutch) 68, 70, 87, 91–
118 *passim*
West Indies, last Royalist stronghold 38;
reduced by Sir George Ayscue 48;
Rupert and the revolted fleet in 48–
51; French and Dutch possessions in
48–51; H. appointed to command of
squadron to suppress the buccaneers,
which Narbrough undertakes 199
Wetwang, Captain 150
Wiamba: *see* Winneba
Wight, Isle of 24, 63, 126, 128, 137,
167 ff, 186–194, 196–7, 199, 201–4,
206 ff
William of Orange (afterwards William
III) 200
Williamson, Sir Joseph 165, 172–3, 177,
183, 190
Willoughby of Parham, Lord 24–5, 28
Wilson, Professor C. H., quoted 81
Winchester 170
Windward Coast 99
Winneba 108, 119
Wreckage, profits of 188, 208

Yarmouth (I.O.W.) 13–14, 65, 167;
H.'s house at 190; 191, 202, 207–9
York, Duke of: *see* James II